The
Anti-Stalin Campaign
and International
Communism

A Selection of Documents
Edited by the RUSSIAN INSTITUTE
Columbia University

New York and London

COLUMBIA UNIVERSITY PRESS

Foreword

THE FOLLOWING selection of documents concerns a limited subject and a limited period of time: the response of the Communist parties in the major Western states to the secret Khrushchev report of February 24-25, 1956, in the weeks since its publication, on June 4, by the U. S. Department of State. The subject is, of course, closely linked to two larger questions which go back to the origins of the Soviet Union and the international Communist movement: the question of leadership within the Communist Parties and the question of the relations between the Communist Party of the Soviet Union and other Communist Parties. Both these questions came to be active issues after Stalin's death in March 1953, as is evidenced by the perceptible, if somewhat fluctuating, decrease in the volume of praise for Stalin, by the public emphasis on collective leadership, and by the Soviet approach to Tito's regime in Yugoslavia. The XXth Party Congress of the CPSU led to an intensification of these trends, in the growing criticism of the "cult of the individual" (or "personality cult"—*Kult lichnosti*), in the disbanding of the Cominform, and in the stress upon a variety of roads to "socialism." Quite evidently the Communist world was in a state of flux well before the June revelation of the secret Khrushchev report.

Still, the publication of this report by a non-Communist government appears to mark a new stage, because of the extensive and harsh indictment of Stalin which the report contains, because of the manner in which it has been made public, as well as because of the many questions which its appearance and contents raise but do not answer.

The repercussions in a number of Communist Parties have been unprecedented in recent Communist history and have included explicit criticisms of the present Soviet leaders. Whatever the future course of developments— a number of party delegations are presently visiting Moscow and several party congresses are scheduled for later in the year—these repercussions are of sufficient intrinsic interest to warrant early publication of a selection of principal documents to indicate their temper and progress.

It will be noted that, apart from statements of the CPSU, the documents relate only to the Communist parties of Italy, France, Great Britain and the United States, though there have been some corresponding repercussions in the smaller countries of Western Europe. Thus far there has been little open reaction in the Communist parties of Asia. In the Communist Parties of the Soviet orbit of Eastern Europe there have been no public expressions of dissent from the position taken by the CPSU on this question. In general, the problem has appeared most acute in those European countries, and the United States, where the Communist parties, while having varying degrees of political strength, are not in power.

With the exception of one article by a left-wing Socialist—Pietro Nenni—the articles are reproduced in their entirety. Except for the first document, Khrushchev's secret report, for which no Soviet text is currently available, all translations are from the original printed text.

In the interests of time the materials, while provided with brief introductions, have not been annotated. A biographical listing appears at the end of the selection. I wish to thank Professor Alexander Dallin for his care and labor in preparing the text for publication.

July 16, 1956   HENRY L. ROBERTS
                                   Director, Russian Institute
                                   Columbia University

Note on the Revised Edition
THE REVISED edition of *The Anti-Stalin Campaign and International Communism* has made it possible to carry the documentation through the end of August 1956.
August 31, 1956   H.L.R.

Contents

Contents

1

Secret Speech of Khrushchev Concerning the "Cult of the Individual," Delivered at the Twentieth Congress of the Communist Party of the Soviet Union

February 25, 1956

ON FEBRUARY 24-25, 1956, Nikita S. Khrushchev, as First Secretary of the Communist Party of the Soviet Union, delivered a report on Stalin and the "cult of the individual," to a closed session of the Party's Twentieth Congress in Moscow. Foreign Communists were barred from this session.

Information concerning this speech soon became the subject of rumors in Moscow, and different versions of the speech were reported by foreign journalists from about March 10 on. These reports became the subject of discussions in Communist as well as non-Communist quarters abroad. Within the Soviet Union attacks on Joseph Stalin appeared in milder and less systematic form, beginning with an editorial in *Pravda* on March 28, 1956. Indirect confirmation of the existence of the Khrushchev speech may be inferred from subsequent Soviet statements and publications (see Documents 5 and 11 below).

On June 4, the United States Department of State released a text of the Khrushchev speech with the following introduction:

The Department of State has recently obtained from a confidential source a copy of a document which purports to be a version of the speech of Party First Secretary N. S. Krushchev at a session of the XXth Party Congress of the Communist Party of the Soviet Union on February 25, 1956. This session was limited in attendance to the delegates from the USSR.

The document is being released in response to many inquiries. This version is understood to have been prepared for the guidance of the party leadership of a Communist Party outside of the USSR. The Department of State does not vouch for the authenticity of the document and in releasing it intends that the document speak for itself.

COMRADES! In the report of the Central Committee of the Party at the XXth Congress, in a number of speeches by delegates to the Congress, as also formerly during the plenary CC/CPSU sessions, quite a lot has been said about the cult of the individual and about its harmful consequences.

After Stalin's death the Central Committee of the Party began to implement a policy of explaining concisely and consistently that it is impermissible and foreign to the spirit of Marxism-Leninism to elevate one person, to transform him into a superman possessing supernatural characteristics akin to those of a god. Such a man supposedly knows everything, sees everything, thinks for everyone, can do anything, is infallible in his behavior.

Such a belief about a man, and specifically about Stalin, was cultivated among us for many years.

The objective of the present report is not a thorough evaluation of Stalin's life and activity. Concerning Stalin's merits, an entirely sufficient number of books, pamphlets and studies had already been written in his lifetime. The role of Stalin in the preparation and execution of the Socialist Revolution, in the Civil War, and in the fight for the construction of Socialism in our country is universally known. Everyone knows this well. At the present we are concerned with a question which has immense importance for the Party now and for the future— [we are concerned] with how the cult of the person of Stalin has been gradually growing, the cult which became at a certain specific stage the source of a whole series of exceedingly serious and grave perversions of Party principles, of Party democracy, of revolutionary legality.

Because of the fact that not all as yet realize fully the practical consequences resulting from the cult of the individual, the great harm caused by the violation of the principle of collective direction of the Party and because of the accumulation of immense and limitless power in the hands of one person—the Central Committee of the Party considers it absolutely necessary to make the material pertaining to this matter available to the XXth Congress of the Communist Party of the Soviet Union.

Allow me first of all to remind you how severely the classics of Marxism-Leninism denounced every manifestation of the cult of the individual. In a letter to the German political worker, Wilhelm Bloss, Marx stated: "From my antipathy to any cult of the individual, I never made public during the existence of the International the numerous addresses from various countries which recognized my merits and which annoyed me. I did not even reply to them, except sometimes to rebuke their authors. Engels and I first joined the secret society of Communists on the condition that everything making for superstitious worship of authority would be deleted from its statute. Lassalle subsequently did quite the opposite."

Sometime later Engels wrote: "Both Marx and I have always been against any public manifestation with regard to individuals, with the exception of cases when it had an important purpose; and we most strongly opposed such manifestations which during our lifetime concerned us personally."

The great modesty of the genius of the revolution, Vladimir Ilyich Lenin, is known. Lenin had always stressed the role of the people as the creator of history, the directing and organizational role of the Party as a living and creative organism, and also the role of the Central Committee.

Marxism does not negate the role of the leaders of the workers' class in directing the revolutionary liberation movement.

While ascribing great importance to the role of the leaders and organizers of the masses, Lenin at the same time mercilessly stigmatized every manifestation of the cult of the individual, inexorably combated the foreign-to-Marxism views about a "hero" and a "crowd" and countered all efforts to oppose a "hero" to the masses and to the people.

Lenin taught that the Party's strength depends on its indissoluble unity with the masses, on the fact that behind the Party follow the people—workers, peasants and intelligentsia. "Only he will win and retain the power," said Lenin, "who believes in the people, who submerges himself in the fountain of the living creativeness of the people."

Lenin spoke with pride about the Bolshevik Communist Party as the leader and teacher of the people; he called for the presentation of all the most important questions before the opinion of knowledgeable workers, before the opinion of their Party; he said: "We believe in it, we see in it the wisdom, the honor, and the conscience of our epoch."

Lenin resolutely stood against every attempt aimed at belittling or weakening the directing role of the Party in the structure of the Soviet State. He worked out Bolshevik principles of Party direction and norms of Party life, stressing that the guiding principle of Party leadership is its collegiality. Already during the pre-revolutionary years Lenin called the Central Committee of the Party a collective of leaders and the guardian and interpreter of Party principles. "During the period between congresses," pointed out Lenin, "the Central Committee guards and interprets the principles of the Party."

Underlining the role of the Central Committee of the Party and its authority, Vladimir Ilyich pointed out: "Our Central Committee constituted itself as a closely centralized and highly authoritative group. . . ."

During Lenin's life the Central Committee of the Party was a real expression of collective leadership of the Party and of the nation. Being a militant Marxist-revolutionist, always unyielding in matters of principle, Lenin never imposed by force his views upon his co-workers. He tried to convince; he patiently explained his opinions to others.

Lenin always diligently observed that the norms of Party life were realized, that the Party statute was enforced, that the Party congresses and the plenary sessions of the Central Committee took place at the proper intervals.

In addition to the great accomplishments of V. I. Lenin for the victory of the working class and of the working peasants, for the victory of our Party and for the application of the ideas of scientific Communism to life, his acute mind expressed itself also in this, that he detected in Stalin in time those negative characteristics which resulted later in grave consequences. Fearing for the future fate of the Party and of the Soviet nation, V. I. Lenin made a completely correct characterization of Stalin, pointing out that it was necessary to consider the question of transferring Stalin from the position of the Secretary General because of the fact that Stalin is excessively rude, that he does not have a proper attitude toward his comrades, that he is capricious and abuses his power.

In December 1922 in a letter to the Party Congress Vladimir Ilyich wrote: "After taking over the position of Secretary General Comrade Stalin accumulated in his hands immeasurable power and I am not certain whether he will be always able to use this power with the required care."

This letter—a political document of tremendous importance, known in the Party history as Lenin's "testament"—was distributed among the delegates to the XXth Party Congress.* You have read it, and will undoubtedly read

* Lenin's "testament" and other documents cited by Khrushchev were "distributed to the delegates at the XXth Party Congress" and subsequently circulated as supplements to the above version of the Khrushchev speech. On June 30, the Department of State made available these documents

it again more than once. You might reflect on Lenin's plain words, in which expression is given to Vladimir Ilyich's anxiety concerning the Party, the people, the State, and the future direction of Party policy.

Vladimir Ilyich said: "Stalin is excessively rude, and this defect, which can be freely tolerated in our midst and in contacts among us Communists, becomes a defect which cannot be tolerated in one holding the position of the Secretary General. Because of this, I propose that the comrades consider the method by which Stalin would be removed from this position and by which another man would be selected for it, a man, who above all, would differ from Stalin in only one quality, namely, greater tolerance, greater loyalty, greater kindness and more considerate attitude toward the comrades, a less capricious temper, etc."

This document of Lenin's was made known to the delegates at the XIIIth Party Congress, who discussed the question of transferring Stalin from the position of Secretary General. The delegates declared themselves in favor of retaining Stalin in this post, hoping that he would heed the critical remarks of Vladimir Ilyich and would be able to overcome the defects which caused Lenin serious anxiety.

Comrades! The Party Congress should become acquainted with two new documents, which confirm Stalin's character as already outlined by Vladimir Ilyich Lenin in his "testament." These documents are a letter from Nadezhda Konstantinovna Krupskaya to Kamenev, who was at that time head of the Political Bureau, and a personal letter from Vladimir Ilyich Lenin to Stalin.

---

which it had secured from a confidential source. Since they deal with the period of 1922-1923, they are not reproduced in this collection.—*Editor.*

I will now read these documents:

Lev Borisovich!

Because of a short letter which I had written in words dictated to me by Vladimir Ilyich by permission of the doctors, Stalin allowed himself yesterday an unusually rude outburst directed at me. This is not my first day in the Party. During all these thirty years I have never heard from any comrade one word of rudeness. The business of the Party and of Ilyich are not less dear to me than to Stalin. I need at present the maximum of self-control. What one can and what one cannot discuss with Ilyich—I know better than any doctor, because I know what makes him nervous and what does not, in any case I know better than Stalin. I am turning to you and to Grigory as to much closer comrades of V. I. and I beg you to protect me from rude interference with my private life and from vile invectives and threats. I have no doubt as to what will be the unanimous decision of the Control Commission, with which Stalin sees fit to threaten me; however, I have neither the strength nor the time to waste on this foolish quarrel. And I am a living person and my nerves are strained to the utmost.

N. KRUPSKAYA

Nadezhda Konstantinovna wrote this letter on December 23, 1922. After two and a half months, in March 1923, Vladimir Ilyich Lenin sent Stalin the following letter:

The Letter of V. I. Lenin

To Comrade Stalin.

Copies for: Kamenev and Zinoviev.

Dear Comrade Stalin!

You permitted yourself a rude summons of my wife to the telephone and a rude reprimand of her. Despite the fact that she told you that she agreed to forget what was said, nevertheless Zinoviev and Kamenev heard about it from her. I have no intention to forget so easily that which is being done against me, and I need not stress here that I consider as directed against me that which is being done against my wife. I ask you, therefore, that you weigh carefully whether you are agreeable to retracting your words and apologizing or whether you prefer the severance of relations between us.

[*Commotion in the hall*]

Sincerely,

LENIN

March 5, 1923

Comrades! I will not comment on these documents. They speak eloquently for themselves. Since Stalin could behave in this manner during Lenin's life, could thus behave toward Nadezhda Konstantinovna Krupskaya, whom the Party knows well and values highly as a loyal friend of Lenin and as an active fighter for the cause of the Party since its creation—we can easily imagine how Stalin treated other people. These negative characteristics of his developed steadily and during the last years acquired an absolutely insufferable character.

As later events have proven, Lenin's anxiety was justified: in the first period after Lenin's death Stalin still paid attention to his [i.e., Lenin's] advice, but later he began to disregard the serious admonitions of Vladimir Ilyich.

When we analyze the practice of Stalin in regard to the direction of the Party and of the country, when we pause to consider everything which Stalin perpetrated, we must be convinced that Lenin's fears were justified. The negative characteristics of Stalin, which, in Lenin's time, were only incipient, transformed themselves during the last years into a grave abuse of power by Stalin, which caused untold harm to our Party.

We have to consider seriously and analyze correctly this matter in order that we may preclude any possibility of a repetition in any form whatever of what took place during the life of Stalin, who absolutely did not tolerate collegiality in leadership and in work, and who practiced brutal violence, not only toward everything which opposed him, but also toward that which seemed to his capricious and despotic character, contrary to his concepts.

Stalin acted not through persuasion, explanation, and patient co-operation with people, but by imposing his concepts and demanding absolute submission to his opinion. Whoever opposed this concept or tried to prove his viewpoint, and the correctness of his position, was doomed to removal from the leading collective and to subsequent moral and physical annihilation. This was especially true during the period following the XVIIth Party Congress, when many prominent Party leaders and rank-and-file Party workers, honest and dedicated to the cause of Communism, fell victim to Stalin's despotism.

We must affirm that the Party had fought a serious fight against the Trotskyites, rightists and bourgeois nationalists, and that it disarmed ideologically all the enemies of Leninism. This ideological fight was carried on successfully, as a result of which the Party became strengthened and tempered. Here Stalin played a positive role.

The Party led a great political ideological struggle against those in its own ranks who proposed anti-Leninist theses, who represented a political line hostile to the Party and to the cause of socialism. This was a stubborn and a difficult fight but a necessary one, because the political line of both the Trotskyite-Zinovievite bloc and of the Bukharinites led actually toward the restoration of capitalism and capitulation to the world bourgeoisie. Let us consider for a moment what would have happened if in 1928-1929 the political line of right deviation had prevailed among us, or orientation toward "cotton-dress industrialization," or toward the kulak, etc. We would not now have a powerful heavy industry, we would not have the kolkhozes, we would find ourselves disarmed and weak in a capitalist encirclement.

It was for this reason that the Party led an inexorable ideological fight and explained to all Party members and to the non-Party masses the harm and the danger of the anti-Leninist proposals of the Trotskyite opposition and the rightist opportunists. And this great work of explaining the Party line bore fruit; both the Trotskyites and the rightist opportunists were politically isolated; the overwhelming Party majority supported the Leninist line and the Party was able to awaken and organize the working masses to apply the Leninist Party line and to build socialism.

Worth noting is the fact that even during the progress of the furious ideological fight against the Trotskyites, the Zinovievites, the Bukharinites and others, extreme repressive measures were not used against them. The fight was on ideological grounds. But some years later when socialism in our country was fundamentally constructed, when the exploiting classes were generally liquidated, when the

Soviet social structure had radically changed, when the
social basis for political movements and groups hostile to
the Party had violently contracted, when the ideological
opponents of the Party were long since defeated politically
—then the repression directed against them began.

It was precisely during this period (1935-1937-1938)
that the practice of mass repression through the government apparatus was born, first against the enemies of
Leninism—Trotskyites, Zinovievites, Bukharinites, long
since politically defeated by the Party, and subsequently
also against many honest Communists, against those Party
cadres who had borne the heavy load of the Civil War
and the first and most difficult years of industrialization
and collectivization, who actively fought against the Trotskyites and the rightists for the Leninist Party line.

Stalin originated the concept "enemy of the people."
This term automatically rendered it unnecessary that the
ideological errors of a man or men engaged in a con-
troversy be proven; this term made possible the usage
of the most cruel repression, violating all norms of revolutionary legality, against anyone who in any way dis-
agreed with Stalin, against those who were only suspected
of hostile intent, against those who had bad reputations.
This concept, "enemy of the people," actually eliminated
the possibility of any kind of ideological fight or the
making of one's views known on this or that issue, even
those of a practical character. In the main, and in actu-
ality, the only proof of guilt used, against all norms of
current legal science, was the "confession" of the accused
himself; and, as subsequent probing proved, "confessions"
were acquired through physical pressures against the
accused.

This led to glaring violations of revolutionary legality, and to the fact that many entirely innocent persons, who in the past had defended the Party line, became victims.

We must assert that in regard to those persons who in their time had opposed the Party line, there were often no sufficiently serious reasons for their physical annihilation. The formula, "enemy of the people," was specifically introduced for the purpose of physically annihilating such individuals.

It is a fact that many persons, who were later annihilated as enemies of the Party and people, had worked with Lenin during his life. Some of these persons had made errors during Lenin's life, but, despite this, Lenin benefited by their work, he corrected them and he did everything possible to retain them in the ranks of the Party; he induced them to follow him.

In this connection the delegates to the Party Congress should familiarize themselves with an unpublished note by V. I. Lenin directed to the Central Committee's Political Bureau in October 1920. Outlining the duties of the Control Commission, Lenin wrote that the Commission should be transformed into a real "organ of Party and proletarian conscience."

As a special duty of the Control Commission there is recommended a deep, individualized relationship with, and sometimes even a type of therapy for, the representatives of the so-called opposition—those who have experienced a psychological crisis because of failure in their Soviet or Party career. An effort should be made to quiet them, to explain the matter to them in a way used among comrades, to find for them (avoiding the method of issuing orders) a task for which they are psychologically fitted. Advice and rules relating to this matter are to be formulated by the Central Committee's Organizational Bureau, etc.

Everyone knows how irreconcilable Lenin was with the ideological enemies of Marxism, with those who deviated from the correct Party line. At the same time, however, Lenin, as is evident from the given document, in his practice of directing the Party demanded the most intimate Party contact with people who had shown indecision or temporary nonconformity with the Party line, but whom it was possible to return to the Party path. Lenin advised that such people should be patiently educated without the application of extreme methods.

Lenin's wisdom in dealing with people was evident in his work with cadres.

An entirely different relationship with people characterized Stalin. Lenin's traits—patient work with people; stubborn and painstaking education of them; the ability to induce people to follow him without using compulsion, but rather through the ideological influence on them of the whole collective—were entirely foreign to Stalin. He [Stalin] discarded the Leninist method of convincing and educating; he abandoned the method of ideological struggle for that of administrative violence, mass repressions, and terror. He acted on an increasingly larger scale and more stubbornly through punitive organs, at the same time often violating all existing norms of morality and of Soviet laws.

Arbitrary behavior by one person encouraged and permitted arbitrariness in others. Mass arrests and deportations of many thousands of people, execution without trial and without normal investigation created conditions of insecurity, fear and even desperation.

This, of course, did not contribute toward unity of the Party ranks and of all strata of working people, but on the contrary brought about annihilation and the expulsion from the Party of workers who were loyal but inconvenient to Stalin.

Our Party fought for the implementation of Lenin's plans for the construction of socialism. This was an ideological fight. Had Leninist principles been observed during the course of this fight, had the Party's devotion to principles been skillfully combined with a keen and solicitous concern for people, had they not been repelled and wasted but rather drawn to our side—we certainly would not have had such a brutal violation of revolutionary legality and many thousands of people would not have fallen victim of the method of terror. Extraordinary methods would then have been resorted to only against those people who had in fact committed criminal acts against the Soviet system.

Let us recall some historical facts.

In the days before the October Revolution two members of the Central Committee of the Bolshevik Party—Kamenev and Zinoviev—declared themselves against Lenin's plan for an armed uprising. In addition, on October 18 they published in the Menshevik newspaper, *Novaya Zhizn,* a statement declaring that the Bolsheviks were making preparations for an uprising and that they considered it adventuristic. Kamenev and Zinoviev thus disclosed to the enemy the decision of the Central Committee to stage the uprising, and that the uprising had been organized to take place within the very near future.

This was treason against the Party and against the revolution. In this connection, V. I. Lenin wrote: "Kamenev and Zinoviev revealed the decision of the Central Committee of their Party on the armed uprising to Rodzyanko and Kerensky. . . ." He put before the Central Committee the question of Zinoviev's and Kamenev's expulsion from the Party.

However, after the Great Socialist October Revolution, as is known, Zinoviev and Kamenev were given leading positions. Lenin put them in positions in which they carried out most responsible Party tasks and participated actively in the work of the leading Party and Soviet organs. It is known that Zinoviev and Kamenev committed a number of other serious errors during Lenin's life. In his "testament" Lenin warned that "Zinoviev's and Kamenev's October episode was of course not an accident." But Lenin did not pose the question of their arrest and certainly not their shooting.

Or let us take the example of the Trotskyites. At present, after a sufficiently long historical period, we can speak about the fight with the Trotskyites with complete calm and can analyze this matter with sufficient objectivity. After all, around Trotsky were people whose origin cannot by any means be traced to bourgeois society. Part of them belonged to the Party intelligentsia and a certain part were recruited from among the workers. We can name many individuals who in their time joined the Trotskyites; however, these same individuals took an active part in the workers' movement before the revolution, during the Socialist October Revolution itself, and also in the consolidation of the victory of this greatest of revolutions. Many of them broke with Trotskyism and returned to Leninist positions. Was it necessary to annihilate such people? We are deeply convinced that had Lenin lived such an extreme method would not have been used against many of them.

Such are only a few historical facts. But can it be said that Lenin did not decide to use even the most severe means against enemies of the revolution when this was actually necessary? No, no one can say this. Vladimir Ilyich demanded uncompromising dealings with the enemies of the revolution and of the working class and when necessary resorted ruthlessly to such methods. You will recall only V. I. Lenin's fight with the Socialist Revolutionary organizers of the anti-Soviet uprising, with the counter-revolutionary kulaks in 1918 and with others, when Lenin without hesitation used the most extreme methods against the enemies. Lenin used such methods, however, only against actual class enemies and not against those who blunder, who err, and whom it was possible to lead through ideological influence, and even retain in the leadership.

Lenin used severe methods only in the most necessary cases, when the exploiting classes were still in existence and were vigorously opposing the revolution, when the struggle for survival was decidedly assuming the sharpest forms, even including a civil war.

Stalin, on the other hand, used extreme methods and mass repressions at a time when the revolution was already victorious, when the Soviet state was strengthened, when the exploiting classes were already liquidated and Socialist relations were rooted solidly in all phases of national economy, when our Party was politically consolidated and had strengthened itself both numerically and ideologically. It is clear that here Stalin showed in a whole series of cases his intolerance, his brutality and his abuse of power. Instead of proving his political correctness and mobilizing the masses, he often chose the path of repression and physical annihilation, not only against actual enemies, but also against individuals who had not committed any crimes against the Party and the Soviet government. Here we see no wisdom but only a demonstration of the brutal force which had once so alarmed V. I. Lenin.

Lately, especially after the unmasking of the Beria gang, the Central Committee has looked into a series of matters fabricated by this gang. This revealed a very ugly picture of brutal willfulness connected with the incorrect behavior of Stalin. As facts prove, Stalin, using his unlimited power, allowed himself many abuses, acting in the name of the Central Committee, not asking for the opinion of the Committee members nor even of the members of the Central Committee's Political Bureau; often he did not inform them about his personal decisions concerning very important Party and government matters.

Considering the question of the cult of an individual we must first of all show everyone what harm this caused to the interests of our Party.

Vladimir Ilyich Lenin had always stressed the Party's role and significance in the direction of the socialist government of workers and peasants; he saw in this the chief precondition for a successful building of socialism in our country.   Pointing to the great responsibility of the Bolshevik Party, as a ruling party in the Soviet state, Lenin called for the most meticulous observance of all norms of Party life; he called for the realization of the principles of collegiality in the direction of the Party and the state.

Collegiality of leadership flows from the very nature of our Party, a party built on the principles of democratic centralism.   "This means," said Lenin, "that all Party matters are accomplished by all Party members— directly or through representatives—who without any exceptions are subject to the same rules; in addition, all administrative members, all directing collegia, all holders of Party positions are elective, they must account for their activities and are recallable."

It is known that Lenin himself offered an example of the most careful observance of these principles.   There was no matter so important that Lenin himself decided it without asking for advice and approval of the majority of the Central Committee members or of the members of the Central Committee's Political Bureau.

In the most difficult period for our Party and our country, Lenin considered it necessary regularly to convoke congresses, Party conferences, and plenary sessions of the Central Committee at which all the most important questions were discussed and where resolutions, carefully worked out by the collective of leaders, were approved.

We can recall, for an example, the year 1918 when the country was threatened by the attack of the imperialistic interventionists.   In this situation the VIIth Party Con-

gress was convened in order to discuss a vitally important
matter which could not be postponed—the matter of peace.
In 1919, while the Civil War was raging, the VIIIth Party
Congress convened which adopted a new Party program,
decided such important matters as the relationship with
the peasant masses, the organization of the Red Army,
the leading role of the Party in the work of the Soviets,
the correction of the social composition of the Party, and
other matters. In 1920 the IXth Party Congress was convened which laid down guiding principles pertaining to
the Party's work in the sphere of economic construction.
In 1921, the Xth Party Congress accepted Lenin's New
Economic Policy and the historical resolution called
"About Party Unity."

During Lenin's life Party Congresses were convened
regularly; always, when a radical turn in the development of the Party and the country took place, Lenin
considered it absolutely necessary that the Party discuss
at length all the basic matters pertaining to internal and
foreign policy and to questions bearing on the development of Party and government.

It is very characteristic that Lenin addressed to the
Party Congress as the highest Party organ his last articles,
letters and remarks. During the period between congresses the Central Committee of the Party, acting as
the most authoritative leading collective, meticulously
observed the principles of the Party and carried out its
policy.

So it was during Lenin's life.

Were our Party's holy Leninist principles observed after
the death of Vladimir Ilyich?

Whereas during the first few years after Lenin's death Party Congresses and Central Committee plenums took place more or less regularly, later, when Stalin began increasingly to abuse his power, these principles were brutally violated. This was especially evident during the last 15 years of his life. Was it a normal situation when over 13 years elapsed between the XVIIIth and XIXth Party Congresses, years during which our Party and our country had experienced so many important events? These events demanded categorically that the Party should have passed resolutions pertaining to the country's defense during the Patriotic War and to peacetime construction after the war. Even after the end of the war a Congress was not convened for over 7 years.

Central Committee plenums were hardly ever called. It should be sufficient to mention that during all the years of the Patriotic War not a single Central Committee plenum took place. It is true that there was an attempt to call a Central Committee plenum in October 1941, when Central Committee members from the whole country were called to Moscow. They waited two days for the opening of the plenum, but in vain. Stalin did not even want to meet and to talk to the Central Committee members. This fact shows how demoralized Stalin was in the first months of the war and how haughtily and disdainfully he treated the Central Committee members.

In practice Stalin ignored the norms of Party life and trampled on the Leninist principle of collective Party leadership.

Stalin's willfulness *vis-à-vis* the Party and its Central Committee became fully evident after the XVIIth Party Congress which took place in 1934.

Having at its disposal numerous data showing brutal willfulness toward Party cadres, the Central Committee has created a Party Commission under the control of the Central Committee Presidium; it was charged with investigating what made possible the mass repressions against the majority of the Central Committee members and candidates elected at the XVIIth Congress of the All-Union Communist Party (Bolsheviks).

The Commission has become acquainted with a large quantity of materials in the NKVD archives and with other documents and has established many facts pertaining to the fabrication of cases against Communists, to false accusations, to glaring abuses of socialist legality—which resulted in the death of innocent people. It became apparent that many Party, Soviet and economic activists who were branded in 1937-1938 as "enemies" were actually never enemies, spies, wreckers, etc., but were always honest Communists; they were only so stigmatized, and often, no longer able to bear barbaric tortures, they charged themselves (at the order of the investigative judges—falsifiers) with all kinds of grave and unlikely crimes. The Commission has presented to the Central Committee Presidium lengthy and documented materials pertaining to mass repressions against the delegates to the XVIIth Party Congress and against members of the Central Committee elected at that Congress. These materials have been studied by the Presidium of the Central Committee.

It was determined that of the 139 members and candidates of the Party's Central Committee who were elected at the XVIIth Congress, 98 persons, i.e., 70 percent,

were arrested and shot (mostly in 1937-1938). *(Indignation in the hall.)*

What was the composition of the delegates to the XVIIth Congress? It is known that 80 percent of the voting participants of the XVIIth Congress joined the Party during the years of conspiracy before the Revolution and during the Civil War; this means before 1921. By social origin the basic mass of the delegates to the Congress were workers (60 percent of the voting members).

For this reason, it was inconceivable that a Congress so composed would have elected a Central Committee, a majority of which would prove to be enemies of the Party. The only reason why 70 percent of the Central Committee members and candidates elected at the XVIIth Congress were branded as enemies of the Party and of the people was that honest Communists were slandered, accusations against them were fabricated, and revolutionary legality was gravely undermined.

The same fate met not only the Central Committee members but also the majority of the delegates to the XVIIth Party Congress. Of 1966 delegates with either voting or advisory rights, 1,108 persons were arrested on charges of anti-revolutionary crimes, i.e., decidedly more than a majority. This very fact shows how absurd, wild and contrary to common sense were the charges of counter-revolutionary crimes made out, as we now see, against a majority of participants at the XVIIth Party Congress. *(Indignation in the hall.)*

We should recall that the XVIIth Party Congress is historically known as the Congress of Victors. Delegates to

the Congress were active participants in the building of
our socialist state; many of them suffered and fought for
Party interests during the pre-revolutionary years in the
conspiracy and at the Civil War fronts; they fought their
enemies valiantly and often nervelessly looked into the
face of death. How then can we believe that such people
could prove to be "two-faced" and had joined the camps
of the enemies of socialism during the era after the political liquidation of Zinovievites, Trotskyites and rightists
and after the great accomplishments of socialist construction?

This was the result of the abuse of power by Stalin, who
began to use mass terror against the Party cadres.

What is the reason that mass repressions against activists
increased more and more after the XVIIth Party Congress?
It was because at that time Stalin had so elevated himself
above the Party and above the nation that he ceased to
consider either the Central Committee or the Party. While
he still reckoned with the opinion of the collective before
the XVIIth Congress, after the complete political liquidation of the Trotskyites, Zinovievites and Bukharinites,
when as a result of that fight and socialist victories the
Party achieved unity, Stalin ceased to an ever greater
degree to consider the members of the Party's Central Committee and even the members of the Political Bureau.
Stalin thought that now he could decide all things alone
and all he needed were statisticians; he treated all others
in such a way that they could only listen to and praise him.

After the criminal murder of S. M. Kirov, mass repressions and brutal acts of violation of socialist legality began.

On the evening of December 1, 1934, on Stalin's initiative (without the approval of the Political Bureau—which was passed two days later, casually) the secretary of the Presidium of the Central Executive Committee, Yenukidze, signed the following directive.

I. Investigative agencies are directed to speed up the cases of those accused of the preparation or execution of acts of terror.

II. Judicial organs are directed not to hold up the execution of death sentences pertaining to crimes of this category in order to consider the possibility of pardon, because the Presidium of the Central Executive Committee [of the] USSR does not consider as possible the receiving of petitions of this sort.

III. The organs of the Commissariat of Internal Affairs [NKVD] are directed to execute death sentences against criminals of the above-mentioned category immediately after the passage of sentences.

This directive became the basis for mass acts of abuse against socialist legality. During many of the fabricated court cases the accused were charged with "the preparation" of terroristic acts; this deprived them of any possibility that their cases might be re-examined, even when they stated before the court that their "confessions" were secured by force, and when, in a convincing manner, they disproved the accusations against them.

It must be asserted that to this day the circumstances surrounding Kirov's murder hide many things which are inexplicable and mysterious and demand a most careful examination. There are reasons for the suspicion that the killer of Kirov, Nikolayev, was assisted by someone from among the people whose duty it was to protect the person

of Kirov. A month and a half before the killing, Nikolayev was arrested on the grounds of suspicious behavior,
but he was released and not even searched. It is an unusually suspicious circumstance that when the Chekist
assigned to protect Kirov was being brought for an interrogation, on December 2, 1934, he was killed in a car
"accident" in which no other occupants of the car were
harmed. After the murder of Kirov, top functionaries of
the Leningrad NKVD were given very light sentences, but
in 1937 they were shot. We can assume that they were
shot in order to cover the traces of the organizers of Kirov's
killing. (*Movement in the hall.*)

Mass repressions grew tremendously from the end of
1936 after a telegram from Stalin and Zhdanov, dated
from Sochi on September 25, 1936, was addressed to
Kaganovich, Molotov and other members of the Political
Bureau. The content of the telegram was as follows:

"We deem it absolutely necessary and urgent that Comrade Yezhov be nominated to the post of People's Commissar for Internal Affairs. Yagoda has definitely proved
himself to be incapable of unmasking the Trotskyite-Zinovievite bloc. The OGPU is 4 years behind in this matter.
This is noted by all Party workers and by the majority of
the representatives of the NKVD." Strictly speaking we
should stress that Stalin did not meet with and therefore
could not know the opinion of party workers.

This Stalinist formulation that the "NKVD is 4 years
behind" in applying mass repression and that there is a
necessity for "catching up" with the neglected work
directly pushed the NKVD workers on the path of mass
arrests and executions.

We should state that this formulation was also forced on the February-March plenary session of the Central Committee of the All-Union Communist Party (Bolsheviks) in 1937. The plenary resolution approved it on the basis of Yezhov's report, "Lessons flowing from the harmful activity, diversion and espionage of the Japanese-German-Trotskyite agents," stating:

The Plenum of the Central Committee of the All-Union Communist Party (Bolsheviks) considers that all facts revealed during the investigation into the matter of an anti-Soviet Trotskyite center and of its followers in the provinces show that the People's Commissariat of Internal Affairs has fallen behind at least 4 years in the attempt to unmask these most inexorable enemies of the people.

The mass repressions at this time were made under the slogan of a fight against the Trotskyites. Did the Trotskyites at this time actually constitute such a danger to our Party and to the Soviet state? We should recall that in 1927 on the eve of the XVth Party Congress only some 4,000 votes were cast for the Trotskyite-Zinovievite opposition, while there were 724,000 for the Party line. During the 10 years which passed between the XVth Party Congress and the February-March Central Committee Plenum Trotskyism was completely disarmed; many former Trotskyites had changed their former views and worked in the various sectors building socialism. It is clear that in the situation of socialist victory there was no basis for mass terror in the country.

Stalin's report at the February-March Central Committee Plenum in 1937, "Deficiencies of Party work and methods for the liquidation of the Trotskyites and of other

two-facers," contained an attempt at theoretical justification of the mass terror policy under the pretext that as we
march forward toward socialism, class war must allegedly
sharpen. Stalin asserted that both history and Lenin
taught him this.

Actually Lenin taught that the application of revolutionary violence is necessitated by the resistance of the exploiting classes, and this referred to the era when the exploiting
classes existed and were powerful. As soon as the nation's
political situation had improved, when in January 1920
the Red Army took Rostov and thus won a most important
victory over Denikin, Lenin instructed Dzerzhinsky to stop
mass terror and to abolish the death penalty. Lenin justified this important political move of the Soviet state in
the following manner in his report at the session of the
All-Union Central Executive Committee on February 2,
1920:

> We were forced to use terror because of the terror practiced
> by the Entente, when strong world powers threw their hordes
> against us, not avoiding any type of combat. We would not
> have lasted two days had we not answered these attempts of
> officers and White Guardists in a merciless fashion; this meant
> the use of terror, but this was forced upon us by the terrorist
> methods of the Entente.
>
> But as soon as we attained a decisive victory, even before the
> end of the war, immediately after taking Rostov, we gave up the
> use of the death penalty and thus proved that we intend to
> execute our own program in the manner that we promised. We
> say that the application of violence flows out of the decision to
> smother the exploiters, the big landowners and the capitalists; as
> soon as this was accomplished we gave up the use of all extraordi-
> nary methods. We have proved this in practice.

Stalin deviated from these clear and plain precepts of Lenin. Stalin put the Party and the NKVD up to the use of mass terror when the exploiting classes had been liquidated in our country and when there were no serious reasons for the use of extraordinary mass terror.

This terror was actually directed not at the remnants of the defeated exploiting classes but against the honest workers of the Party and of the Soviet state; against them were made lying, slanderous and absurd accusations concerning "two-facedness," "espionage," "sabotage," preparation of fictitious "plots," etc.

At the February-March Central Committee Plenum in 1937 many members actually questioned the rightness of the established course regarding mass repressions under the pretext of combating "two-facedness."

Comrade Postyshev most ably expressed these doubts. He said:

I have philosophized that the severe years of fighting have passed; Party members who have lost their backbones have broken down or have joined the camp of the enemy; healthy elements have fought for the Party. These were the years of industrialization and collectivization. I never thought it possible that after this severe era had passed Karpov and people like him would find themselves in the camp of the enemy. (Karpov was a worker in the Ukrainian Central Committee whom Postyshev knew well.) And now, according to the testimony, it appears that Karpov was recruited in 1934 by the Trotskyites. I personally do not believe that in 1934 an honest Party member who had trod the long road of unrelenting fight against enemies, for the Party and for Socialism, would now be in the camp of the enemies. I do not believe it . . . I cannot imagine how it would be possible to travel with the Party during the difficult years and then, in 1934, join the Trotskyites. It is an odd thing. . . .

(*Movement in the hall.*)

Using Stalin's formulation, namely that the closer we
are to socialism, the more enemies we will have, and using
the resolution of the February-March Central Committee
Plenum passed on the basis of Yezhov's report—the
provocateurs who had infiltrated the state security organs
together with conscienceless careerists began to protect
with the Party name the mass terror against Party cadres,
cadres of the Soviet state and the ordinary Soviet citizens.
It should suffice to say that the number of arrests based
on charges of counter-revolutionary crimes had grown ten
times between 1936 and 1937.

It is known that brutal willfulness was practiced against
leading Party workers. The Party Statute, approved at
the XVIIth Party Congress, was based on Leninist principles expressed at the Xth Party Congress. It stated that
in order to apply an extreme method such as exclusion
from the Party against a Central Committee member,
against a Central Committee candidate, and against a
member of the Party Control Commission, "it is necessary to call a Central Committee Plenum and to invite
to the Plenum all Central Committee candidate members
and all members of the Party Control Commission"; only
if two thirds of the members of such a general assembly
of responsible Party leaders find it necessary, only then
can a Central Committee member or candidate be expelled.

The majority of the Central Committee members and
candidates elected at the XVIIth Congress and arrested in
1937-1938 were expelled from the Party illegally through
the brutal abuse of the Party Statute, because the question of their expulsion was never studied at the Central
Committee Plenum.

Now when the cases of some of these so-called "spies" and "saboteurs" were examined it was found that all their cases were fabricated. Confessions of guilt of many arrested and charged with enemy activity were gained with the help of cruel and inhuman tortures.

At the same time Stalin, as we have been informed by members of the Political Bureau of that time, did not show them the statements of many accused political activists when they retracted their confessions before the military tribunal and asked for an objective examination of their cases. There were many such declarations, and Stalin doubtlessly knew of them.

The Central Committee considers it absolutely necessary to inform the Congress of many such fabricated "cases" against the members of the Party's Central Committee elected at the XVIIth Party Congress.

An example of vile provocation, of odious falsification and of criminal violation of revolutionary legality is the case of the former candidate for the Central Committee Political Bureau, one of the most eminent workers of the Party and of the Soviet government, Comrade Eikhe, who was a Party member since 1905. *(Commotion in the hall.)*

Comrade Eikhe was arrested on April 29, 1938 on the basis of slanderous materials, without the sanction of the Prosecutor of the USSR, which was finally received 15 months after the arrest.

Investigation of Eikhe's case was made in a manner which most brutally violated Soviet legality and was accompanied by willfulness and falsification.

Eikhe was forced under torture to sign ahead of time a protocol of his confession prepared by the investigative judges, in which he and several other eminent Party workers were accused of anti-Soviet activity.

On October 1, 1939, Eikhe sent his declaration to Stalin in which he categorically denied his guilt and asked for an examination of his case. In the declaration he wrote:

There is no more bitter misery than to sit in the jail of a government for which I have always fought.

A second declaration of Eikhe has been preserved which he sent to Stalin on October 27, 1939; in it he cited facts very convincingly and countered the slanderous accusations made against him, arguing that this provocatory accusation was on the one hand the work of real Trotskyites whose arrests he had sanctioned as First Secretary of the West Siberian Krai Party Committee and who conspired in order to take revenge on him, and, on the other hand, the result of the base falsification of materials by the investigative judges.

Eikhe wrote in his declaration:

. . . . On October 25 of this year I was informed that the investigation in my case has been concluded and I was given access to the materials of this investigation. Had I been guilty of only one hundredth of the crimes with which I am charged, I would not have dared to send you this pre-execution declaration; however, I have not been guilty of even one of the things with which I am charged and my heart is clean of even the shadow of baseness. I have never in my life told you a word of falsehood and now, finding my two feet in the grave, I am also not lying. My whole case is a typical example of provocation, slander and violation of the elementary basis of revolutionary legality. . . .

. . . . The confessions which were made part of my file are not only absurd but contain some slander toward the Central Committee of the All-Union Communist Party (Bolsheviks) and toward the Council of People's Commissars because correct resolutions of the Central Committee of the All-Union Communist Party (Bolsheviks) and of the Council of People's Commissars which were not made on my initiative and without my participation are presented as hostile acts of counter-revolutionary organizations made at my suggestion. . . .

I am now alluding to the most disgraceful part of my life and to my really grave guilt against the Party and against you. This is my confession of counter-revolutionary activity. . . . The case is as follows: not being able to suffer the tortures to which I was submitted by Ushakov and Nikolayev—and especially by the first one—who utilized the knowledge that my broken ribs have not properly mended and have caused me great pain—I have been forced to accuse myself and others.

The majority of my confession has been suggested or dictated by Ushakov, and the remainder is my reconstruction of NKVD materials from western Siberia for which I assumed all responsibility. If some part of the story which Ushakov fabricated and which I signed did not properly hang together, I was forced to sign another variation. The same thing was done to Rukhimovich, who was at first designated as a member of the reserve net and whose name later was removed without telling me anything about it; the same was also done with the leader of the reserve net, supposedly created by Bukharin in 1935. At first I wrote my name in, and then I was instructed to insert Mezhlauk. There were other similar incidents.

. . . I am asking and begging you that you again examine my case and this not for the purpose of sparing me but in order to unmask the vile provocation which like a snake wound itself around many persons in a great degree due to my meanness and criminal slander. I have never betrayed you or the Party. I know that I perish because of vile and mean work of the enemies of the Party and of the people, who fabricated the provocation against me.

It would appear that such an important declaration was worth an examination by the Central Committee. This, however, was not done and the declaration was transmitted

to Beria while the terrible maltreatment of the Political
Bureau candidate, Comrade Eikhe, continued.

On February 2, 1940 Eikhe was brought before the
court. Here he did not confess any guilt and said as follows:

In all the so-called confessions of mine there is not one letter
written by me with the exception of my signatures under the
protocols which were forced from me. I have made my confession under pressure from the investigative judge who from the
time of my arrest tormented me. After that I began to write
all this nonsense. . . . The most important thing for me is to tell
the court, the Party and Stalin that I am not guilty. I have never
been guilty of any conspiracy. I will die believing in the truth
of Party policy as I have believed in it during my whole life.

On February 4 Eikhe was shot. (*Indignation in the
hall.*) It has been definitely established now that Eikhe's
case was fabricated; he has been posthumously rehabilitated.

Comrade Rudzutak, candidate member of the Political
Bureau, member of the Party since 1905, who spent 10
years in a Tsarist hard labor camp, completely retracted
in court the confession which was forced from him. The
protocol of the session of the Collegium of the Supreme
Military Court contains the following statement by Rudzutak:

. . . . The only plea which he places before the court is that the
Central Committee of the All-Union Communist Party (Bolsheviks) be informed that there is in the NKVD an as yet not
liquidated center which is craftily manufacturing cases, which
forces innocent persons to confess; there is no opportunity to
prove one's nonparticipation in crimes to which the confessions
of various persons testify. The investigative methods are such

that they force people to lie and to slander entirely innocent persons in addition to those who already stand accused. He asks the Court that he be allowed to inform the Central Committee of the All-Union Communist Party (Bolsheviks) about all this in writing. He assures the Court that he personally had never any evil designs in regard to the policy of our Party because he had always agreed with the Party policy pertaining to all spheres of economic and cultural activity.

This declaration of Rudzutak was ignored, despite the fact that Rudzutak was in his time the chief of the Central Control Commission which was called into being in accordance with Lenin's concept for the purpose of fighting for Party unity. . . . In this manner fell the chief of this highly authoritative Party organ, a victim of brutal willfulness: he was not even called before the Central Committee's Political Bureau because Stalin did not want to talk to him. Sentence was pronounced on him in 20 minutes and he was shot. (*Indignation in the hall.*)

After careful examination of the case in 1955 it was established that the accusation against Rudzutak was false and that it was based on slanderous materials. Rudzutak has been rehabilitated posthumously.

The way in which the former NKVD workers manufactured various fictitious "anti-Soviet centers" and "blocs" with the help of provocatory methods is seen from the confession of Comrade Rozenblum, Party member since 1906, who was arrested in 1937 by the Leningrad NKVD.

During the examination in 1955 of the Komarov case Rozenblum revealed the following fact: when Rozenblum was arrested in 1937 he was subjected to terrible torture during which he was ordered to confess false information

concerning himself and other persons. He was then
brought to the office of Zakovsky, who offered him freedom on condition that he make before the court a false
confession fabricated in 1937 by the NKVD concerning
"sabotage, espionage and diversion in a terroristic center
in Leningrad." (*Movement in the hall.*) With unbelievable cynicism Zakovsky told about the vile "mechanism"
for the crafty creation of fabricated "anti-Soviet plots."

"In order to illustrate it to me," stated Rozenblum,

Zakovsky gave me several possible variants of the organization
of this center and of its branches. After he detailed the organization to me, Zakovsky told me that the NKVD would prepare the
case of this center, remarking that the trial would be public.

Before the court were to be brought 4 or 5 members of
this center: Chudov, Ugarov, Smorodin, Pozern, Shaposhnikova
(Chudov's wife) and others together with 2 or 3 members from
the branches of this center. . . .

. . . . The case of the Leningrad center has to be built solidly
and for this reason witnesses are needed. Social origin (of
course, in the past) and the Party standing of the witness will
play more than a small role.

"You, yourself," said Zakovsky,

will not need to invent anything. The NKVD will prepare for
you a ready outline for every branch of the center; you will have
to study it carefully and to remember well all questions and
answers which the Court might ask. This case will be ready in
4-5 months, or perhaps a half year. During all this time you
will be preparing yourself so that you will not compromise the
investigation and yourself. Your future will depend on how
the trial goes and on its results. If you begin to lie and to
testify falsely, blame yourself. If you manage to endure it,
you will save your head and we will feed and clothe you at the
government's cost until your death.

This is the kind of vile things which were then practiced. *(Movement in the hall.)*

Even more widely was the falsification of cases practiced in the provinces. The NKVD headquarters of the Sverdlov oblast "discovered" the so-called "Ural uprising staff"—an organ of the bloc of rightists, Trotskyites, Socialist Revolutionaries, church leaders—whose chief supposedly was the Secretary of the Sverdlov Oblast Party Committee and member of the Central Committee, All-Union Communist Party (Bolsheviks), Kabakov, who had been a Party member since 1914. The investigative materials of that time show that in almost all krais, oblasts and republics there supposedly existed "rightist Trotskyite, espionage-terror and diversionary-sabotage organizations and centers" and that the heads of such organizations as a rule—for no known reason—were first secretaries of oblast or republic Communist Party committees or Central Committees. *(Movement in the hall.)*

Many thousands of honest and innocent Communists have died as a result of this monstrous falsification of such "cases," as a result of the fact that all kinds of slanderous "confessions" were accepted, and as a result of the practice of forcing accusations against oneself and others. In the same manner were fabricated the "cases" against eminent Party and state workers— Kossior, Chubar, Postyshev, Kosarev, and others.

In those years repressions on a mass scale were applied which were based on nothing tangible and which resulted in heavy cadre losses to the Party.

The vicious practice was condoned of having the NKVD prepare lists of persons whose cases were under the juris-

diction of the Military Collegium and whose sentences
were prepared in advance. Yezhov would send these lists
to Stalin personally for his approval of the proposed
punishment. In 1937-1938, 383 such lists containing the
names of many thousands of Party, Soviet, Komsomol,
Army and economic workers were sent to Stalin. He
approved these lists.

A large part of these cases are being reviewed now and
a great part of them are being voided because they were
baseless and falsified. Suffice it to say that from 1954
to the present time the Military Collegium of the Supreme
Court has rehabilitated 7,679 persons, many of whom
were rehabilitated posthumously.

Mass arrests of Party, Soviet, economic and military
workers caused tremendous harm to our country and to
the cause of socialist advancement.

Mass repressions had a negative influence on the moral-
political condition of the Party, created a situation of
uncertainty, contributed to the spreading of unhealthy
suspicion, and sowed distrust among Communists. All
sorts of slanderers and careerists were active.

Resolutions of the January Plenum of the Central Committee, All-Union Communist Party (Bolsheviks), in 1938
had brought some measure of improvement to the Party
organizations. However, widespread repression also
existed in 1938.

Only because our Party has at its disposal such great
moral-political strength was it possible for it to survive
the difficult events in 1937-1938 and to educate new
cadres. There is, however, no doubt that our march
forward toward socialism and toward the preparation of

the country's defense would have been much more successful were it not for the tremendous loss in the cadres suffered as a result of the baseless and false mass repressions in 1937-1938.

We are justly accusing Yezhov for the degenerate practices of 1937. But we have to answer these questions: Could Yezhov have arrested Kossior, for instance, without the knowledge of Stalin? Was there an exchange of opinions or a Political Bureau decision concerning this? No, there was not, as there was none regarding other cases of this type. Could Yezhov have decided such important matters as the fate of such eminent Party figures? No, it would be a display of naivete to consider this the work of Yezhov alone. It is clear that these matters were decided by Stalin, and that without his orders and his sanction Yezhov could not have done this.

We have examined the cases and have rehabilitated Kossior, Rudzutak, Postyshev, Kosarev and others. For what causes were they arrested and sentenced? The review of evidence shows that there was no reason for this. They, like many others, were arrested without the Prosecutor's knowledge. In such a situation there is no need for any sanction, for what sort of a sanction could there be when Stalin decided everything. He was the chief prosecutor in these cases. Stalin not only agreed to, but on his own intiative issued, arrest orders. We must say this so that the delegates to the Congress can clearly undertake and themselves assess this and draw the proper conclusions.

Facts prove that many abuses were made on Stalin's orders without reckoning with any norms of Party and

Soviet legality. Stalin was a very distrustful man, sickly suspicious; we knew this from our work with him. He could look at a man and say: "Why are your eyes so shifty today," or "Why are you turning so much today and avoiding to look me directly in the eyes?" The sickly suspicion created in him a general distrust even toward eminent Party workers whom he had known for years. Everywhere and in everything he saw "enemies," "two-facers" and "spies."

Possessing unlimited power he indulged in great willfulness and choked a person morally and physically. A situation was created where one could not express one's own will.

When Stalin said that one or another should be arrested, it was necessary to accept on faith that he was an "enemy of the people." Meanwhile, Beria's gang, which ran the organs of state security, outdid itself in proving the guilt of the arrested and the truth of materials which it falsified. And what proofs were offered? The confessions of the arrested, and the investigative judges accepted these "confessions." And how is it possible that a person confesses to crimes which he has not committed? Only in one way —because of application of physical methods of pressuring him, tortures, bringing him to a state of unconsciousness, deprivation of his judgment, taking away of his human dignity. In this manner were "confessions" acquired.

When the wave of mass arrests began to recede in 1939, and the leaders of territorial Party organizations began to accuse the NKVD workers of using methods of physical

pressure on the arrested, Stalin dispatched a coded telegram on January 20, 1939 to the committee secretaries of
oblasts and krais, to the Central Committees of republic
Communist Parties, to the Peoples Commissars of Internal
Affairs and to the heads of NKVD organizations. This
telegram stated:

The Central Committee of the All-Union Communist Party (Bolsheviks) explains that the application of methods of physical
pressure in NKVD practice is permissible from 1937 on in
accordance with permission of the Central Committee of the All-
Union Communist Party (Bolsheviks). . . . It is known that all
bourgeois intelligence services use methods of physical influence
against the representatives of the socialist proletariat and that
they use them in their most scandalous form. The question arises
as to why the socialist intelligence service should be more humani-
tarian against the mad agents of the bourgeoisie, against the
deadly enemies of the working class and the kolkhoz workers.
The Central Committee of the All-Union Communist Party (Bolsheviks) considers that physical pressure should still be used
obligatorily, as an exception applicable to known and obstinate
enemies of the people, as a method both justifiable and appropriate.

Thus, Stalin had sanctioned in the name of the Central
Committee of the All-Union Communist Party (Bolsheviks)
the most brutal violation of socialist legality, torture and
oppression, which led as we have seen to the slandering and
self-accusation of innocent people.

Not long ago—only several days before the present Congress—we called to the Central Committee Presidium session and interrogated the investigative judge Rodos, who
in his time investigated and interrogated Kossior, Chubar
and Kosarev. He is a vile person, with the brain of a bird,
and morally completely degenerate. And it was this man

who was deciding the fate of prominent Party workers; he
was making judgments also concerning the politics in these
matters, because having established their "crime," he provided therewith materials from which important political
implications could be drawn.

The question arises whether a man with such an intellect
could alone make the investigation in a manner to prove
the guilt of people such as Kossior and others. No, he
could not have done it without proper directives. At the
Central Committee Presidium session he told us: "I was
told that Kossior and Chubar were people's enemies and
for this reason, I, as an investigative judge, had to make
them confess that they are enemies." (*Indignation in the
hall.*)

He could do this only through long tortures, which he
did, receiving detailed instructions from Beria. We must
say that at the Central Committee Presidium session he
cynically declared: "I thought that I was executing the
orders of the Party." In this manner Stalin's orders concerning the use of methods of physical pressure against
the arrested were in practice executed.

These and many other facts show that all norms of correct Party solution of problems were invalidated and
everything was dependent upon the willfulness of one man.

The power accumulated in the hands of one person,
Stalin, led to serious consequences during the Great Patriotic War.

When we look at many of our novels, films and historical
"scientific studies," the role of Stalin in the Patriotic War
appears to be entirely improbable. Stalin had foreseen

everything. The Soviet Army, on the basis of a strategic plan prepared by Stalin long before, used the tactics of so-called "active defense," i.e., tactics which, as we know, allowed the Germans to come up to Moscow and Stalingrad. Using such tactics the Soviet Army, supposedly, thanks only to Stalin's genius, turned to the offensive and subdued the enemy. The epic victory gained through the armed might of the Land of the Soviets, through our heroic people, is ascribed in this type of novel, film and "scientific study" as being completely due to the strategic genius of Stalin.

We have to analyze this matter carefully because it has a tremendous significance not only from the historical, but especially from the political, educational and practical point of view.

What are the facts of this matter?

Before the war our press and all our political-educational work was characterized by its bragging tone: when an enemy violates the holy Soviet soil, then for every blow of the enemy we will answer with three blows and we will battle the enemy on his soil and we will win without much harm to ourselves. But these positive statements were not based in all areas on concrete facts, which would actually guarantee the immunity of our borders.

During the war and after the war Stalin put forward the thesis that the tragedy which our nation experienced in the first part of the war was the result of the "unexpected" attack of the Germans against the Soviet Union. But, Comrades, this is completely untrue. As soon as Hitler came to power in Germany he assigned to himself the task of liquidating Communism. The Fascists were

saying this openly; they did not hide their plans. In
order to attain this aggressive end all sorts of pacts and
blocs were created, such as the famous Berlin-Rome-Tokyo
axis. Many facts from the pre-war period clearly showed
that Hitler was going all out to begin a war against the
Soviet state and that he had concentrated large armed
units, together with armored units, near the Soviet borders.

Documents which have now been published show that
by April 3, 1941, Churchill, through his ambassador to
the USSR, Cripps, personally warned Stalin that the
Germans had begun regrouping their armed units with
the intent of attacking the Soviet Union. It is self-evident
that Churchill did not do this at all because of his friendly
feeling toward the Soviet nation. He had in this his
own imperialistic goals—to bring Germany and the USSR
into a bloody war and thereby to strengthen the position
of the British Empire. Just the same, Churchill affirmed
in his writings that he sought to "warn Stalin and call
his attention to the danger which threatened him."
Churchill stressed this repeatedly in his dispatches of
April 18 and in the following days. However, Stalin
took no heed of these warnings. What is more, Stalin
ordered that no credence be given to information of this
sort, in order not to provoke the initiation of military
operations.

We must assert that information of this sort concerning
the threat of German armed invasion of Soviet territory
was coming in also from our own military and diplomatic
sources; however, because the leadership was conditioned
against such information, such data was dispatched with
fear and assessed with reservation.

Thus, for instance, information sent from Berlin on May 6, 1941, by the Soviet military attaché, Capt. Vorontsov, stated: "Soviet citizen Bozer . . . communicated to the deputy naval attaché that according to a statement of a certain German officer from Hitler's Headquarters, Germany is preparing to invade the USSR on May 14 through Finland, the Baltic countries and Latvia. At the same time Moscow and Leningrad will be heavily raided and paratroopers landed in border cities . . . ."

In his report of May 22, 1941, the deputy military attaché in Berlin, Khlopov, communicated that ". . . the attack of the German army is reportedly scheduled for June 15, but it is possible that it may begin in the first days of June . . . ."

A cable from our London Embassy dated June 18, 1941 stated: "As of now Cripps is deeply convinced of the inevitability of armed conflict between Germany and the USSR which will begin not later than the middle of June. According to Cripps, the Germans have presently concentrated 147 divisions (including air force and service units) along the Soviet borders. . . ."

Despite these particularly grave warnings, the necessary steps were not taken to prepare the country properly for defense and to prevent it from being caught unawares.

Did we have time and the capabilities for such preparations? Yes, we had the time and capabilities. Our industry was already so developed that it was capable of supplying fully the Soviet army with everything that it needed. This is proven by the fact that although during the war we lost almost half of our industry and important industrial and food production areas as the result of enemy occupation of the Ukraine, Northern Caucasus and other western parts of the country, the Soviet people was still able to organize the production of military equipment in the eastern parts of the country, install there equipment taken from the Western industrial areas, and to supply our armed forces with everything which was necessary to destroy the enemy.

Had our industry been mobilized properly and in time to supply the army with the necessary materiel, our wartime losses would have been decidedly smaller. Such mobilization had not been, however, started in time. And already in the first days of the war it became evident that our army was badly armed, that we did not have enough artillery, tanks and planes to throw the enemy back.

Soviet science and technology produced excellent models of tanks and artillery pieces before the war. But mass production of all this was not organized and as a matter of fact we started to modernize our military equipment only on the eve of the war. As a result, at the time of the enemy's invasion of the Soviet land we did not have sufficient quantities either of old machinery which was no longer used for armament production or of new machinery which we had planned to introduce into armament production. The situation with antiaircraft artillery was especially bad; we did not organize the production of anti-tank ammunition. Many fortified regions had proven to be indefensible as soon as they were attacked, because the old arms had been withdrawn and new ones were not yet available there.

This pertained, alas, not only to tanks, artillery and planes. At the outbreak of the war we did not even have sufficient numbers of rifles to arm the mobilized manpower. I recall that in those days I telephoned to Comrade Malenkov from Kiev and told him, "People have volunteered for the new army and demand arms. You must send us arms."

Malenkov answered me, "We cannot send you arms. We are sending all our rifles to Leningrad and you have to arm yourselves." (*Movement in the hall.*)

Such was the armament situation.

In this connection we cannot forget, for instance, the following fact. Shortly before the invasion of the Soviet Union by the Hitlerite army, Kirponos, who was Chief of the Kiev Special Military District (he was later killed at the front), wrote to Stalin that the German armies were at the Bug River, were preparing for an attack and in the very near future would probably start their offensive. In this connection Kirponos proposed that a strong defense be organized, that 300,000 people be evacuated from the border areas and that several strong points be organized there: anti-tank ditches, trenches for the soldiers, etc.

Moscow answered this proposition with the assertion that this would be a provocation, that no preparatory defensive work should be undertaken at the borders, that the Germans were not to be given any pretext for the initiation of military action against us. Thus, our borders were insufficiently prepared to repel the enemy.

When the Fascist armies had actually invaded Soviet territory and military operations began, Moscow issued the order that the German fire was not to be returned. Why? It was because Stalin, despite evident facts, thought

that the war had not yet started, that this was only a provocative action on the part of several undisciplined sections of the German army, and that our reaction might
serve as a reason for the Germans to begin the war.

The following fact is also known. On the eve of the
invasion of the territory of the Soviet Union by the Hitlerite army a certain German citizen crossed our border and
stated that the German armies had received orders to start
the offensive against the Soviet Union on the night of June
22, at 3 o'clock. Stalin was informed about this immediately, but even this warning was ignored.

As you see, everything was ignored: warnings of certain army commanders, declarations of deserters from the
enemy army, and even the open hostility of the enemy.
Is this an example of the alertness of the Chief of the
Party and of the state at this particularly significant historical moment?

And what were the results of this carefree attitude,
this disregard of clear facts? The result was that already
in the first hours and days the enemy had destroyed in
our border regions a large part of our air force, artillery
and other military equipment; he annihilated large numbers of our military cadres and disorganized our military
leadership; consequently we could not prevent the enemy
from marching deep into the country.

Very grievous consequences, especially in reference to
the beginning of the war, followed Stalin's annihilation
of many military commanders and political workers during 1937-1941 because of his suspiciousness and through
slanderous accusations. During these years repressions

were instituted against certain parts of military cadres beginning literally at the company and battalion commander level and extending to the higher military centers; during this time the cadre of leaders who had gained military experience in Spain and in the Far East was almost completely liquidated.

The policy of large-scale repression against the military cadres led also to undermined military discipline, because for several years officers of all ranks and even soldiers in the Party and Komsomol cells were taught to "unmask" their superiors as hidden enemies. *(Movement in the hall.)* It is natural that this caused a negative influence on the state of military discipline in the first war period.

And, as you know, we had before the war excellent military cadres which were unquestionably loyal to the Party and to the Fatherland. Suffice it to say that those of them who managed to survive despite severe tortures to which they were subjected in the prisons, have from the first war days shown themselves real patriots and heroically fought for the glory of the Fatherland; I have here in mind such comrades as Rokossovsky (who, as you know, had been jailed), Gorbatov, Meretskov (who is a delegate at the present Congress), Podlas (he was an excellent commander who perished at the front), and many, many others. However, many such commanders perished in camps and jails and the army saw them no more.

All this brought about the situation which existed at the beginning of the war and which was the great threat to our Fatherland.

It would be incorrect to forget that after the first severe disaster and defeats at the front, Stalin thought that this was the end. In one of his speeches in those days he said: "All that which Lenin created we have lost forever."

After this Stalin for a long time actually did not direct the military operations and ceased to do anything whatever. He returned to active leadership only when some members of the Political Bureau visited him and told him that it was necessary to take certain steps immediately in order to improve the situation at the front.

Therefore, the threatening danger which hung over our Fatherland in the first period of the war was largely due to the faulty methods of directing the nation and the Party by Stalin himself.

However, we speak not only about the moment when the war began, which led to serious disorganization of our army and brought us severe losses. Even after the war began, the nervousness and hysteria which Stalin demonstrated, interfering with actual military operations, caused our army serious damage.

Stalin was very far from an understanding of the real situation which was developing at the front. This was natural because during the whole Patriotic War he never visited any section of the front or any liberated city except for one short ride on the Mozhaisk Highway during a stabilized situation at the front. To this incident were dedicated many literary works full of fantasies of all sorts and so many paintings. Simultaneously, Stalin was interfering with operations and issuing orders which did not take into consideration the real situation at a given section of the front and which could not help but result in huge personnel losses.

I will allow myself in this connection to bring out one characteristic fact which illustrates how Stalin directed operations at the fronts. There is present at this Congress Marshal Bagramyan who was once the Chief of Operations in the Headquarters of the Southwestern front and who can corroborate what I will tell you.

When there developed an exceptionally serious situation for our army in 1942 in the Kharkov region, we had correctly decided to drop an operation whose objective was to encircle Kharkov, because the real situation at that time would have threatened our army with fatal consequences if this operation were continued.

We communicated this to Stalin, stating that the situation demanded changes in operational plans so that the enemy would be prevented from liquidating a sizable concentration of our army.

Contrary to common sense, Stalin rejected our suggestion and issued the order to continue the operation aimed at the encirclement of Kharkov, despite the fact that at this time many army concentrations were themselves actually threatened with encirclement and liquidation.

I telephoned to Vasilevsky and begged him,

"Alexander Mikhailovich, take a map (Vasilevsky is present here) and show Comrade Stalin the situation which has developed." We should note that Stalin planned operations on a globe. *(Animation in the hall.)* Yes, comrades, he used to take the globe and trace the front-line on it. I said to Comrade Vasilevsky: "Show him the situation on a map; in the present situation we can-

not continue the operation which was planned. The old
decision must be changed for the good of the cause."

Vasilevsky replied saying that Stalin had already
studied this problem and that he, Vasilevsky, would not
see Stalin further concerning this matter, because the
latter didn't want to hear any arguments on the subject
of this operation.

After my talk with Vasilevsky I telephoned to Stalin
at his villa. But Stalin did not answer the telephone
and Malenkov was at the receiver. I told Comrade
Malenkov that I was calling from the front and that I
wanted to speak personally to Stalin. Stalin informed
me through Malenkov that I should speak with Malenkov.
I stated for the second time that I wished to inform Stalin
personally about the grave situation which had arisen for
us at the front. But Stalin did not consider it convenient
to raise the phone and again stated that I should speak
to him through Malenkov, although he was only a few
steps from the telephone.

After "listening" in this manner to our plea Stalin said,
"Let everything remain as it is!"

And what was the result of this? The worst that we
had expected. The Germans surrounded our army concentrations and consequently we lost hundreds of thousands of our soldiers. This is Stalin's military "genius";
this is what it cost us. *(Movement in the hall.)*

On one occasion after the war, during a meeting of
Stalin with members of the Political Bureau, Anastas
Ivanovich Mikoyan mentioned that Khrushchev must have
been right when he telephoned concerning the Kharkov
operation and that it was unfortunate that his suggestion
had not been accepted.

You should have seen Stalin's fury! How could it be admitted that he, Stalin, had not been right! He is after all a "genius," and a genius cannot help but be right! Everyone can err, but Stalin considered that he never erred, that he was always right. He never acknowledged to anyone that he made any mistake, large or small, despite the fact that he made not a few mistakes in the matter of theory and in his practical activity. After the Party Congress we shall probably have to re-evaluate many wartime military operations and to present them in their true light.

The tactics on which Stalin insisted without knowing the essence of the conduct of battle operations cost us much blood until we succeeded in stopping the opponent and going over to the offensive.

The military know that already by the end of 1941 instead of great operational maneuvers flanking the opponent and penetrating behind his back, Stalin demanded incessant frontal attacks and the capture of one village after another. Because of this we paid with great losses until our generals, on whose shoulders rested the whole weight of conducting the war, succeeded in changing the situation and shifting to flexible maneuver operations, which immediately brought serious changes at the front favorable to us.

All the more shameful was the fact that after our great victory over the enemy which cost us so much, Stalin began to downgrade many of the commanders who contributed so much to the victory over the enemy, because Stalin excluded every possibility that services rendered at the front should be credited to anyone but himself.

Stalin was very much interested in the assessment of Comrade Zhukov as a military leader. He asked me often for my opinion of Zhukov. I told him then, "I have known Zhukov for a long time; he is a good general and a good military leader."

After the war Stalin began to tell all kinds of nonsense about Zhukov, among others the following, "You praised Zhukov, but he does not deserve it. It is said that before each operation at the front Zhukov used to behave as follows: he used to take a handful of earth, smell it and say, 'We can begin the attack,' or the opposite, 'The planned operation cannot be carried out.' " I stated at that time, "Comrade Stalin, I do not know who invented this, but it is not true."

It is possible that Stalin himself invented these things for the purpose of minimizing the role and military talents of Marshal Zhukov.

In this connection Stalin very energetically popularized himself as a great leader; in various ways he tried to inculcate in the people the version that all victories gained by the Soviet nation during the Great Patriotic War were due to the courage, daring and genius of Stalin and to no one else. Exactly like Kuzma Kryuchkov* he put one dress on 7 people at the same time. (*Animation in the hall.*)

In the same vein, let us take, for instance, our historical and military films and some literary creations; they make us feel sick. Their true objective is the propagation of the theme of praising Stalin as a military genius. Let us recall the film, "The Fall of Berlin." Here only Stalin

* A famous Cossack who performed heroic feats against the Germans (Translator's comment).

rders in the hall in which there are many
d only one man approaches him and
...ething to him—that is Poskrebyshev, his loyal
...ield-bearer. *(Laughter in the hall.)*

And where is the military command? Where is the Political Bureau? Where is the Government? What are they doing and with what are they engaged? There is nothing about them in the film. Stalin acts for everybody; he does not reckon with anyone; he asks no one for advice. Everything is shown to the nation in this false light. Why? In order to surround Stalin with glory, contrary to the facts and contrary to historical truth.

The question arises: And where are the military on whose shoulders rested the burden of the war? They are not in the film; with Stalin in, no room was left for them.

Not Stalin, but the Party as a whole, the Soviet Government, our heroic army, its talented leaders and brave soldiers, the whole Soviet nation—these are the ones who assured the victory in the Great Patriotic War. *(Tempestuous and prolonged applause.)*

The Central Committee members, ministers, our economic leaders, leaders of Soviet culture, directors of territorial Party and Soviet organizations, engineers, and technicians—every one of them in his own place of work generously gave of his strength and knowledge toward ensuring victory over the enemy.

Exceptional heroism was shown by our hard core—surrounded by glory is our whole working class, our kolkhoz peasantry, the Soviet intelligentsia, who under the leadership of Party organizations overcame untold

hardships and, bearing the hardships of war, devoted a
their strength to the cause of the defense of the Fatherland.

Great and brave deeds during the war were accomplished by our Soviet women who bore on their backs the
heavy load of production work in the factories, on the
kolkhozes, and in various economic and cultural sectors;
many women participated directly in the Great Patriotic
War at the fronts; our brave youth contributed immeasurably at the front and at home to the defense of the Soviet
Fatherland and to the annihilation of the enemy.

Immortal are the services of the Soviet soldiers, of our
commanders and political workers of all ranks; after the
loss of a considerable part of the army in the first war
months they did not lose their heads and were able to
reorganize during the progress of combat; they created
and toughened during the progress of the war a strong
and heroic army and not only stood off pressure of the
strong and cunning enemy but also smashed him.

The magnificent and heroic deeds of hundreds of millions of people of the East and of the West during the
fight against the threat of Fascist subjugation which loomed
before us will live centuries and millenia in the memory
of thankful humanity. *(Thunderous applause.)*

The main role and the main credit for the victorious
ending of the war belongs to our Communist Party, to the
armed forces of the Soviet Union, and to the tens of millions of Soviet people raised by the Party. *(Thunderous
and prolonged applause.)*

Comrades, let us reach for some other facts. The Soviet
Union is justly considered as a model of a multi-national
state because we have in practice assured the equality

and friendship of all nations which live in our great Fatherland.

All the more monstrous are the acts whose initiator was Stalin and which are rude violations of the basic Leninist principles of the nationality policy of the Soviet state. We refer to the mass deportations from their native places of whole nations, together with all Communists and Komsomols without any exception; this deportation action was not dictated by any military considerations.

Thus, already at the end of 1943, when there occurred a permanent breakthrough at the fronts of the Great Patriotic War benefiting the Soviet Union, a decision was taken and executed concerning the deportation of all the Karachai from the lands on which they lived. In the same period, at the end of December 1943, the same lot befell the whole population of the Autonomous Kalmyk Republic. In March 1944 all the Chechen and Ingush peoples were deported and the Chechen-Ingush Autonomous Republic was liquidated. In April 1944, all Balkars were deported to faraway places from the territory of the Kabardino-Balkar Autonomous Republic and the Republic itself was renamed the Autonomous Kabardin Republic. The Ukrainians avoided meeting this fate only because there were too many of them and there was no place to which to deport them. Otherwise, he would have deported them also. *(Laughter and animation in the hall.)*

Not only a Marxist-Leninist but also no man of common sense can grasp how it is possible to make whole nations responsible for inimical activity, including women, children, old people, Communists and Komsomols, to use mass repression against them, and to expose them to misery

and suffering for the hostile acts of individual persons
or groups of persons.

After the conclusion of the Patriotic War the Soviet
nation stressed with pride the magnificent victories gained
through great sacrifices and tremendous efforts. The country experienced a period of political enthusiasm. The
Party came out of the war even more united; in the fire of
the war Party cadres were tempered and hardened. Under
such conditions nobody could have even thought of the
possibility of some plot in the Party.

And it was precisely at this time that the so-called "Leningrad Affair" was born. As we have now proven, this
case was fabricated. Those who innocently lost their lives
included Comrades Voznesensky, Kuznetsov, Rodionov,
Popkov, and others.

As is known, Voznesensky and Kuznetsov were talented
and eminent leaders. Once they stood very close to Stalin.
It is sufficient to mention that Stalin made Voznesensky first
deputy to the Chairman of the Council of Ministers and
Kuznetsov was elected Secretary of the Central Committee.
The very fact that Stalin entrusted Kuznetsov with the
supervision of the state security organs shows the trust
which he enjoyed.

How did it happen that these persons were branded as
enemies of the people and liquidated?

Facts prove that the "Leningrad Affair" is also the result
of willfulness which Stalin exercised against Party cadres.

Had a normal situation existed in the Party's Central
Committee and in the Central Committee Political Bureau,
affairs of this nature would have been examined there in
accordance with Party practice, and all pertinent facts

assessed; as a result such an affair as well as others would not have happened.

We must state that after the war the situation became even more complicated. Stalin became even more capricious, irritable and brutal; in particular his suspicion grew. His persecution mania reached unbelievable dimensions. Many workers were becoming enemies before his very eyes. After the war Stalin separated himself from the collective even more. Everything was decided by him alone without any consideration for anyone or anything.

This unbelievable suspicion was cleverly taken advantage of by the abject provocateur and vile enemy, Beria, who had murdered thousands of Communists and loyal Soviet people. The elevation of Voznesensky and Kuznetsov alarmed Beria. As we have now proven, it had been precisely Beria who had "suggested" to Stalin the fabrication by him and by his confidants of materials in the form of declarations and anonymous letters, and in the form of various rumors and talks.

The Party's Central Committee has examined this so-called "Leningrad Affair"; persons who innocently suffered are now rehabilitated and honor has been restored to the glorious Leningrad Party organization. Abakumov and others who had fabricated this affair were brought before a court; their trial took place in Leningrad and they received what they deserved.

The question arises: Why is it that we see the truth of this affair only now, and why did we not do something earlier, during Stalin's life, in order to prevent the loss of innocent lives? It was because Stalin personally supervised the "Leningrad Affair," and the majority of the

Political Bureau members did not, at that time, know all of the circumstances in these matters, and could not therefore intervene.

When Stalin received certain materials from Beria and Abakumov, without examining these slanderous materials, he ordered an investigation of the "Affair" of Voznesensky and Kuznetsov. With this their fate was sealed. Instructive in the same way is the case of the Mingrelian nationalist organization which supposedly existed in Georgia. As is known, resolutions by the Central Committee [of the] Communist Party of the Soviet Union, were made concerning this case in November 1951 and in March 1952. These resolutions were made without prior discussion with the Political Bureau. Stalin had personally dictated them. They made serious accusations against many loyal Communists. On the basis of falsified documents it was proven that there existed in Georgia a supposedly nationalistic organization whose objective was the liquidation of the Soviet power in that Republic with the help of imperialist powers.

In this connection, a number of responsible Party and Soviet workers were arrested in Georgia. As was later proven, this was a slander directed against the Georgian Party Organization.

We know that there have been at times manifestations of local bourgeois nationalism in Georgia as in several other republics. The question arises: Could it be possible that in the period during which the resolutions referred to above were made, nationalist tendencies grew so much that there was a danger of Georgia's leaving the Soviet Union and joining Turkey? (*Animation in the hall, laughter.*)

This is, of course, nonsense. It is impossible to imagine how such assumptions could enter anyone's mind. Everyone knows how Georgia has developed economically and culturally under Soviet rule.

Industrial production of the Georgian Republic is 27 times greater than it was before the revolution. Many new industries have arisen in Georgia which did not exist there before the revolution: iron smelting, an oil industry, a machine construction industry, etc. Illiteracy has long since been liquidated, which, in pre-revolutionary Georgia, included 78 percent of the population.

Could the Georgians, comparing the situation in their Republic with the hard situation of the working masses in Turkey, be aspiring to join Turkey? In 1955 Georgia produced 18 times as much steel per person as Turkey. Georgia produces 9 times as much electrical energy per person as Turkey. According to the available 1950 census, 65 percent of Turkey's total population are illiterate, and of the women, 80 percent are illiterate. Georgia has 19 institutions of higher learning which have about 39,000 students; this is 8 times more than in Turkey (for each 1,000 inhabitants). The prosperity of the working people has grown tremendously in Georgia under Soviet rule.

It is clear that as the economy and culture develop, and as the socialist consciousness of the working masses in Georgia grows, the source from which bourgeois nationalism draws its strength evaporates.

As it developed, there was no nationalistic organization in Georgia. Thousands of innocent people fell victim of willfulness and lawlessness. All of this happened under

the "genial" leadership of Stalin, "the great son of the
Georgian nation," as Georgians liked to refer to Stalin.
(*Animation in the hall.*)

The willfulness of Stalin showed itself not only in
decisions concerning the internal life of the country but
also in the international relations of the Soviet Union.

The July Plenum of the Central Committee studied in
detail the reasons for the development of conflict with
Yugoslavia. It was a shameful role which Stalin played
here. The "Yugoslav Affair" contained no problems which
could not have been solved through Party discussions
among comrades. There was no significant basis for the
development of this "affair"; it was completely possible
to have prevented the rupture of relations with that
country. This does not mean, however, that the Yugoslav
leaders did not make mistakes or did not have shortcomings. But these mistakes and shortcomings were magnified
in a monstrous manner by Stalin, which resulted in a
break of relations with a friendly country.

I recall the first days when the conflict between the
Soviet Union and Yugoslavia began artificially to be
blown up. Once, when I came from Kiev to Moscow, I
was invited to visit Stalin who, pointing to the copy of a
letter lately sent to Tito, asked me, "Have you read this?"
Not waiting for my reply he answered, "I will shake my
little finger—and there will be no more Tito. He will fall."

We have dearly paid for this "shaking of the little
finger." This statement reflected Stalin's mania for greatness, but he acted just that way: "I will shake my little
finger—and there will be no Kossior"; "I will shake my
little finger once more and Postyshev and Chubar will be

no more"; "I will shake my little finger again—and Voznesensky, Kuznetsov and many others will disappear."

But this did not happen to Tito. No matter how much or how little Stalin shook, not only his little finger but everything else that he could shake, Tito did not fall. Why? The reason was that, in this case of disagreement with the Yugoslav comrades, Tito had behind him a state and a people who had gone through a severe school of fighting for liberty and independence, a people which gave support to its leaders.

You see to what Stalin's mania for greatness led. He had completely lost consciousness of reality; he demonstrated his suspicion and haughtiness not only in relation to individuals in the USSR, but in relation to whole parties and nations.

We have carefully examined the case of Yugoslavia and have found a proper solution which is approved by the peoples of the Soviet Union and of Yugoslavia as well as by the working masses of all the People's Democracies and by all progressive humanity. The liquidation of the abnormal relationship with Yugoslavia was done in the interest of the whole camp of socialism, in the interest of strengthening peace in the whole world.

Let us also recall the "Affair of the Doctor-Plotters." *(Animation in the hall.)* Actually there was no "Affair" outside of the declaration of the woman doctor Timashuk, who was probably influenced or ordered by someone (after all, she was an unofficial collaborator of the organs of state security) to write Stalin a letter in which she declared that doctors were applying supposedly improper methods of medical treatment.

Such a letter was sufficient for Stalin to reach an
immediate conclusion that there were doctor-plotters in the
Soviet Union. He issued orders to arrest a group of
eminent Soviet medical specialists. He personally issued
advice on the conduct of the investigation and the method
of interrogation of the arrested persons. He said that the
academician Vinogradov should be put in chains, another
one should be beaten. Present at this Congress as a delegate is the former Minister of State Security, Comrade
Ignatiev. Stalin told him curtly, "If you do not obtain
confessions from the doctors we will shorten you by a
head." *(Tumult in the hall.)*

Stalin personally called the investigative judge, gave
him instructions, advised him on which investigative
methods should be used; these methods were simple—beat,
beat and, once again, beat.

Shortly after the doctors were arrested we members of
the Political Bureau received protocols with the doctors'
confessions of guilt. After distributing these protocols
Stalin told us, "You are blind like young kittens; what will
happen without me? The country will perish because you
do not know how to recognize enemies."

The case was so presented that no one could verify the
facts on which the investigation was based. There was no
possibility of trying to verify facts by contacting those who
had made the confessions of guilt.

We felt, however, that the case of the arrested doctors
was questionable. We knew some of these people personally because they had once treated us. When we examined this "case" after Stalin's death, we found it to be
fabricated from beginning to end.

This ignominious "case" was set up by Stalin; he did not, however, have the time in which to bring it to an end (as he conceived that end), and for this reason the doctors are still alive. Now all have been rehabilitated; they are working in the same places they were working before; they treat top individuals, not excluding members of the government; they have our full confidence; and they execute their duties honestly, as they did before.

In organizing the various dirty and shameful cases, a very base role was played by the rabid enemy of our Party, an agent of a foreign intelligence service—Beria, who had stolen into Stalin's confidence. In what way could this provocateur gain such a position in the Party and in the state, so as to become the First Deputy Chairman of the Council of Ministers of the Soviet Union and a member of the Central Committee Political Bureau? It has now been established that this villain had climbed up the government ladder over an untold number of corpses.

Were there any signs that Beria was an enemy of the Party? Yes, there were. Already in 1937, at a Central Committee Plenum, former People's Commissar of Health Protection, Kaminsky, said that Beria worked for the Mussavat intelligence service. But the Central Committee Plenum had barely concluded when Kaminsky was arrested and then shot. Had Stalin examined Kaminsky's statement? No, because Stalin believed in Beria, and that was enough for him. And when Stalin believed in anyone or anything, then no one could say anything which was contrary to his opinion; anyone who would dare to express opposition would have met the same fate as Kaminsky.

There were other signs also. The declaration which Comrade Snegov made at the Party's Central Committee

is interesting. (Parenthetically speaking, he was also rehabilitated not long ago, after 17 years in prison camps.)
In this declaration Snegov writes:

In connection with the proposed rehabilitation of the former
Central Committee member, Kartvelishvili-Lavrentiev, I have
entrusted to the hands of the representative of the Committee
of State Security a detailed deposition concerning Beria's role
in the disposition of the Kartvelishvili case and concerning the
criminal motives by which Beria was guided.

In my opinion it is indispensable to recall an important fact
pertaining to this case and to communicate it to the Central Committee, because I did not consider it as proper to include it in the
investigation documents.

On October 30, 1931, at the session of the Organizational Bureau of the Central Committee, All-Union Communist Party (Bolsheviks), Kartvelishvili, Secretary of the Trans-Caucasian Krai
Committee made a report. All members of the Executive of the
Krai Committee were present; of them I alone am alive. During
this session J. V. Stalin made a motion at the end of his speech
concerning the organization of the Secretariat of the Trans-
Caucasian Krai Committee composed of the following: First
Secretary, Kartvelishvili; Second Secretary, Beria (it was then
for the first time in the Party's history that Beria's name was mentioned as a candidate for a Party position). Kartvelishvili
answered that he knew Beria well and for that reason refused
categorically to work together with him. Stalin proposed then
that this matter be left open and that it be solved in the process
of the work itself. Two days later a decision was arrived at that
Beria would receive the Party post and that Kartvelishvili would be
deported from the Trans-Caucasus.

This fact can be confirmed by Comrades Mikoyan and
Kaganovich who were present at that session.

The long unfriendly relations between Kartvelishvili and Beria were widely known; they date back to the time when Comrade Sergo* was active in the Trans-Caucasus; Kartvelishvili was the closest assistant of Sergo. The unfriendly relationship impelled Beria to fabricate a "case" against Kartvelishvili.

It is a characteristic thing that in this "case" Kartvelishvili was charged with a terroristic act against Beria.

The indictment in the Beria case contains a discussion of his crimes. Some things shculd, however, be recalled, especially since it is possible that not all delegates to the Congress have read this document. I wish to recall Beria's bestial disposition of the cases of Kedrov, Golubiev, and Golubiev's adopted mother, Baturina—persons who wished to inform the Central Committee concerning Beria's treacherous activity. They were shot without any trial and the sentence was passed ex-post facto, after the execution.

Here is what the old Communist, Comrade Kedrov, wrote to the Central Committee through Comrade Andreyev (Comrade Andreyev was then a Central Committee secretary):

I am calling to you for help from a gloomy cell of the Lefortosky prison. Let my cry of horror reach your ears; do not remain deaf; take me under your protection; please, help remove the nightmare of interrogations and show that this is all a mistake.

I suffer innocently. Please believe me. Time will testify to the truth. I am not an agent-provocateur of the Tsarist Okhrana; I am not a spy; I am not a member of an anti-Soviet organization

*Translator's note: "Sergo" was the popular nickname for Ordzhonikidze.

of which I am being accused on the basis of denunciations. I am also not guilty of any other crimes against the Party and the government. I am an old Bolshevik, free of any stain; I have honestly fought for almost 40 years in the ranks of the Party for the good and the prosperity of the nation. . . .

. . . Today I, a 62-year-old man, am being threatened by the investigative judges with more severe, cruel and degrading methods of physical pressure. They [the judges] are no longer capable of becoming aware of their error and of recognizing that their handling of my case is illegal and impermissible. They try to justify their actions by picturing me as a hardened and raving enemy and are demanding increased repressions. But let the Party know that I am innocent and that there is nothing which can turn a loyal son of the Party into an enemy, even right up to his last dying breath.

But I have no way out. I cannot divert from myself the hastily approaching new and powerful blows.

Everything, however, has its limits. My torture has reached the extreme. My health is broken, my strength and my energy are waning, the end is drawing near. To die in a Soviet prison, branded as a vile traitor to the Fatherland—what can be more monstrous for an honest man. And how monstrous all this is! Unsurpassed bitterness and pain grips my heart. No! No! This will not happen; this cannot be—I cry. Neither the Party, nor the Soviet government, nor the People's Commissar, L. P. Beria, will permit this cruel irreparable injustice. I am firmly certain that given a quiet, objective examination, without any foul rantings, without any anger and without the fearful tortures, it would be easy to prove the baselessness of the charges. I believe deeply that truth and justice will triumph. I believe. I believe.

The old Bolshevik, Comrade Kedrov, was found innocent by the Military Collegium. But despite this, he was shot at Beria's order. (*Indignation in the hall.*)

Beria also handled cruelly the family of Comrade Ordzhonikidze. Why? Because Ordzhonikidze had tried to prevent Beria from realizing his shameful plans. Beria had cleared from his way all persons who could possibly interfere with him. Ordzhonikidze was always an opponent of Beria, which he told to Stalin. Instead of examining this affair and taking appropriate steps, Stalin allowed the liquidation of Ordzhonikidze's brother and brought Ordzhonikidze himself to such a state that he was forced to shoot himself. (*Indignation in the hall.*) Such was Beria.

Beria was unmasked by the Party's Central Committee shortly after Stalin's death. As a result of the particularly detailed legal proceedings it was established that Beria had committed monstrous crimes and Beria was shot.

The question arises why Beria, who had liquidated tens of thousands of Party and Soviet workers, was not unmasked during Stalin's life? He was not unmasked earlier because he had utilized very skillfully Stalin's weaknesses; feeding him with suspicions, he assisted Stalin in everything and acted with his support.

Comrades! The cult of the individual acquired such monstrous size chiefly because Stalin himself, using all conceivable methods, supported the glorification of his own person. This is supported by numerous facts. One of the most characteristic examples of Stalin's self-glorification and of his lack of even elementary modesty is the edition of his *Short Biography*, which was published in 1948.

This book is an expression of the most dissolute flattery, an example of making a man into a godhead, of transforming him into an infallible sage, "the greatest leader," "sublime strategist of all times and nations." Finally no other words could be found with which to lift Stalin up to the heavens.

We need not give here examples of the loathsome adulation filling this book. All we need to add is that they all were approved and edited by Stalin personally and some of them were added in his own handwriting to the draft text of the book.

What did Stalin consider essential to write into this book? Did he want to cool the ardor of his flatterers who were composing his *Short Biography?* No! He marked the very places where he thought that the praise of his services was insufficient.

Here are some examples characterizing Stalin's activity, added in Stalin's own hand:

In this fight against the skeptics and capitulators, the Trotskyites, Zinovievites, Bukharinites and Kamenevites, there was definitely welded together, after Lenin's death, that leading core of the Party . . .* that upheld the great banner of Lenin, rallied the Party behind Lenin's behests, and brought the Soviet people into the broad road of industrializing the country and collectivising the rural economy. The leader of this core and the guiding force of the Party and the State was Comrade Stalin.

Thus writes Stalin himself! Then he adds:

Although he performed his task of leader of the Party and the people with consummate skill and enjoyed the unreserved support of the entire Soviet people, Stalin never allowed his work to be marred by the slightest hint of vanity, conceit or self-adulation.

Where and when could a leader so praise himself? Is this worthy of a leader of the Marxist-Leninist type? No.

---

* Translator's note: Omitted portion of list as found in "Joseph Stalin; A Short Biography" (Moscow: Foreign Languages Publishing House, 1949, p. 89) is as follows: ". . . consisting of Stalin, Molotov, Kalinin, Voroshilov, Kuibyshev, Frunze, Dzerzhinsky, Kaganovich, Ordzhonikidze, Kirov, Yaroslavsky, Mikoyan, Andreyev, Shvernik, Zhdanov, Shkiryatov and others."

Precisely against this did Marx and Engels take such a strong position. This also was always sharply condemned by Vladimir Ilyich Lenin.

In the draft text of his book appeared the following sentence: "Stalin is the Lenin of today." This sentence appeared to Stalin to be too weak, so in his own handwriting he changed it to read: "Stalin is the worthy continuer of Lenin's work, or, as it is said in our Party, Stalin is the Lenin of today." You see how well it is said, not by the nation but by Stalin himself.

It is possible to give many such self-praising appraisals written into the draft text of that book in Stalin's hand. Especially generously does he endow himself with praises pertaining to his military genius, to his talent for strategy.

I will cite one more insertion made by Stalin concerning the theme of the Stalinist military genius.

"The advanced Soviet science of war received further development," he writes,

at Comrade Stalin's hands. Comrade Stalin elaborated the theory of the permanently operating factors that decide the issue of wars, of active defense and the laws of counter-offensive and offensive, of the co-operation of all services and arms in modern warfare, of the role of big tank masses and air forces in modern war, and of the artillery as the most formidable of the armed services. At the various stages of the war Stalin's genius found the correct solutions that took account of all the circumstances of the situation.

(*Movement in the hall.*) And further, writes Stalin:

Stalin's military mastership was displayed both in defense and offense. Comrade Stalin's genius enabled him to divine the enemy's plans and defeat them. The battles in which Comrade Stalin directed the Soviet armies are brilliant examples of operational military skill.

In this manner was Stalin praised as a strategist. Who did this? Stalin himself, not in his role as a strategist but in the role of an author-editor, one of the main creators of his self-adulatory biography.

Such, comrades, are the facts. We should rather say shameful facts.

And one additional fact from the same *Short Biography* of Stalin. As is known, *The Short Course of the History of the All-Union Communist Party (Bolsheviks)* was written by a commission of the Party Central Committee.

This book, parenthetically, was also permeated with the cult of the individual and was written by a designated group of authors. This fact was reflected in the following formulation on the proof copy of the *Short Biography* of Stalin:

A commission of the Central Committee, All-Union Communist Party (Bolsheviks), under the direction of Comrade Stalin and with his most active personal participation, has prepared a *Short Course of the History of the All-Union Communist Party (Bolsheviks).*

But even this phrase did not satisfy Stalin; the following sentence replaced it in the final version of the *Short Biography:*

"In 1938 appeared the book, *History of the All-Union Communist Party (Bolsheviks), Short Course,* written by Comrade Stalin and approved by a commission of the Central Committee, All-Union Communist Party (Bolsheviks)." Can one add anything more? *(Animation in the hall.)*

As you see, a surprising metamorphosis changed the work created by a group into a book written by Stalin. It is not necessary to state how and why this metamorphosis took place.

A pertinent question comes to our mind: If Stalin is the author of this book, why did he need to praise the person of Stalin so much and to transform the whole post-October historical period of our glorious Communist Party solely into an action of "the Stalin genius"?

Did this book properly reflect the efforts of the Party in the socialist transformation of the country, in the construction of socialist society, in the industrialization and collectivization of the country, and also other steps taken by the Party which undeviatingly traveled the path outlined by Lenin? This book speaks principally about Stalin, about his speeches, about his reports. Everything without the smallest exception is tied to his name.

And when Stalin himself asserts that he himself wrote the *Short Course of the History of the All-Union Communist Party (Bolsheviks)*, this calls at least for amazement. Can a Marxist-Leninist thus write about himself, praising his own person to the heavens?

Or let us take the matter of the Stalin Prizes. (*Movement in the hall.*) Not even the tsars created prizes which they named after themselves.

Stalin recognized as the best a text of the national anthem of the Soviet Union which contains not a word about the Communist Party; it contains, however, the following unprecedented praise of Stalin:

> Stalin brought us up in loyalty to the people,
> He inspired us to great toil and acts.

In these lines of the anthem is the whole educational, directional and inspirational activity of the great Leninist

Party ascribed to Stalin. This is, of course, a clear
deviation from Marxism-Leninism, a clear debasing and
belittling of the role of the Party. We should add for
your information that the Presidium of the Central Committee has already passed a resolution concerning the
composition of a new text of the anthem, which will reflect
the role of the people, and the role of the Party. (*Loud,
prolonged applause.*)

And was it without Stalin's knowledge that many of
the largest enterprises and towns were named after him?
Was it without his knowledge that Stalin monuments were
erected in the whole country—these "memorials to the
living"? It is a fact that Stalin himself had signed on
July 2, 1951, a resolution of the USSR Council of Ministers concerning the erection on the Volga-Don Canal of an
impressive monument to Stalin; on September 4 of the
same year he issued an order making 33 tons of copper
available for the construction of this impressive monument. Anyone who has visited the Stalingrad area must
have seen the huge statue which is being built there, and
that on a site which hardly any people frequent. Huge
sums were spent to build it at a time when people of this
area had lived since the war in huts. Consider yourself,
was Stalin right when he wrote in his biography that
". . . he did not allow in himself . . . even a shadow of
conceit, pride, or self-adoration"?

At the same time Stalin gave proofs of his lack of
respect for Lenin's memory. It is not a coincidence that,
despite the decision taken over 30 years ago to build a
Palace of Soviets as a monument to Vladimir Ilyich, this

Palace was not built, its construction was always postponed, and the project allowed to lapse.

We cannot forget to recall the Soviet government resolution of August 14, 1925, concerning "the founding of Lenin prizes for educational work." This resolution was published in the press, but until this day there are no Lenin prizes. This, too, should be corrected. (*Tumultuous, prolonged applause.*)

During Stalin's life, thanks to known methods which I have mentioned, and quoting facts, for instance, from the *Short Biography* of Stalin—all events were explained as if Lenin played only a secondary role, even during the October Socialist Revolution. In many films and in many literary works, the figure of Lenin was incorrectly presented and inadmissibly depreciated.

Stalin loved to see the film, "The Unforgettable Year of 1919," in which he was shown on the steps of an armored train and where he was practically vanquishing the foe with his own sabre. Let Kliment Yefremovich, our dear friend, find the necessary courage and write the truth about Stalin; after all, he knows how Stalin had fought. It will be difficult for Comrade Voroshilov to undertake this, but it would be good if he did it. Everyone will approve of it, both the people and the Party. Even his grandsons will thank him. (*Prolonged applause.*)

In speaking about the events of the October Revolution and about the Civil War, the impression was created that Stalin always played the main role, as if everywhere and always Stalin had suggested to Lenin what to do and how to do it. However, this is slander of Lenin. (*Prolonged applause.*)

I will probably not sin against the truth when I say that 99 percent of the persons present here heard and knew very little about Stalin before the year 1924, while Lenin was known to all; he was known to the whole Party, to the whole nation, from the children up to the graybeards. (*Tumultuous, prolonged applause.*)

All this has to be thoroughly revised, so that history, literature, and the fine arts properly reflect V. I. Lenin's role and the great deeds of our Communist Party and of the Soviet people—the creative people. (*Applause.*)

Comrades! The cult of the individual has caused the employment of faulty principles in Party work and in economic activity; it brought about rude violation of internal Party and Soviet democracy, sterile administration, deviations of all sorts, covering up of shortcomings and varnishing of reality. Our nation gave birth to many flatterers and specialists in false optimism and deceit.

We should also not forget that due to the numerous arrests of Party, Soviet and economic leaders, many workers began to work uncertainly, showed over-cautiousness, feared all which was new, feared their own shadows and began to show less initiative in their work.

Take, for instance, Party and Soviet resolutions. They were prepared in a routine manner often without considering the concrete situation. This went so far that Party workers, even during the smallest sessions, read their speeches. All this produced the danger of formalizing the Party and Soviet work and of bureaucratizing the whole apparatus.

Stalin's reluctance to consider life's realities and the fact that he was not aware of the real state of affairs in the provinces can be illustrated by his direction of agriculture.

All those who interested themselves even a little in the national situation saw the difficult situation in agriculture, but Stalin never even noted it. Did we tell Stalin about this? Yes, we told him, but he did not support us. Why? Because Stalin never traveled anywhere, did not meet city and kolkhoz workers; he did not know the actual situation in the provinces.

He knew the country and agriculture only from films. And these films had dressed up and beautified the existing situation in agriculture.

Many films so pictured kolkhoz life that the tables were bending from the weight of turkeys and geese. Evidently Stalin thought that it was actually so.

Vladimir Ilyich Lenin looked at life differently; he was always close to the people; he used to receive peasant delegates, and often spoke at factory gatherings; he used to visit villages and talk with the peasants.

Stalin separated himself from the people and never went anywhere. This lasted tens of years. The last time he visited a village was in January 1928 when he visited Siberia in connection with grain deliveries. How then could he have known the situation in the provinces?

And when he was once told during a discussion that our situation on the land was a difficult one and that the situation of cattle breeding and meat production was especially bad, a commission was formed which was charged with the preparation of a resolution called, "Means toward further

development of animal breeding in kolkhozes and sovkhozes." We worked out this project.

Of course, our propositions of that time did not contain
all possibilities, but we did charter ways in which animal
breeding on the kolkhozes and sovkhozes would be raised.
We had proposed then to raise the prices of such products
in order to create material incentives for the kolkhoz, MTS
and sovkhoz workers in the development of cattle breeding.
But our project was not accepted and in February 1953
was laid aside entirely.

What is more, while reviewing this project Stalin proposed that the taxes paid by the kolkhozes and by the kolkhoz workers should be raised by 40 billion rubles; according to him the peasants are well-off and the kolkhoz
worker would need to sell only one more chicken to pay
his tax in full.

Imagine what this meant. Certainly 40 billion rubles
is a sum which the kolkhoz workers did not realize for all
the products which they sold to the government. In 1952,
for instance, the kolkhozes and the kolkhoz workers received 26,280 million rubles for all their products delivered and sold to the government.

Did Stalin's position then rest on data of any sort whatever? Of course not.

In such cases facts and figures did not interest him. If
Stalin said anything, it meant it was so—after all, he was
a "genius" and a genius does not need to count, he only
needs to look and can immediately tell how it should be.
When he expresses his opinion, everyone has to repeat it
and to admire his wisdom.

But how much wisdom was contained in the proposal
to raise the agricultural tax by 40 billion rubles? None,

absolutely none, because the proposal was not based on an actual assessment of the situation but on the fantastic ideas of a person divorced from reality. We are currently beginning slowly to work our way out of a difficult agricultural situation. The speeches of the delegates to the XXth Congress please us all; we are glad that many delegates deliver speeches, that there are conditions for the fulfillment of the Sixth Five-Year Plan for animal husbandry, not during the period of five years, but within two to three years. We are certain that the commitments of the new Five-Year Plan will be accomplished successfully. *(Prolonged applause.)*

Comrades! If we sharply criticize today the cult of the individual which was so widespread during Stalin's life and if we speak about the many negative phenomena generated by this cult which is so alien to the spirit of Marxism-Leninism, various persons may ask: How could it be? Stalin headed the Party and the country for 30 years and many victories were gained during his lifetime. Can we deny this? In my opinion, the question can be asked in this manner only by those who are blinded and hopelessly hypnotized by the cult of the individual, only by those who do not understand the essence of the revolution and of the Soviet state, only by those who do not understand, in a Leninist manner, the role of the Party and of the nation in the development of the Soviet society.

The socialist revolution was attained by the working class and by the poor peasantry with the partial support of middle-class peasants. It was attained by the people under the leadership of the Bolshevik Party. Lenin's great service consisted of the fact that he created a militant

Party of the working class, but he was armed with Marxist understanding of the laws of social development and with the science of proletarian victory in the fight with capitalism, and he steeled this Party in the crucible of revolutionary struggle of the masses of the people. During this fight the Party consistently defended the interests of the people, became its experienced leader, and led the working masses to power, to the creation of the first socialist state.

You remember well the wise words of Lenin that the Soviet state is strong because of the awareness of the masses that history is created by the millions and tens of millions of people.

Our historical victories were attained thanks to the organizational work of the Party, to the many provincial organizations, and to the self-sacrificing work of our great nation. These victories are the result of the great drive and activity of the nation and of the Party as a whole; they are not at all the fruit of the leadership of Stalin, as the situation was pictured during the period of the cult of the individual.

If we are to consider this matter as Marxists and as Leninists, then we have to state unequivocally that the leadership practice which came into being during the last years of Stalin's life became a serious obstacle in the path of Soviet social development.

Stalin often failed for months to take up some unusually important problems concerning the life of the Party and of the state whose solution could not be postponed. During Stalin's leadership our peaceful relations with other nations were often threatened, because one-man decisions could cause and often did cause great complications.

In the last years, when we managed to free ourselves of the harmful practice of the cult of the individual and took several proper steps in the sphere of internal and external policies, everyone saw how activity grew before their very eyes, how the creative activity of the broad working masses developed, how favorably all this acted upon the development of economy and of culture. (*Applause.*)

Some comrades may ask us: Where were the members of the Political Bureau of the Central Committee? Why did they not assert themselves against the cult of the individual in time? And why is this being done only now?

First of all we have to consider the fact that the members of the Political Bureau viewed these matters in a different way at different times. Initially, many of them backed Stalin actively because Stalin was one of the strongest Marxists and his logic, his strength and his will greatly influenced the cadres and Party work.

It is known that Stalin, after Lenin's death, especially during the first years, actively fought for Leninism against the enemies of Leninist theory and against those who deviated. Beginning with Leninist theory, the Party, with its Central Committee at the head, started on a great scale the work of socialist industrialization of the country, agricultural collectivization and the cultural revolution. At that time Stalin gained great popularity, sympathy and support. The Party had to fight those who attempted to lead the country away from the correct Leninist path; it had to fight Trotskyites, Zinovievites and rightists, and the bourgeois nationalists. This fight was indispensable. Later, however, Stalin, abusing his power more and more, began to fight eminent Party and government leaders and to use

terroristic methods against honest Soviet people. As we
have already shown, Stalin thus handled such eminent
Party and government leaders as Kossior, Rudzutak, Eikhe,
Postyshev and many others.

Attempts to oppose groundless suspicions and charges
resulted in the opponent falling victim of the repression.
This characterized the fall of Comrade Postyshev.

In one of his speeches Stalin expressed his dissatisfaction
with Postyshev and asked him, "What are you actually?"

Postyshev answered clearly, "I am a Bolshevik, Comrade Stalin, a Bolshevik."

This assertion was at first considered to show a lack of
respect for Stalin; later it was considered a harmful act
and consequently resulted in Postyshev's annihilation and
branding without any reason as a "people's enemy."

In the situation which then prevailed I have talked often
with Nikolai Alexandrovich Bulganin; once when we two
were traveling in a car, he said, "It has happened sometimes that a man goes to Stalin on his invitation as a friend.
And when he sits with Stalin, he does not know where he
will be sent next, home or to jail."

It is clear that such conditions put every member of the
Political Bureau in a very difficult situation. And when we
also consider the fact that in the last years the Central
Committee plenary sessions were not convened and that
the sessions of the Political Bureau occurred only occasion-
ally, from time to time, then we will understand how difficult it was for any member of the Political Bureau to take
a stand against one or another injust or improper procedure, against serious errors and shortcomings in the practices of leadership.

As we have already shown, many decisions were taken either by one person or in a roundabout way, without collective discussions. The sad fate of Political Bureau member, Comrade Voznesensky, who fell victim to Stalin's repressions, is known to all. It is a characteristic thing that the decision to remove him from the Political Bureau was never discussed but was reached in a devious fashion. In the same way came the decision concerning the removal of Kuznetsov and Rodionov from their posts.

The importance of the Central Committee's Political Bureau was reduced and its work was disorganized by the creation within the Political Bureau of various commissions—the so-called "quintets," "sextets," "septets" and "novenaries." Here is, for instance, a resolution of the Political Bureau of October 3, 1946.

Stalin's Proposal:

1. The Political Bureau Commission for Foreign Affairs ("Sextet") is to concern itself in the future, in addition to foreign affairs, also with matters of internal construction and domestic policy.

2. The Sextet is to add to its roster the Chairman of the State Commission of Economic Planning of the USSR, Comrade Voznesensky, and is to be known as a Septet.

Signed: Secretary of the Central Committee, J. Stalin.

What a terminology of a card player! *(Laughter in the hall.)* It is clear that the creation within the Political Bureau of this type of commission—"quintets," "sextets," "septets," and "novenaries,"—was against the principle of collective leadership. The result of this was that some members of the Political Bureau were in this way kept away from participation in reaching the most important state matters.

One of the oldest members of our Party, Kliment Yefremovich Voroshilov, found himself in an almost impossible situation. For several years he was actually deprived of the right of participation in Political Bureau sessions. Stalin forbade him to attend the Political Bureau sessions and to receive documents. When the Political Bureau was in session and Comrade Voroshilov heard about it, he telephoned each time and asked whether he would be allowed to attend. Sometimes Stalin permitted it, but always showed his dissatisfaction. Because of his extreme suspicion, Stalin toyed also with the absurd and ridiculous suspicion that Voroshilov was an English agent. *(Laughter in the hall.)* It's true—an English agent. A special tapping device was installed in his home to listen to what was said there. *(Indignation in the hall.)*

By unilateral decision Stalin had also separated one other man from the work of the Political Bureau—Andrei Andreyevich Andreyev. This was one of the most unbridled acts of willfulness.

Let us consider the first Central Committee Plenum after the XIXth Party Congress when Stalin, in his talk at the Plenum, characterized Vyacheslav Mikhailovich Molotov and Anastas Ivanovich Mikoyan and suggested that these old workers of our Party were guilty of some baseless charges. It is not excluded that had Stalin remained at the helm for another several months, Comrades Molotov and Mikoyan would probably have not delivered any speeches at this Congress.

Stalin evidently had plans to finish off the old members of the Political Bureau. He often stated that Political Bureau members should be replaced by new ones.

His proposal, after the XIXth Congress concerning the selection of 25 persons to the Central Committee Presidium, was aimed at the removal of the old Political Bureau members and the bringing in of less experienced persons so that these would extol him in all sorts of ways.

We can assume that this was also a design for the future annihilation of the old Political Bureau members and in this way a cover for all shameful acts of Stalin, acts which we are now considering.

Comrades! In order not to repeat errors of the past, the Central Committee has declared itself resolutely against the cult of the individual. We consider that Stalin was excessively extolled. However, in the past Stalin doubtlessly performed great services to the Party, to the working class, and to the international workers' movement.

This question is complicated by the fact that all this which we have just discussed was done during Stalin's life under his leadership and with his concurrence; here Stalin was convinced that this was necessary for the defense of the interests of the working classes against the plotting of the enemies and against the attack of the imperialist camp. He saw this from the position of the interest of the working class, of the interest of the laboring people, of the interest of the victory of socialism and Communism. We cannot say that these were the deeds of a giddy despot. He considered that this should be done in the interest of the Party; of the working masses, in the name of the defense of the revolution's gains. In this lies the whole tragedy!

Comrades! Lenin had often stressed that modesty is an absolutely integral part of a real Bolshevik. Lenin himself was the living personification of the greatest modesty. We cannot say that we have been following this Leninist example in all respects. It is enough to point out that many towns, factories and industrial enterprises, kolkhozes and sovkhozes, Soviet institutions and cultural institutions have been referred to by us with a title—if I may express it so—of private property of the names of these or those government or Party leaders who were still active and in good health. Many of us participated in the action of assigning our names to various towns, rayons, undertakings and kolkhozes. We must correct this. (*Applause.*)

But this should be done calmly and slowly. The Central Committee will discuss this matter and consider it carefully in order to prevent errors and excesses. I can remember how the Ukraine learned about Kossior's arrest. The Kiev radio used to start its programs thus: "This is radio [in the name of] Kossior." When one day the programs began without naming Kossior, everyone was quite certain that something had happened to Kossior, that he probably had been arrested.

Thus, if today we begin to remove the signs everywhere and to change names, people will think, that these comrades in whose honor the given enterprises, kolkhozes or cities are named, also met some bad fate and that they have also been arrested. (*Animation in the hall.*)

How is the authority and the importance of this or that leader judged? On the basis of how many towns, industrial enterprises and factories, kolkhozes and sovkhozes carry his name. Is it not about time that we eliminate this "private property" and "nationalize" the factories, the industrial enterprises, the kolkhozes and the sovkhozes? (*Laughter, applause, voices: "That is right."*) This will benefit our cause. After all the cult of the individual is manifested also in this way.

We should in all seriousness consider the question of the cult of the individual. We cannot let this matter get out of the Party, especially not to the press. It is for this reason that we are considering it here at a closed Congress session. We should know the limits; we should not give ammunition to the enemy; we should not wash our dirty linen before their eyes. I think that the delegates to the Congress will understand and assess properly all these proposals. *(Tumultuous applause.)*

Comrades: We must abolish the cult of the individual decisively, once and for all; we must draw the proper conclusions concerning both ideological-theoretical and practical work.

It is necessary for this purpose:

First, in a Bolshevik manner to condemn and to eradicate the cult of the individual as alien to Marxism-Leninism and not consonant with the principles of Party leadership and the norms of Party life, and to fight inexorably all attempts at bringing back this practice in one form or another.

To return to and actually practice in all our ideological work the most important theses of Marxist-Leninist science about the people as the creator of history and as the creator of all material and spiritual good of humanity, about the decisive role of the Marxist Party in the revolutionary fight for the transformation of society, about the victory of Communism.

In this connection we will be forced to do much work in order to examine critically from the Marxist-Leninist viewpoint and to correct the widely spread erroneous views connected with the cult of the individual in the sphere of history, philosophy, economy and of other sciences, as well as in literature and the fine arts. It is especially necessary that in the immediate future we compile a serious textbook of the history of our Party which will be edited in accordance with scientific Marxist objectivism, a textbook of the history of Soviet society, a book pertaining to the events of the Civil War and the Great Patriotic War.

Secondly, to continue systematically and consistently the work done by the Party's Central Committee during the last years, a work characterized by minute observation in all Party organizations, from the bottom to the top, of the Leninist principles of Party leadership, characterized, above all, by the main principle of collective leadership, characterized by the observation of the norms of Party life described in the Statutes of our Party, and finally, characterized by the wide practice of criticism and self-criticism.

Thirdly, to restore completely the Leninist principles of Soviet socialist democracy, expressed in the Constitution of the Soviet Union, to fight willfulness of individuals abusing their power. The evil caused by acts violating revolutionary socialist legality which have accumulated during a long time as a result of the negative influence of the cult of the individual has to be completely corrected.

Comrades! The XXth Congress of the Communist Party of the Soviet Union has manifested with a new strength the unshakable unity of our Party, its cohesiveness around the Central Committee, its resolute will to accomplish the great task of building Communism. *(Tumultuous applause.)* And the fact that we present in all their ramifications the basic problems of overcoming the cult of the individual which is alien to Marxism-Leninism, as well as the problem of liquidating its burdensome consequences, is an evidence of the great moral and political strength of our Party. *(Prolonged applause.)*

We are absolutely certain that our Party, armed with the historical resolutions of the XXth Congress, will lead the Soviet people along the Leninist path to new successes, to new victories. *(Tumultuous, prolonged applause.)*

Long live the victorious banner of our Party—Leninism! *(Tumultuous, prolonged applause ending in ovation. All rise.)*

2

"The Khrushchev Speech: An Editorial"

DAILY WORKER, New York

June 6, 1956

ONE OF the first parties abroad in which reports of the Moscow attacks on Stalinism evoked public discussion was the Communist Party of the United States. As early as March 18, the foreign editor of the Sunday *Worker* rebuked Moscow: the collective leadership claimed that the glorification of Stalin "led to a cult—in which they all participated; but they did not explain why they did." He added that the Congress had failed to answer all the questions which it had raised regarding Stalin. A week later, the party's New York State committee chairman, George B. Charney, was quoted as admitting that there was a sharp split of Communist opinion into three camps. There were the "defenders" of Stalin, those who now turned against the late dictator, and those seeking a mildly critical middle position. (*The New York Times*, March 24, 1956.)

Unlike other Communist parties abroad, the CPUSA (like the British Party) opened the pages of its organ, particularly the "letters-to-the-editor" columns, to spokesmen of all three positions —including some who argued that "this criticism of Stalin is the most terrible instrument in the hands of the capitalists and . . . is causing a split in the Communist Party all over the world. Where was Khrushchev when all those 'crimes' were committed?" (April 1.)

The Party leadership, from William Z. Foster down, publicly at least, followed the public pronouncements of the XXth Party Congress. "The essence of Stalin's errors," wrote Foster, "is that he multiplied, complicated, and intensified [a number of] mistakes by his virtual liquidation of collective leadership and by the atmosphere of omniscience and extreme adulation with which he surrounded himself." Nonetheless, there remained "the basic fact that over the years the USSR has made the most tremendous progress in the building of Socialism." ("Lessons from the Stalin Question," *Daily Worker*, March 28, 1956.) Why was the re-evaluation of Stalin delayed until now? Foster replied (echoing statements from Poland and East Germany, and in effect anticipating the CC/CPSU position of June 30, see Document 11): "In view of the existing situation when Stalin was alive, with his tremendous prestige in the Communist Party and among the masses, it would have been extremely difficult, if not impossible, to have gone through with any such revaluation." Besides, "when all of Stalin's shortcomings and leadership excesses have been exposed and explained, he will still stand as a fighter who performed great services in the building of Soviet and world Socialism." ("Why the Stalin Revaluation Takes Place at This Time," *Daily Worker*, April 10, 1956.)

Editorially, the *Daily Worker* chose the issue of anti-Semitism to publicize its dissent from the Moscow line. After a Yiddish-language newspaper in Warsaw confirmed the "framing" and execution of a number of Jewish figures in Soviet public life, the New York Communist newspaper declared: "We register our strong dissatisfaction that the Soviet leaders have not offered any explanation of what took place." ("Grievous Deeds," *Daily Worker*, April 13, 1956. See also William Z. Foster, "Stalin's Excesses and Distortions," *ibid.*, April 19, 1956.)

No explanation was forthcoming, and the issue remained in abeyance until the publication by the U. S. State Department of the Khrushchev speech on June 4. Two days later, the *Daily Worker* responded with the following editorial.

THE SHATTERING revelations made by Khrushchev show what a gigantic transformation is taking place in the Soviet Union. The report is part of an effort—not at all completed—to correct what was a monstrous perversion of socialist principles under Stalin's brutal rule.

The State Department would have us believe there is no change taking place in the Soviet Union. They timed the release of Khrushchev's report, however, with Tito's visit to the USSR. Apparently Washington thought this was a bold propaganda counterstroke. Unwittingly, thereby, they refuted their claim that nothing is changing in the Soviet Union.

As Walter Lippmann put it yesterday in the *Herald Tribune*:

Tito's visit to Moscow does not fit very well into the standardized assumption that nothing really changes in the Soviet Union, and that the passing of Stalin has made no difference. If that assumption were true, we should have to read the reconciliation which is now being celebrated in Moscow as meaning that Tito is returning his country to its former position of a satellite. This is just what is not happening.

The State Department is dead wrong when it suggests that the evils of the Stalin era are inherent in socialism. The fact is that the development of those evils created a peril for socialism. The repression, the injustice, the frameup, the torture are a gross perversion of socialist principles. Khrushchev noted this in his report. Socialism requires government of the people, by the people and for the people, in economic as well as in political life. It therefore flourishes in freedom and is endangered by repression and injustice. This is indicated by the overhauling of the Soviet legal system and the correction that has been taking place there for over three years since the death of Stalin.

The exposure of Stalin's misrule, of his crimes against socialism and humanity is a measure of how much this was a departure from socialist ideas, and from what Lenin taught.

The timing of the State Department's release of the Khrushchev report helps explain why they published it. Even by their own admission they had the documents for some time.

They released it now because they're worried that the cold war is dying an ignominious death. There's a crisis of foreign policy because of the State Department's sorry efforts to maintain the cold war. With the Gallup Poll showing a majority of Americans favoring an invitation to Bulganin and Khrushchev to visit our country, the State Department wants to keep down mutual exchange to an absolute minimum.

The State Department is so concerned about the Soviet Union's reduction of its armed forces that they hoped to divert attention from the whole issue of disarmament.

We do not hesitate to state that we don't like the way Khrushchev's speech was made public. The leaders of the Soviet Union probably had their reasons for letting the contents come out piece-meal and in a round-about way. In our opinion they made a mistake and should have published the speech immediately and made it available throughout the world.

We also express our concern that in the long list of crimes mentioned in the speech, there was silence on those committed against Jewish culture and Jewish cultural leaders. To date, this series of outrages has not been publicized in the socialist countries except in the columns of a Jewish-language paper in Warsaw.

We do not consider the speech to be the last word on just how Stalin's terror control came into existence and maintained itself for 20 years and of the role of the other Communist leaders.

One of the conclusions this paper began to draw when the XXth Congress was still in progress back in March was that the revaluation and correction of the Stalin regime represented a long overdue turning point not only for the Soviet Union and for other countries of socialism but likewise for Communist movements everywhere.

The blind and uncritical attitude of the *Daily Worker* in past years to the repressions in the Soviet Union only did grave damage to our goal of promoting a socialist movement in this country. It created obstacles in what we consider was a notable contribution over the years in defending the genuine socialist achievements in the USSR and its policy for peace.

This paper has attempted to express the need for an effective Marxist movement in this country to base itself on the conditions found in America, on the traditions of the American working class and of the people as a whole. Its decisions and policies must be independent ones and must arise from the needs of the American working people. At the same time, the struggle for socialism in America can be effective only if it is carried on in the spirit of international working-class solidarity—genuine internationalism, based on equality, fervent support of the socialist achievements of other people coupled with fraternal, open and frank criticism wherever it may be due.

We dedicate ourselves to unrelenting struggle against the monopolists in our country who build up their fantastic profits out of the sweat of the American workers, out of a run-away armaments and H-bomb race, out of exploitation, discrimination and injustice.

We dedicate ourselves to building a people's coalition against the policies of these monopolists and to helping bring about a new political alignment to the end that peace and democracy and civil rights should prevail and that the forces of atomic energy and automation may become boons to our people instead of threats.

We dedicate ourselves to helping the American working people find the American road to a complete re-organization of our society.

This will be a society of democratic socialism in which the civil and political rights of the individual and of groups will be guaranteed under the Constitution. It will be a society in which the American people will own the resources and giant factories which they have built with their own hands and will at last, in friendship with the peoples of the whole world, determine their own destiny in their own way.

The present situation, in our opinion, underlines the urgency of the outlook put forward by Eugene Dennis at the National Committee meeting of the Communist Party of a new "mass party of socialism in our country" and of the need to "create the conditions for such a necessary and historic development." We believe that the situation calls for an all-out effort and cooperation of all socialist-minded forces, in order to bring about such a new party without unnecessary delay, and as quickly as circumstances will permit.

3

Palmiro Togliatti:
"9 Domande sullo Stalinismo"

NUOVI ARGOMENTI, No. 20

June 16, 1956

THE INITIAL reaction of a number of numerically small Communist Parties in Europe to the release of the Khrushchev speech in Washington stressed the endeavors of U. S. propaganda, rather than the substance of the report (e.g., the Luxembourg *Zeitung,* June 6, and the Netherlands *De Waarheid,* June 7, accused the Department of State of "broadcasting falsified statements . . . merely for the purpose of creating confusion and distrust"). The Danish Communist organ insisted that the text "contained nothing new of significance," that "serious errors of judgment" had been committed, and that it was "completely correct to bring these mistakes into the open" (*Land og Folk,* June 7). In Norway, the Party granted that "the text of Khrushchev's speech will both frighten and shock those who read it." The causes of the "startling abuse," it maintained, "were the complex of circumstances arising from the heritage of tsarism and from the strained situation in which the Soviet Union found itself when it had to solve problems which meant life or death to the whole Soviet state and the building of socialism." At the same time, it praised the present leadership for baring these facts and launching "a new era for the whole socialist world, and thus also for all of humanity" (*Friheten,* June 8).

A distinctly new tone and argumentation were introduced for
the first time in the public press by the replies of the Italian
Communist leader, Palmiro Togliatti, to nine questions regarding
the XXth Party Congress, submitted to him (and other prominent
personalities) by the Italian periodical *Nuovi Argomenti*. The
extensive interview was promptly re-published by the Communist
newspaper *L'Unità*, and widely reported by Communist organs
outside the Soviet Union. It marked the end of several months'
effort by the Italian Communist Party to re-establish Party harmony after a faction led by Senator Umberto Terracini had
sharply assailed the present Soviet leaders. "It is stated," Terracini was reported to have declared, "that things [in Moscow] have
changed, but the truth is that the only thing that has changed is
the men in the Kremlin. . . . The truth of yesterday is not the truth
of today. In this way many truths become doubtful and the
responsibilities become collective." (*The New York Times*, March
30, 1956.) On the other hand, a section within the Italian party
reportedly pressed for a more radical policy, implicitly rejecting
the guidance issuing forth from Moscow. Publicly, if there were
reservations about the propriety of positions adopted at the XXth
Party Congress in Moscow, the Italian Communist Party maintained its silence until publication of the Togliatti text reproduced
below.

*1. In your opinion, what is the meaning of the condemna-
tion of the personality cult in the USSR? What are its
internal, external, political, social, economic, psychological, and historical causes?*

In my opinion, the condemnation of the personality cult
made by the Communists in the Soviet Union and the
criticisms leveled against Stalin's work mean exactly what
has been said and is being repeated by the Soviet Communist leaders: neither more nor less than that. Let us be
on guard, therefore, against two mistaken notions.

The first mistaken notion, gross and even ridiculous,
is to believe—or pretend to believe—that in formulating
that condemnation and those criticisms the Soviet Com-

munists have adopted, if not the attitudes of anti-Communism, at least the attitudes of those who have never approved of or understood their actions; that is, that they have scrapped, or are about to scrap all their positions of principle and practice, their entire past, everything that they have affirmed, supported, defended, and carried out in so many decades of their work. I understand very well that this is the interpretation given to the XXth Congress by the standard-bearers of anti-Communism, but there is no reason why we should listen to them today any more than we did yesterday. Moreover, they show what their game is, forcing it to the point of exasperation, as always, and thus showing their bad faith. I do not rule out, however, and I wish to say this openly, that there are also those who in perfect good faith are slipping into such an attitude and are beginning to ask whether, in view of those criticisms against Stalin, and in view of the fact that Stalin was the principal exponent of Communist policy for an entire period, one should not today doubt the correctness of all the main phases of that policy, beginning, let us say, with the decided opposition to the plans of imperialism during the post-war period and going back, through Yalta and Teheran, to the 1939 non-aggression pact with Germany, the war in Spain, etc.; and, in other fields, to the directives for socialist economic development and the fight against those who opposed it, and finally, once having started—why not?—go back to the decisive action of the October Revolution, namely, the seizure of power by the workers', peasants', and soldiers' soviets, the dissolution of the Constituent Assembly, and the establishment of a new political structure of society. To those who in good faith would be inclined to understand the situation in this manner we should say that they are mistaken. Naturally, it is always possible to discuss, and they will be discussed for a long time, all the actions through which the Soviet

Communists conquered power and established their present
social order, without doubt, for the purpose of determining
their character, content and consequences, and in order to
evaluate them historically in the most exact manner possible. Our Soviet comrades today are ridding their his-
toriography of errors and exaggerations which had been
introduced in it to extoll not only the merits but also the
personality of Stalin, and this will make it possible to
arrive at an ever more exact historical judgment. It is not
to be ruled out, in fact it is easily foreseeable that many
judgments will be corrected, that the criticisms will be
directed to specific weaknesses, specific errors, and specific
negative aspects of the action carried out at specific
moments. It would be a serious mistake, however, to think
that this particular revision, which aims at placing all the
men and all the events in their proper light, entails, on the
part of the Soviet Communists, a radical rejection, or a
radical and destructive criticism of their action as it has
now developed for over half a century. This action remains, in its development through the successive phases
which everyone knows, the first great historical model of
subsequent revolutionary activity for the advent of the
working class to leadership in society and for the construction of a Socialist society.

The second error consists in considering the criticisms
against Stalin and the denunciation of the cult of his person
as episodes in a personal struggle or struggle of groups
which is supposedly developing among Communist Party
and Soviet state leaders, and which, in substance, allegedly
is only a struggle for power. The influential press of
the capitalist countries has particularly devoted itself
to this sort of interpretation, which extends to everything
that happens in the Soviet Union. For this purpose, it

has its specialists who, for any shift involving the head of this or that department, of this or that organization, are capable of weighing exactly how many grams of political influence this or that leader has lost, by how many meters this or that group of men has advanced toward absolute power, and so forth. The silliest things are said when the attempt is made to proceed from subtle hypothetical evaluations to the differences, and even to the struggle between civilians and the military, for example, [or] between technicians and party men, etc. The technician and the party man often are one and the same in the Soviet Union. As for the military, everyone knows that in all internal party struggles which have occurred from the time of the revolution there has never been a position taken by the armed forces as such. One must therefore leave these things to the amateurs who concern themselves with trifles and political gossip. We cannot, nor do we want to rule out the possibility that in the elaboration of the more recent political actions and judgments of the Soviet leaders there may have been points of divergence, debates, or even heated discussions among them. Thus must operate a living political organism whose internal activity is not stifled by the cult of a single person. However, there is not one fact, or even an indication, which might substantiate the representation of a secret struggle for power which is supposedly taking place through the criticisms leveled against Stalin and the cult of his person. On the contrary, in this connection it is possible to go even beyond that. It is sufficient to have known superficially what role Stalin played not only in the minds of the party cadres and members, but also among the great mass of people, to understand how difficult was the situation which developed after his death, and especially how difficult and dangerous is the task of correcting the errors committed by him, of denouncing those errors, and of proceeding along a road which is new in many respects. This obvious difficulty explains why the open denunciation of the errors previously committed could not be made soon after Stalin's death. Not only would it not have been understood, but perhaps it would have caused negative, dangerous, and uncontrollable reactions. On the other hand, correction of the errors pertaining first to the method of governing, and then to the errors in other fields evidently began at once. It is likewise evident, however, that this correction could not have been effected by a ruling group beset by a secret personal or group struggle for power. This is demonstrated by the very elimination of Beria, one of those principally responsible for the bloody consequences of the most serious errors committed under Stalin's direction. It was possible, in fact, for it [the correction of errors] to take place rapidly, without shocks within the ruling group and without any conflict between the different sectors of public administration.

To sum up this point, it is necessary then to accustom oneself to thinking that the criticisms against Stalin and the cult of his person mean to our Soviet comrades exactly what they have said up to now. And what is that, precisely? That as a result of Stalin's errors and the cult of his person, negative elements had accumulated and unfavorable, even positively bad, situations had developed in different sectors of the life of Soviet society and in different sectors of the activity of the Party and of the state. It is not a simple matter, however, to reduce all these negative points to a single general concept, because even in such a case, one runs the risk of excessive, arbitrary, and false generalizations, i.e., the risk of judging as bad, rejecting, and criticizing the entire Soviet economic, social and cultural reality, which would be a return to the usual reactionary idiocies.

The least arbitrary of the generalizations is the one which sees in Stalin's errors a progressive encroachment by personal power on the collective entities of a democratic origin and nature and, as a result of this, the pile-up of phenomena of bureaucracy, of violation of legality, of stagnation, and, also, partially, of degeneration at different points of the social organism. However, it must be said at once that this encroachment was partial and probably had its most serious manifestations at the summit of the leading organs of the state and Party. This was the origin of a tendency to restrict democratic life, initiative, and dynamic thought and action in numerous fields (technical and economic development, cultural activity, literature, art, etc.), but it cannot be stated categorically that there has arisen from this the destruction of those fundamental features of Soviet society from which it derives its democratic and socialist character and which make this society superior in quality to the modern capitalist societies. Soviet society could not fall into such errors, while, on the other hand, the bourgeois capitalist regimes fall into errors and situations which are much more serious. Those errors could not become a permanent and general part of its civil, economic, and political life. If they had lasted longer,

perhaps the breaking point might have been reached,
although even this hypothesis should be taken with caution,
because a break would certainly have brought more harm
than good to the masses and to the entire socialist movement; this danger was known not only to those men who
could have engineered this break but also to wide strata
of society.

I do not mean to say by this that the consequences of
Stalin's errors were not extremely serious. They were very
serious; they touched many fields, and I do not think it
will be easy to overcome them, nor to do so quickly. In
substance, it may be said that a large part of the leading
cadres of Soviet society (Party, state, economy, culture,
etc.) had become torpid in the cult of Stalin, losing or
lessening its critical and creative ability in thought and
action. For this reason it was absolutely necessary that
Stalin's errors be denounced, and that it be done in such
a way as to jolt them and to reactivate the entire life of
the organisms on which the complex system of socialist
society rests. Thus there will be a new democratic progress of this society, and that will be a powerful contribution
to a better understanding among all peoples, to an international detente, to the advance of socialism, and to peace.

2. *Do you believe that criticism of the personality cult
in the USSR will lead to institutional changes?*

3. *The legitimacy of power is the great problem of
public law, and modern political thought tends to indicate
that the people's will is the wellspring of legitimacy.
Parliamentary democracies of the Western type believe
that the people's will must have a plurality of parties to
express itself. Do you believe that power is legitimate in*

a single-party system with elections offering no choice between government and opposition?

I may be mistaken, but in my opinion there are not to be foreseen today any institutional changes in the Soviet Union, nor do the criticisms formulated openly at the XXth Congress imply the necessity for such changes. This does not mean that very profound modifications ought not to occur, some of which, incidentally, are already in progress.

First of all, what is meant by institutional changes? I believe that individuals who speak of them mean changes in the political structure which would usher Soviet society into at least some of the forms of political organization intrinsic in the so-called Western regimes, or would place a new emphasis on some of the institutions intrinsic in these regimes. If the problem is posed thus, my answer is negative.

Let us, if we must, begin by examining the legitimacy of power and of its source, but let us try to free ourselves from the hypocritical formalism with which this problem is treated by the apologists for Western civilization. We have read *State and Revolution* and, fortunately for us, we have not forgotten the substance of that teaching. Criticism of Stalin's errors will not make us forget it. The truth of the matter is that in the so-called Western civilizations, the source of legitimate power is not at all the will of the people. The people's will is at best only one of the contributing factors, periodically expressing itself in elections, in determining some government policies. However, elections (Italy is a typical example for some aspects) are marked by a complex system of pressure, intimidation, coercion, falsification, and legal and illegal subterfuges, which seriously limit and falsify the expression of the people's will. And this system works not only to the advantage of and in the hands of those in power at the moment, but also for whoever holds the real power in society, afforded by wealth, ownership of the means of production and trade, and by the end products, beginning with the actual direction of political life and going to the unfailing protection of the religious authorities and of all the other nerve centers of power which exist in a capitalist society. We maintain that today, because of the developments and the present strength of the democratic and socialist movement, very large rents can be torn in this system which hinders the free expression of the people's will, and, therefore, an increasingly wider breach can be opened to the expression of this will. For this reason we move on democratic grounds, and without leaving these grounds we believe that new developments are always possible. This does not mean, however, that we do not see things as they are, and that we should make a fetish, the universal and absolute model of democracy, out of the way democratic life is lived in the Western World (it is bad enough without going so far as to end up in Spain, or Turkey, or Latin America, or Portugal, or come upon the discriminatory electoral system of the U.S.A.)! As a matter of fact, we still believe that a democracy of the Western type is a limited and imperfect democracy which is false in many ways and needs to be developed and perfected through a series of economic and political reforms. Therefore, even if we should reach the conclusion that the XXth Congress opens a new process of democratic development in the Soviet Union, we are far from thinking, and believe that it is wrong to think, that this development can or must be made by a return to institutions of the "Western" type.

The legitimacy of power in the Soviet Union has its main source in the Revolution. This gave power to the working class, which was a minority but which, by solving the great national and social problems facing it, succeeded in gradually rallying around itself all the popular masses, transforming the economic structure of the country, creating, managing and advancing a new society built on socialist principles. To forget the Revolution, to lose sight of the new social structure, to forget, that is, all that is intrinsic in the Soviet Union, and then make a purely outward comparison with the forms of political life in the capitalist countries—this is a trick and nothing more.

This first recall to reality is insufficient. Soviet society since its beginning has had a democratic political structure founded specifically on the existence and operation of the soviets (workers', peasants', laborers' and soldiers' councils). The system of the soviets as such is much more democratic and advanced than any system of traditional democracy for two reasons. The first is that it causes democratic life to penetrate into every constituent part of society, beginning at the basic workers' unit and going step by step up to the large municipal, regional, and national assemblies. The second is that it brings the elementary cells of democratic life closer to the productive units and therefore overcomes the negative aspect of the traditional democratic organizations, which consists in separating the world of production from politics and, therefore, in the external, formal nature of freedom. Is it possible that there was in the operation of the Soviet system a halt, an obstacle by which Soviet democracy was limited? It is not only possible; it was openly admitted at the XXth Congress. Soviet democratic life was limited, partly suffocated, by the ascendancy of a bureaucratic and authoritarian method of leadership, and by violations of the legality of the regime. In theory such a thing is possible because a socialist regime is not in itself free of errors and danger. Whoever thinks this would be falling into a naive infantilism. Socialist society is not only a society composed of men, but also a developing society in which there exist objective and subjective contrasts, and it is subject to the tides of history. In practice, we shall attempt to see how and why a limitation of Soviet democratic life could have come about, but whatever the answer to this question, there is for us no doubt that we will never need to return to the forms of organization of the capitalist societies.

The multi-party or single-party system may not in itself be considered a distinguishing element between bourgeois and socialist societies, just as in itself it does not mark the difference between a democratic and a non-democratic society. In the Soviet Union two parties shared the power for a certain period of time after the Revolution, with a Soviet government and dictatorship of the proletariat. In China today there is more than one party in power, and yet the government is known as a democratic dictatorship. In the People's Democracies too, there are still parties which are not Communist, although not in all these countries. In the countries which are still capitalist and in which the workers' and peoples' movement is very strong and developed, the hypothesis of profound socialist transformations, which could be carried out with the existence of several parties and on the initiative of some of them, should by no means be excluded. However, to think of a multi-party system in the Soviet Union today seems impossible to us. Where would they [the parties] come from? By decision from above? That would be a fine democratic process. It must be realized that there is not only a social homogeneity because the capitalist classes have disappeared, not only a political homogeneity expressed in the workers' and peasants' alliance, but also a form of unity in civil life and in political leadership which is unknown and perhaps not even understood here in the "Western" world. The very notion of a party in the Soviet Union is something different from what we mean by this term. The party works and struggles to realize and develop socialism, but its work is essentially of a positive and constructive nature, not argumentative against a hypothetical domestic political opponent. The "opponent" against whom it fights is the objective difficulty to be overcome, the difference to be resolved by working, the reality to be mastered, the remnants of the old to be destroyed for the progress of the new, and so forth. The dialectic of conflict, which is essential for the development of society, is no longer expressed by the contests between various parties, either of the government or of the opposition, because there is no longer an objective basis (for things) or a subjective basis (in the spirit of men) for this kind of contest. It is expressed within

the unitarian system which comprises a whole series of
co-ordinated organizations (party, soviets, trade unions,
etc.). Stalin is criticized for having hindered this expression within the system. The correction consists in restoring it to normal, not in denying the system or in demolishing
it.

But while I believe it absurd that the system be demol-
ished for the sake of going back, I do believe that modifications, even radical ones, can and must be introduced in
it, on the basis of our experience, on the basis of the success achieved in every field, and on the basis of having
more effective guarantees against errors like those of
Stalin. Our attention must be fixed on this point and,
therefore, we must follow and study the new measures
which the Soviet Union is gradually taking, both the Party
and the government. The most interesting and important
so far are the measures which more and more decentralize
the economic leadership. Centralization, even in its
extreme forms, was a necessity of the periods in which
it was essential to make very radical changes quickly, to
destroy the foundations of capitalism, to lay the ground-
work for a socialist economy, to cope with urgent economic, political, and military necessities. Centralization,
however, is not *per se* a mandatory form of socialist
economic administration, especially in its extreme forms.
A greater or smaller degree of centralization, and therefore of direction from above, is dictated by the complex
of objective conditions, but it determines a greater or
lesser degree of peripheral democratic life, of activity
and initiative by the masses; and as far as we are concerned, the activity of the masses and their effective par-

ticipation in criticism and control and, therefore, in the administration of the entire economic and social organism are the true signs of democracy. Here [in Italy] in a multi-party regime, in a regime of dialectics between the government and the opposition, etc., this activity of the masses does not exist in any form or measure, or only in a very limited and completely indirèct form and measure. That is why we say that this [Italy] is not yet a true democracy, and we do not understand why the Soviet peoples should move backward just for the sake of correcting the bad things done by Stalin.

I should like to say a few more things regarding effective guarantees against the repetition of errors like those made by Stalin. In this country I know that we put forth the idea of the "independence of the magistrature" (that is, of the division of powers) as a sure remedy against any violation of legality. I tell you sincerely, I do not believe in this remedy. A judge must have an independent position, and the Soviet Constitution guarantees it to him, as do many other constitutions. But the violation of this standard always happens as a matter of fact rather than law. Moreover, a judge is not and cannot be a citizen who lives outside of society, of its conflicts, and of the currents which permeate and dominate it. Ten years ago no judge would have dreamed of sentencing a heroic partisan leader to life imprisonment—to life imprisonment!— for having killed, under war conditions, someone reported to him as a spy. This has been done. Can we call these judges "independent"? They are probably formally independent of direct ministerial injunction, but not independent of the campaign which DeGasperi and all the others conducted for ten years to smear the partisan movement, put it under indictment, and have its members convicted. Judges are part of the ruling class and influenced by currents of opinion in it, whether these be just or unjust. They tell us now that in the USSR, in Stalin's time, there were trials which ended in illegal and unjust sentences. The judges who decided those sentences were very probably not citizens who betrayed their own consciences. They were citizens who were convinced that the mistaken doctrines of Stalin, which had spread among the people and concerned the presence of "enemies of the people" everywhere to be destroyed, were just. Therefore, even though theoretically independent, they judged in that manner. The only true guarantee lies in the justice of the political policies of the Party and government, and this can be assured by a proper democratic life both in the Party and in the State, and by permanent and close contact with the popular masses in all walks of public life. The judge also will be that much more just, the more he is in close contact with the people.

4. *It has already been remarked that there is no common political language between the East and the West. Personality cult is known as tyranny in the West; the errors which lead to purges, trials and convictions are called crimes.*

Conversely, the East calls opposition treason; discussion is called deviation, and so on. A different language always means substantial differences. To what do you attribute this diversity of language?

This assertion about diversity of political language between West and East, if you will allow me, is pure reactionary foolishness. It was one of the arguments of "sanfedismo" [pro-Vatican association in southern Italy after the French Revolution], and it still is. Again I will refer to a quaint text, the *New Democratic Philosophic Dictionary Indispensable for Anyone Who Yearns to Understand the New Revolutionary Language*, published in Venice in 1799. Liberty, patriotism, equality, rights, etc., the entire political terminology of its time expressing the great ideas which were newly affirmed and made victorious by the bourgeois revolutions, is analyzed in this 200-page "sanfedista" [pro-Vatican] manual to prove that those great words expressed great things in the past, during the time of absolute governments, and still express them to anyone who keeps faith with the past, whereas in the mouths of the revolutionaries of France, where the abhorred revolution had triumphed, they expressed different and opposite things. For the revolutionary, liberty means "absolute power for bums, thieves and thugs of every nation to despoil and massacre the honest and hard-working segment of the citizenry which has something." Equality is a word without meaning, "the biggest foolishness, without a factual idea." Democratic means "atheist, assassin, a rascal in the government." And so on. This reference to the "sanfedista" polemic of the past centuries, which in its own way applied the doctrine of diversity of political languages, can serve thoroughly to clarify the question. It is not that two different languages are spoken in different parts of the world, but that the social groups, incapable of approving or even understanding the radical social and political changes which are taking place and to which they are hostile, would like to create abysses of misunderstanding between the various parts of the world, to the detriment of the progressive part. But they are not succeeding.

Political terminology in use in the West and East is absolutely the same. Tyranny has the same meaning here and there. In specific periods of the Stalin regime there were instances of tyranny, and criminal acts were perpetrated by the government which were morally repugnant. No one denies this. Democracy means, here as well as there, government by the people, in the interest of the people, equality for all the people, and so on. In their first constitutions, when the Russian Communists established a marked difference in the importance of the workers' and the peasants' vote, they were well aware that this was not strictly a democratic practice. But they adopted it because they desired that the leadership function, obtained through the revolution, be formally and legally guaranteed for the working class, saving the country from foreign invasion and catastrophe, and creating the initial condition necessary to pave the way for socialism. Once these first steps were accomplished, this practice was abolished. And always this point was clearly made. It was openly stated that once the inequality and differentiation in the vote was removed, democracy was restored. Here in this wonderful West, I am waiting for someone to clarify for me what relationship there is between democracy and the political discrimination between citizens which a government coalition of Christian Democrats and Social Democrats sought to make a part of all government activity, and which today is the general rule of conduct of most state governing bodies, of land and factory owners, of welfare agencies, labor offices, and so forth.

It is completely untrue that in the "East," the term opposition is synonymous with treason, discussion with deviation, etc. In a discussion views can be expressed which do not agree with the existing political line, and this can be called deviation because it is that. Here [in Italy] the expressing of political views contrary to those of the ruling parties instead is termed "ideological terrorism," I have already spoken of the term opposition, and it cannot be classed as treason. Undoubtedly there have been cases, and times, when opposition took forms which could be considered treason, or which could have led to treason. There were long periods of time when the working class, which came to power through revolution, and the Party, which led this class, were confronted by such serious situations and privations, by so many difficulties and so many enemies both from within and without, to be overcome at any price, that unity of political action and control had to be and was maintained through use of extraordinary measures. It would have been too bad if this had not been done. The grave error committed by Stalin was to have illicitly extended this system (worsening it, in fact, because respect for revolutionary legality had always been demanded by Lenin, initially, even if then this legality was limited by force of circumstances) to subsequent situations, when it was no longer required and therefore became only the basis for personal power. And the mistake of his collaborators was in not seeing this in time, in having allowed him to go on until correction was no longer possible without damage to all concerned.

5. *Do you believe that the personal dictatorship of Stalin came about contrary to, and outside, Russian historical and political traditions, or that instead it was a development of these traditions?*

6. *Stalin's personal dictatorship, to maintain and advance itself, made use of a series of coercive measures which in the West, since the French Revolution, has been called "terror." Do you feel that this "terror" was necessary?*

I shall reply to these two questions at the same time because, aside from their concrete formulation, which would limit the inquiry to themes of a particular order, they permit, once this limitation is overcome, facing the question which logically presents itself at this point: that is, how is it that in Soviet society the mistakes denounced at the XXth Congress could have been perpetrated, and how was it possible for a situation to arise and last for a long time in which democratic life and Socialist legality underwent continual, serious, and extended violations? As can well be imagined, to this can be joined the question of co-responsibility for these mistakes of the entire political leadership group, including the comrades who today have taken the initiative, both in denouncing and in correcting the evil which had previously been committed, and the consequences which derived from it.

Two explanations have been advanced regarding co-responsibility. One is the more obvious and was examined by us in the discussion which took place within our party. It was also expounded by Comrade Courtade in a series of articles appearing in *Humanité**, and, if we can believe what the journalists report, also by Comrade Khrushchev in reply to a question put to him at a reception. The removal of Stalin from power when the seriousness of the mistakes that he was committing became apparent, while "legally possible," in practice was impossible because, if the question had been aired, a conflict would have ensued which probably would have compromised the future of the revolution and of the state, against which the weapons of all parts of the world were pointed. It would suffice to have had even superficial contact with Soviet public opinion, in the years Stalin was ruling the country, and to have followed the international situation of those years to realize that this point is very true. Today, for example, the Soviet leaders denounce specific errors, and a moment of lack of confidence by Stalin at the outset of the war. But who in the Soviet Union at that time would have understood and accepted, I won't say the removal of Stalin but only a diminution of his authority? There would have been a collapse if this had been seen or even suspected. And the same holds true for other times. The observation made by Khrushchev

* In the years between 1934 and 1941, when the imperialists were preparing in ever increasing, massive manner their aggression against the USSR, a move against Stalin might have produced unrest which the enemies of Communism would not have failed to exploit. Would not such a move perhaps have opened the road for aggression? Should such a risk have been taken? No honest Communist would dare say so. In practice, perhaps there was little to be done except what was done. It was necessary to "grit one's teeth," and to work for the elevation of socialism, the strengthening of the USSR, and the strengthening of all world Communist parties, and all this despite the tragedies resulting from Stalin's personality cult. (*L'Humanité*, April 26, 1956.) [Togliatti's note.]

explains, it is true, the difficulty confronting those individuals who would have wished to correct the situation,
but at the same time Khrushchev's explanation compli-
cates the over-all picture and increases its seriousness.
We are forced to admit that either the mistakes Stalin
made were unknown to the great mass of the leading
cadres of the nation, and therefore to the people—and
this does not seem likely—or else they were not regarded
as errors by this mass of cadres, and therefore by the
public opinion which they [the cadres] guided and led.
As you see, I rule out the explanation that a change was
impossible solely because of the presence of a military,
police, terror apparatus which controlled the situation
with its means. The same apparatus consisted of, and
was led by, men who in a serious moment of stress, for
example such as Hitler's attack, would have likewise been
subject to elemental reactions if a crisis had developed.
To me it seems much fairer to recognize that Stalin, in
spite of the errors which he was committing, continued to
command the solidarity of the overwhelming majority
of the nation, and above all had the support of his leading cadres and also of the masses. Was this because
Stalin not only erred, but also did good, "he did a great
deal for the Soviet Union," "he was the most convinced
of Marxists, and had the strongest faith in the people"?
[Quotes from Khrushchev's speech.] Comrade Khrushchev
himself recognized this in the declarations referred to
above, correcting in this way the strange but understandable error that was made, I feel, at the XXth Congress
in maintaining silence on the subject of the merits of

Stalin. But this does not explain everything, and it does not explain everything specifically because of the gravity of the mistakes which are being denounced today. The explanation can only be determined through careful and profound investigation of the manner in which the system characterized by Stalin's errors came about. Only in this way will it be possible to understand how these errors are not only something personal, but go deeper into the very roots of Soviet life. If I am not mistaken, another explanation on why the necessary corrections were not made before has been given by Khrushchev, who states that if these could not be made it was because the position of state and Party leaders regarding Stalin's errors was not uniform at all times. There were, then, times when there was full solidarity of the others with Stalin, and this solidarity was the expression, specifically, of the consensus which we discussed above.

Here we must admit openly and without hesitation that while the XXth Congress greatly aided the proper understanding and solution of many serious and new problems confronting the democratic and socialist movement, and while it marks a most important milestone in the evolution of Soviet society, it is not possible, however, to consider satisfactory the position which was taken at the Congress and which today is being fully developed in the Soviet press regarding the errors of Stalin and the causes and conditions which made them possible.

The basic cause of everything allegedly lies in the "personality cult," and in the cult of one person with specific and serious faults who lacked modesty, leaned toward personal power, who at times erred because of

incompetence, was not loyal in his relations with the other
leaders, who had a megalomania for self-aggrandizement
and excessive self-love, was suspicious in the extreme,
and at the end through the exercise of personal power
reached the point where he detached himself from the
people, neglected his work, and even submitted to an
obvious form of persecution mania. The present Soviet
leaders knew Stalin much better than we (I will, perhaps,
have occasion to speak at some other time of some contacts I had with him), and therefore we must believe
them today when they describe him in this manner. We
can only think, among ourselves, that since this was the
case, aside from the impossibility of a timely change as
already discussed, at least they could have been more
prudent in those public and solemn exaltations of this
man's qualities to which they had accustomed us. It
is true that today they criticize themselves, and this is to
their great credit, but in this criticism they are losing
without doubt a little of their own prestige. But aside
from this, as long as we confine ourselves, in substance,
to denouncing the personal faults of Stalin as the cause
of everything we remain within the realm of the "personality cult." First, all that was good was attributed to
the superhuman, positive qualities of one man: now all
that is evil is attributed to his equally exceptional and
even astonishing faults. In the one case, as well as in
the other, we are outside the criterion of judgment intrinsic
in Marxism. The true problems are evaded, which are
why and how Soviet society could reach and did reach
certain forms alien to the democratic way and to the
legality which it had set for itself, even to the point of

degeneration. This study must be made following the various stages of development of this society, and it is our Soviet comrades above all others who have to do it because they know the situation better than we, who might err because of partial or erroneous knowledge of the facts.

We are reminded, first of all, that Lenin, in his last speeches and writings, stressed the danger of bureaucracy which threatened the new society. It seems to us that undoubtedly Stalin's errors were tied in with an excessive increase in the bureaucratic apparatus in Soviet economic and political life, and perhaps, above all, in Party life. And here it is extremely difficult to distinguish between cause and effect. The one gradually became the expression of the other. Is this excessive bureaucratic burden also a traditional outgrowth of political and organizational forms and customs of Old Russia?

Perhaps this cannot be ruled out and, in fact, I think Lenin says something to this effect; bear in mind, however, that following the revolution the leadership underwent a complete or nearly complete change, and we then are not so much interested in evaluating the residue of the old, as we are in the fact that a new type of bureaucratic leadership was growing from the new leadership class when this class was assuming entirely new tasks.

The first years after the revolution were hard and terrible years marked by superhuman difficulties, foreign intervention, war, and civil war. A maximum of power centralization was required along with severe repressive measures to crush the counter-revolution. In this period, as in time of war, this was inevitable: if a task is not

carried out, the guilty party is brought to speedy justice!
Lenin, in a letter to Dzerzhinsky and now made public,
foresaw that a change of direction would have to be
made when the counter-revolution and foreign invasion
were completely eliminated, which came some years before
his death. It will have to be determined if this change
in course was actually accomplished, or if, almost because
of inertia, a part of that which was destined for amend-
ment or rejection was consolidated. At this time the
fight erupted between groups who were at odds over the
possibilities of socialist economic development, and this
naturally had a widespread influence on all of Soviet life.
This struggle also had all the elements of a real battle,
which was decisive in determining who would assume
power, and which had to be won at any price.

And it was in this period that Stalin assumed a positive role, and the sound forces of the party rallied and
united around him. Now it can be observed that these
forces rallied around Stalin and, guided by him, accepted
such modifications in the function of the Party and of
its directing organisms, i.e., the new functioning of the
apparatus controlled from above, as a result of which
either they could not offer opposition when the evils began
to appear, or else at the outset they did not fully understand that they were evils.

Perhaps we are not in error in asserting that the damag-
ing restrictions placed on the democratic regime, and the
gradual emergence of bureaucratic organizational forms
stemmed from the Party.

More important it seems to me should be a close examination of that which followed, when the first Five-Year

Plan was carried out, and agricultural collectivization was realized. Here we are dealing with fundamental questions. The successes attained were great, in fact, superlative. A large socialist industrial system was created without foreign assistance or loans, through commitment and development of the internal forces of the new society.

The rural social structure was also overhauled, albeit in a less definite way, beset by excessive haste, errors, and significant difficulties. The results were something the world had never seen before and which few outside the Soviet Union would have believed possible. These results confirmed the victory of the October Revolution and the correctness of the political line used against opponents and enemies of every sort. They also marked the beginning of some erroneous trends which had serious and bad after-effects. In the exaltation of the achievements there prevailed, particularly in the then current propaganda but also in the general political line, a tendency to exaggerate, to consider all problems already solved and objective contradictions, difficulties, and differences, which are always inherent in the development of a society, as having been overcome. These objective contradictions, difficulties, and differences often are extremely serious in the building of a socialist society, and cannot be overcome unless they are fully and openly recognized and the working classes are called upon to face and resolve them with their labor and creative work. However, in this period one had the feeling in the Soviet Union that the leaders, even if they were aware of the true conditions, failed to present correctly these problems to the Party and the people. Perhaps this was based upon a fear of detracting

in some way from the greatness and vastness of achievements realized. At a Party school which some students
sent by us attended, a bitter debate lasting for months
took place against those who had praised the "sacrifices"
made by the Russian workers for the success of the Five-
Year Plan. They were not supposed to mention sacrifices;
otherwise what would the workers in the West think? But
there had been sacrifices, because living conditions during
the first Five-Year Plan had been extremely trying, and
the working class does not become frightened when you
tell them that extra effort and sacrifice are necessary to
build socialism; on the contrary, this stimulates and raises
the class spirit of the vanguard. This is a small episode
but it demonstrates, as we were saying, an erroneous orientation in principle, because it is an error of principle
to believe that once the first great successes are achieved
socialist construction goes ahead by itself and not through
the interplay of contradictions of a new type, which must
be solved within the framework of the new society by the
action of the masses and of the party which leads them.

Two main consequences arose from this, I believe. The
first was the stagnation of activity of the masses in the
various places and organizations (Party, labor unions,
factory, soviets) where the new and real difficulties of
the situation should have been faced, and where, instead,
writings and speeches full of pompous statements, of ready-
made slogans, etc. began to become widespread. These
were cold and ineffective because they had lost touch
with life. True creative debate began to disappear little
by little and at the same time the very activity of the
masses diminished, directed more by orders from above

than by its own stimulus. But the second consequence was still more serious. When reality came into play and difficulties came to light as the result of the imbalance and contrasts which still existed everywhere, there occurred little by little, until at last it was the main force, the tendency to consider that, always and in every case, every evil, every obstacle in the application of the plan, every difficulty in supplying provisions, in delivering raw materials, in the development of the various sectors of industry or agriculture, etc.—all was due to sabotage, to the work of class enemies, counter-revolutionary groups operating clandestinely, etc. It is not that these things did not exist; they did indeed exist. The Soviet Union was surrounded by merciless enemies who were ready to resort to any means to damage and to check its rise. But this erroneous trend in judging the objective situation caused a loss of the sense of limits, made them lose the idea of the borderline between good and evil, friend and enemy, incapacity or weakness and conscious hostility and betrayal, contrasts and difficulties which come from things and from the hostile action of one who has sworn to ruin you. Stalin gave a pseudo-scientific formulation to this fearful confusion through his erroneous thesis of the inherent increase in enemies and in the sharpening of the class struggle with the progress of building socialism. This made permanent and aggravated the confusion itself and was the origin of the unheard-of violations of socialist legality which have been denounced publicly today. It is necessary, however, to search more deeply in order to understand how these positions could be accepted and become popular. One of the lines of search will have

to be the one indicated by us, if everything is to be understood. Stalin was at the same time the expression and
the maker of a situation, because he had shown himself the
most expert organizer and leader of a bureaucratic-type
apparatus at the time when this got the better of the
democratic forms of life, as well as because he provided
a doctrinal justification of what was in reality an erroneous
line and on which later was based his personal power, to
the point of taking on degenerate forms. All this explains
the consensus [solidarity] which surrounded him, which
lasted until his demise, and which still perhaps has retained
some effectiveness.

Do not forget that even when this power of his was
established, Soviet society did not want for successes.
These were in the economic, political, cultural, and military fields, as well as in the field of international relations. No one can deny that in 1953 the Soviet Union
was incomparably stronger, better developed in every
direction, more solid internally, and more authoritative
vis-à-vis the rest of the world than, e.g., at the time of
the first Five-Year Plan. How was it possible that so
many errors did not prevent so many successes? To this,
too, the Soviet leaders must give an answer, knowing that
today this is one of the problems which torment the
sincere militants of the international workers' movement.
To what point, from what time, and to what extent did
the mistakes of Stalin compromise the political line of the
Party and create related difficulties; what bearing did these
difficulties have, and how, in spite of those mistakes was
it possible to progress? On the basis of what we know,
we can only make a few general statements which we

are prepared to revise if necessary. It seems to us that it must be recognized that the line followed in building socialism continued to be correct, even if the mistakes which have been denounced are such that they must have seriously limited the success of its application. This, however, is one of the points which will require the greatest explanation because the restriction, and in some cases even the disappearance, of democratic life is an essential question as regards the validity of a political line. It seems irrefutable to us, at any rate, that the bureaucratization of the Party, of the state organisms, of the labor unions, and, above all, of the peripheral organisms which are the most important, must have checked and compressed the democratic functioning of the state and the creative drive of the entire society with real, evident damage resulting therefrom. On the other hand, the very successes achieved, in peace and in war and after the war, are proof of the remarkable capacity for work, enthusiasm, and sacrifice of the popular masses in whatever situation, of their continued adherence to the goals which the policies of the Party placed before the entire nation and which were achieved through their work. It is difficult to say, e.g., what other nation would have been capable of resisting, recovering, and finally winning, with Hitler in the suburbs of Moscow and then on the Volga, and in view of the terrible straits of wartime. It must be concluded, therefore, that the substance of the socialist regime was not lost, because none of its previous conquests was lost, especially not the adhesion to the regime on the part of the masses of workers, peasants, and intellectuals who form Soviet society. This same adhesion proves that, despite everything, this society maintained its fundamentally democratic character.

We have said several times that it is the duty of our Soviet comrades to face some of the questions raised by us and to furnish the necessary elements for a comprehensive answer. Thus far they have developed the criticism of the "personality cult" above all by correcting the erroneous historical and political judgments of facts and people and destroying the myths and legends created for the purpose of exalting one single person. This is very good, but it is not all that one must expect of them. What is more important today is to reply correctly, by a Marxist criterion, to the question of how the mistakes which have been denounced today were interwoven with the development of socialist society, and whether there did not intervene at a certain moment in the very development of this society certain elements of disturbance, mistakes of a general character, against which the whole camp of socialism must be put on guard—I mean all those who are already building socialism according to a path of their own and those who are still seeking their own path. One may readily agree that the central problem is to safeguard the democratic characteristics of socialist society; but what must be studied thoroughly and clarified are the problems pertaining to the interrelation of political democracy and economic democracy, of internal democracy and the leadership function of the party with the democratic operation of the state, and how a mistake made in one of these fields may have repercussions on the entire system.

7. *To what do you attribute the fact that the Communists of the entire world believed the official Stalinist version of the trials and the plots?*

The Communists of the entire world always had limitless faith in the Soviet Communist Party and in its leaders. It is more than obvious what was the source of this faith. The position of the Soviet Communists was correct in the decisive moments of history and on the decisive questions pertaining to the workers' movement and international policy. The 1917 Revolution, in which they came to power, aroused enthusiasm. The correctness of the policy advanced, defended, and followed after the Revolution was based on facts. The superhuman difficulties which they faced and finally overcame were known. The entire world was against them, attacked them with every possible means, abused them. The ruling classes of all nations were united against them. In the opposition parties and even in the workers' movement, there were few persons who expressed at least understanding, if not approbation, of the gigantic task that was being carried out in the Soviet Union. Today all except the most extreme reactionaries are in agreement in recognizing that the creation of the Soviet Union is the greatest event in contemporary history; but, for the most part, it was only, or almost only, the Communists who followed this creation step by step, made it understood, defended it, and defended its authors. It was natural and proper, under these conditions, that a relationship of trust and of profound, complete solidarity should be established between the workers' vanguards in the entire world and that Com-

munist Party, which truly stood in the van of the entire
political and social movement. It is necessary to consider also that in almost every case those who had begun
by criticizing this or that aspect of the Communist policy
of the Soviet Union soon ended by joining the ranks of
the official denouncers of the entire Communist movement and eventually became open or undercover agents
of the most reactionary political forces. Every Communist party, to a greater or lesser degree, did undergo
this same experience. There was created, then, in addition to a relation of faith and complete solidarity with
the Soviet Communists, the firm conviction that this solidarity was the distinctive trait of a truly revolutionary
proletarian movement. And this was fundamentally true.
None of us has to repent for this relationship of faith
and solidarity. It is this which has permitted us, each
fighting and working under the conditions of his own
country, to express and to give a political and organizational form to the new revolutionary impulse which the
October Revolution had awakened in the working class,
which the progress made in the building of a socialist
society in the Soviet Union supported, intensified, and
gradually made more aware of itself. The forms, methods,
and practical ways of these successes, however, were not
the object of discussion among us—up to a certain time
which can be placed, approximately, in the period of the
implementation of the first Five-Year Plan and collectivization of agriculture. In the 10 or 15 years preceding
this period, the debate among the Russian Communists
over the ways to develop the revolution, the possibility

of a socialist transformation, and the forms of such a transformation had spread to the entire workers' movement, especially to the international Communist movement, and this contributed to the defeat of the opposition groups (Trotskyites and rightists). I do not deny that this struggle and this participation had, at certain times, in certain countries, and under certain conditions some negative repercussions on our movement. I refer to the sometimes artificially instigated struggles of groups, to the sometimes exaggerated political judgments, etc. Whoever wants to can review, for example, my speech delivered at the Sixth Congress of the International in 1928 and he will find therein criticism of some of these things, or he can reread what Dimitrov had to say at the Seventh Congress. All in all, however, the political education of our movement was accomplished in these debates, which touched on the most important themes of our ideology and of our policy. Through them, our movement proceeded toward maturity.

Later, our parties spoke less and less of the questions which our Soviet comrades faced in the building of a socialist society because, among other things, our Soviet comrades did not present them to us any longer as problems, as they had before, but almost as stages of a progress already well under way, the course of which did not give rise to any new serious themes. Moreover, we had come to the time when the Communist movement outside the Soviet Union had become so reinforced that it was possible to leave the field of simple agitation and propaganda, to correct many of the mistakes committed before the advent of Hitler to power, and to carry on

broad positive action in the fight against fascism, against
the war that was being prepared, to try to save the Spanish
Republic, for the unity of the workers' and democratic
movement, etc. Conditions were being created which later,
in the course of the war, counseled the dissolution of the
Communist International.

The trials, to which the question refers, I believe are
placed (I shall explain later the significance of this limitation) in this period when there was a struggle in France
for a popular front, in Spain with weapons, and the international policy of the Soviet Union was turning effectively
to the defense of democracy and of peace. The Communist
leaders had no factor which would permit them to doubt
the legality of the judgments, particularly because they
knew that, defeated politically and among the masses, the
leaders of the old opposition groups (Trotskyites and
rightists) were not averse to continuing the struggle by
terrorist means, and that this was also going on outside
the Soviet Union. (At Paris, in 1934, one of our best
militants, Camillo Montanari from Reggio Emilia, was
killed in cold blood by a Trotskyite. There were similar
cases elsewhere.)

The fact that all the accused confessed caused, without
doubt, surprise and discussion even among us, but nothing
more. Besides, it is still not clear, to us, whether the
current denunciations of the violation of legality and
application of illegitimate and morally repugnant prosecuting methods extend to the entire period of the trials,
or only to a given period, more recent than that to which
I have referred. Moreover, the denunciation of excesses
in the use of extraordinary repressive measures and the

decision to correct them had already been stated in a national conference of the CPSU and had met with complete agreement. The ugly thing is that the decision was not respected; on the contrary, in some respects, things later became worse, and this was the unpardonable personal fault of Stalin.

I repeat, with respect to the initial trials—which we were able to consider, the later trials for the most part not being public—my opinion today is that there existed simultaneously two elements: the conspiratorial attempts of the opponents against the regime to commit terrorist acts; and the application of illegal prosecuting methods, censurable on a moral basis. The first, naturally, does not minimize the gravity of the second.

8. *The criticism of the personality cult has been formulated from above without previous consultation of the people by the authorities. Do you consider that this is a proof that Stalinism is not dead, as many assert?*

The judgments which I give and which I have substantially explained bring me to deem it inevitable that the correction and criticism of Stalin's errors should come from above. The very restriction of democratic life in the Party and in the state, a part of and a consequence of these errors, and the solidarity with which Stalin had been surrounded, worked in such a way that criticism from below could have come about only slowly and would have been developed in a confused manner, not without dangerous ruptures. The thing may appear unpleasant, but it is a result of what has happened previously. It was the task of the ruling group, convinced that it was necessary to do away with the evils and to change course, to open the way to the new course by forceful criticism from above, as well as by an initial correction of the more serious mistakes. To re-educate for a normal democratic life on the model that Lenin established during the first years of the revolution; that is, to re-educate to take the initiative in the field of ideas and in practice, to be inquisitive, to engage in lively debate, to attain the degree of tolerance of errors that is indispensable for discovering truth, to attain full independence of judgment and of character, etc., etc., to re-educate thus a party framework of hundreds of thousands of men and women, through them the entire Party, and through the Party an enormous country where living conditions still differ greatly from region to region, is an enormous task which is not to be completed by three years of work nor by a congress. I believe that it might even be an exaggeration to say that everything is only a question of time, of drawing up a new policy and of carrying it out. It does not seem to rule out the fact that new and important debates will enter into this new course of Soviet life, debates which would clearly define the scope of the errors committed and of the indispensable corrections, which would lead to an exact evaluation of principle, policy, and practice with regard to both the errors and the corrections. In short, it seems to me that the errors of Stalin must be corrected, through this broad development, by a method vastly different from that which Stalin himself followed in that period of his life when he abandoned the proper forms of party and State operation. The more this is done, the greater will be the benefits. What we hope is that the corrections will be effected without hesitation and courageously, and that out of this will come, as it must come, a new forward drive of socialist society in all directions, based on a broad and sound democratic base, full of rich, new, vital impulses.

9. *Do you believe that the criticism of the personality cult will bring a change in relations between the USSR and the People's Democracies, between the Russian Communist Party and the Communist parties of the other countries, and, in general, between the USSR and the international workers' movement?*

I hope that there is no longer anyone, at least in Italy, who still believes the foolish myth that the Communist parties receive, step by step, instructions, directives, and orders from Moscow. If such a person still exists, there is no use writing for him because it is evident that his head is too hard and that he is absolutely incapable even of coming close to understanding the problems of the present workers' movement. Therefore, let us write for the others.

In the first years following the First World War, when the Communist International was formed, there is no doubt that the main questions pertaining to the political line of the workers' movement and later of the Communist movement in the individual countries were fully debated at the center, at Moscow, at congresses and other international meetings, out of which precise lines arose. During this period, it can be said that there was a centralized leadership of the Communist movement, and the main responsibility for this fell upon our Russian comrades, assisted by comrades from other countries. Very soon, however, the movement began to go ahead by itself, par-

ticularly where it had good leaders. In 1924, for example, the decision of our party to leave the Aventino
[referring to Roman hills, and used to indicate the opposition of the Italian Deputies to fascism] Assembly of
the opposition forces and return to Parliament was taken
by us in complete opposition to the advice we received
from the leaders of the International. At the time of
the Seventh Congress (1935), the parties which had
become strong and which were united and well directed
already felt that an international center could do no
more than prepare general judgments on the situation
and on the tasks of our movement; the political decisions
and practical action were to be the task of the individual
parties, entrusted fully to their initiative and responsibility. This is the way we acted, in France and in Spain
during the 1934-1939 period of great struggles, during
the war, and even more so after the war. If the Communists advanced in the great wake of the international
policy of the Soviet Union, it is because they were convinced that the policy was correct, and in reality it was.

The Information Bureau, formed in 1947 with tasks
quite different from those of the International, essentially
did two things: the first was good; the second, bad. The
first was to guide properly the entire workers' movement
in its resistance to, and struggle against, the war plans
of imperialism. The second was the unfortunate intervention against the Yugoslav Communists. The Bureau
[Cominform] did nothing else, unless it was to publish
a bulletin which was useful only for information purposes.
Except for the Cominform constituent meeting, we Italians

have never had to discuss our policy at international meetings. All initiative which we took after the war was our own exclusive work, not always fully understood by the leaders of other Communist parties, because [it] was dictated by the very special conditions under which we in Italy are working. Now, then, even the Information Bureau has been dissolved for reasons which have been set forth fully.

The mistakes made by Stalin in the leadership of the Soviet Communist Party certainly also contributed, since they limited the debates and the democratic life to the top echelon of the Party, to making the relations between the Soviet Communists and the Communists of other countries somewhat outward and formal, to creating among them a certain detachment, but without lessening mutual trust because we did not have and could not have any idea of the facts which have now been denounced. This is true insofar as it concerns us. In other parties, especially in the People's Democracies, some of Stalin's errors were repeated after the war in a mechanical manner, just as it was the tendency to transfer and apply mechanically in these countries the entire Soviet experience and practice—always without having proper consideration for the special conditions which, in every country, made and still make mandatory special methods for development, corrections, and adaptation of the Soviet experience.

The criticisms of Stalin at the XXth Congress, unexpected for the most part, have certainly affected the framework of the international Communist movement and also, to a lesser extent, its masses.

The manner in which the enemies have seized upon
these criticisms in order to use them as a weapon against
us has rallied the militants around the Party. Beside
this, it must be said that there was something more than
surprise among them. For some it was grief; for others,
bewilderment. Doubts concerning the past arose, and
so on. These things were inevitable in view of the gravity
of the facts which have been denounced and the method
of the denunciation, since our Soviet comrades, having
limited themselves substantially to denouncing the facts
and undertaking the proper correction, have neglected
up to now the still unfulfilled task of dealing with the
difficult subject of an over-all political and historical
judgment.

I do not believe it will be possible for all this to lead to
a diminution of the mutual trust and solidarity among the
various parties of the Communist movement. However,
undoubtedly, not only the need but also the desire for
increasingly greater autonomy in judgments will come out
of this; and this cannot help but benefit our movement.
The internal political structure of the world Communist
movement has changed today. What the CPSU has done
remains, as I said, as the first great model of building a
socialist society for which the way was opened by a deep,
decisive revolutionary breach. Today, the front of socialist construction in countries where the Communists are the
leading party has been so broadened (amounting to a third
of the human race) that even for this part the Soviet model
cannot and must not any longer be obligatory. In every
country governed by the Communists, the objective and sub-

jective conditions, traditions, the organizational forms of the movement can and must assert their influence in different ways. In the rest of the world there are countries where we wish to start socialism although the Communists are not the leading party. In still other countries, the march toward socialism is an objective for which there is a concentration of efforts coming from various movements, which, however, have not yet reached either an agreement or a reciprocal understanding. The whole system becomes polycentric, and even in the Communist movement itself we cannot speak of a single guide but rather of a progress which is achieved by following paths which are often different. One general problem, common to the entire movement, has arisen from the criticisms of Stalin—the problem of the perils of bureaucratic degeneration, of stifling democratic life, of the confusion between the constructive revolutionary force and the destruction of revolutionary legality, of separation of the economic and political leadership from the life, criticism, and creative activity of the masses. We shall welcome a contest among the Communist parties in power to find the best way to avoid this peril once and for all. It will be up to us to work out our own method and life in order that we, too, may be protected against the evils of stagnation and bureaucratization, in order that we may learn to solve together the problems of freedom for the working masses and of social justice, and hence gain for ourselves ever increasing prestige and membership among the masses.

4

Pietro Nenni:
"Le giunte e il resto"
AVANTI!, Rome
June 17, 1956

ON THE Italian scene—and beyond it, because of the renewed wooing by Communist parties of socialist and other labor organizations—special interest attaches to the position of the Italian Socialist Party (PSI) led by Pietro Nenni. Long a close political ally of the Italian Communists and in 1952 a Stalin Prize winner, Nenni initially attacked the "posthumous trial of Stalin" on the front-page of his newspaper, *Avanti!* (March 22, 1956). In the party's journal, *Mondo Operaio,* Nenni called the demolition of "the so-called Stalin myth" unmotivated and disconcerting. Whatever the reservations and surprises of the new era, he, nonetheless, reportedly favored continued "acceptance" of the Soviet revolution as a whole as well as continued cooperation with the Italian Communist Party (*The New York Times,* March 25, 1956).

After the publication of the secret Khrushchev speech, Nenni responded with an editorial, "From Shock to Comic Strips" (*Avanti!,* June 13). Stating editorially that some readers had construed this as a defense of Stalin, the paper spelled out its position the next day (June 14) in greater detail:

.... *We do not wish to defend Stalin nor cover up his mistakes and faults with a compassionate veil. On the contrary, the first secret report of Khrushchev leaves us perplexed by a basic imbal-*

ance, between the portion which criticizes the man, the personality cult, power abuse, the political and military errors of Stalin (a courageous and just critique in many aspects); and the part concerning the environment, the historical moment, the objective and subjective conditions of the class struggle, which is completely inadequate or even lacking. Vainly, in the lengthy report the reader seeks an answer to why and how so many errors and crimes were committed. An unclear distinction between the Communist system and its practical operations results in Stalin being raised to the symbolic value which Maligno has in certain mystic works, in which the author provides the words and the reader construes the meaning.

An act of courage and clarification cannot halt midway; critical analysis cannot be one-sided if one wishes to be politically constructive and pedagogically correct. It should not leave doubts as to the motivation and the aims that one professes. And the Khrushchev report (at least the version we know) is inadequate, precisely because it lacks a full assumption of responsibility for the criticism, even if the report is considered as an integral part of the overall happenings and debates at the XXth Congress.

Writing from the vantage point of Italian domestic politics, Nenni amplified his views in the editorial of June 17, reproduced below.

AN AMERICAN newspaperman was telling me the day before yesterday with an air of repeating something that was general knowledge: "There is no more socialist unification talk."

I did my best to dissuade him. Not that I believe unification is knocking at the gates. What is knocking at the gates is the need for a policy of socialist unity, and unification can be its conclusive act.

That journalist reflected the opinion of the official circles and the little world of business and the press which is a sub-government, and to whom every new fact swells to the size of a catastrophe. Even the simple resumption of normal relations between our party secretariat and that of the Social Democrats is a disquieting fact in the eyes of these circles. Their reactions are essentially conservative. Their wish is quickly to close the page of a book on which the first word has barely been written, and which goes beyond the fact of the day: the elections of May 27 and the executive council's problem, even if it appears conditioned by this problem in its earliest development.

From this viewpoint Christian-Democrat obstinacy in refusing to include the PSI in the communal executive councils places the Social Democrats at an acid test, following the commitment they have made in a different and opposite direction and in which they have so far shown insistence. It is not only a matter of the executive councils but also of seizing the opportunity to put national and local public life on the right track, so that the great political and social problems of this second decennial of the Republic be faced by adequate forces. It would be a mistake to consider the attitude of the present Christian-Democrat leaders a local matter, as it really reveals the inherent difficulties of collaborating with the Socialists and the Social Democrats when the latter are in a position of strength, and emphasizes the persistent refusal to accept the verdicts of the June 7 and May 27 elections, as they imply the doom and the end of Christian-Democrat monopoly of power. In such case we would have the absurdity of Social Democrats who have gained ground in the election and lost strength in the eyes of Fanfani or even Malagodi, who would then be called upon to hinder the clear and striking wish of the electorate in Milan, Genoa, Turin, Venice, Florence, and that of almost all Italy.

There is method in the haste of those who would bury not only infant socialist reunification, which is not improvised, but also the policy of socialist unity which feeds on the new national and international situation and makes immediately possible, and not just sponsorable, a chain of concrete and common actions by the Italian socialist forces.

It would be of little use, in fact, to have a rapprochement based, for example, on the Milan election results, and be unaware of how those results reflect the new international and national relaxation; against this relaxation there are still pitted considerable forces which thrive on the threat of war and on the hates and fears inherent in it.

If we do not consider this new fact and its development, in which everything points to a thaw in the relations between our country and the Soviet Union, then everything can be reduced to the level of local difficulties which can be solved empirically, or of ministerial difficulties which would be best solved by postponing them until October.

Such is not the case. We are faced with the need to meet the problems of the Italian working class with a new spirit in their entirety and in all their concreteness. Even the Soviet cataclysm invites us and helps us to do it. The fall of the Stalin myth, which was in the eyes of millions of workers the myth of the relentless and victorious revolution, must find a largely positive compensation in a fortified trust in the ability of the workers and the socialist movement to solve its own national and international prob-

lems, in the course of its age-old tradition of democratic
and labor-union struggle, of slow and laborious rise, but
without the far-fetched expectations which were expressed
in the popular saying: "Mustache is coming." As a matter of fact, the last stage of Soviet demolition of the Stalin
myth—of which I will speak at length in the next issue of
Mondo Operaio [Document 8]—is outside the limits of the
cult and the anticult, the myth and the antimyth, in which
it seemed to be intentionally confined by the XXth Moscow
Congress in its public acts. The no longer secret report of
Khrushchev, which made Stalin a sort of modern Ivan the
Terrible, goes beyond an attack on the man and hits the
system, the ideological problems connected with the notion
of dictatorship of the proletariat and its application in the
USSR, hits the Leninist notion of the working party as
well as the Stalinist notion, and attacks the structure of the
state born of the October Revolution. It therefore demands
a critical review of the 40-year period of great struggles
which came of age and developed with all their success,
deviations and degenerations, under the banner of imperialist wars and the Communist Revolution. These problems concern the Communists no less than they concern us
and the Social Democrats. They are only partly new problems, since they have been on our minds for the last 30
years, even though we were unable to solve them systematically; we were caught up in the whirlpool of struggles
which pressed upon us even more than the goal which we
set up; the goal of how to interpret in the light of Soviet
experiences the application of Marx and Engels to the
revolutionary period of transition from capitalism to social-

ism, which the teachers of socialism called the dictatorship
of the proletariat, and which seemed to take place in Russia in the form of a dictatorship by the Communist Party;
which we are inconsiderately told today was the dictatorship of a man, and a bloody dictatorship at that, without
even an explanation or justification of necessity. A frank
and thorough discussion of these problems can lead to a
great good, an alignment of the entire workers' movement
in positions which are more consonant with the democratic
calling of socialism.

Considerations of this kind take us away from the little
problem of the executive councils ["giunte"] and bring
us back to a broader picture, from which I took my cue for
a new policy of socialist unity. But since every day has
its problem and its trouble, today's problem and trouble
is that of drawing conclusions from the May 27 election.
Whereas we are beginning a week which could be decisive,
it is well to note that our patience in supporting the search
for adequate solutions does not imply any concession or
desire to hold up the game. A party like ours may not
have this tendency in either small or big things, because it
is more than ever awake to the importance of the times and
knows how everything is interdependent—minor and major
things, detail and over-all work, means, method, and
finality.

5

Eugene Dennis:
"The U. S. A. and Khrushchev's
Special Report"
DAILY WORKER, New York

June 18, 1956

THE DEVELOPMENT of the American Communist response is exemplified in an article, appearing in the *Daily Worker* of June 12, "Man's Hope," by the Stalin Prize winner Howard Fast. Wrote Fast regarding the Khrushchev speech:

It is a strange and awful document, perhaps without parallel in history; and one must face the fact that it itemizes a record of barbarism and paranoiac blood lust that will be a lasting and shameful memory to civilized man. . . . I, for one, looked hopefully but vainly at the end of the document for a pledge that the last execution has taken place on Soviet soil. I looked for a pledge of civil rights, for the sacred right of habeas corpus, of public appeal to higher courts, of final judgment by one's peers rather than by professional judges. . . .

Instead, I learned that three more executions had been announced from the Soviet Union [Bagirov and associates], and my stomach turned over with the blood-letting, with the madness of vengeance and counter-vengeance, of suspicion and counter-suspicion. I don't think I am alone in this feeling. I think millions of human beings share my disgust at this idiotic behavior—wicked, uncivilized, but above all idiotic.

Fast concluded that, "If Russia has in me a friend, it also has a severe and implacable critic. Never again will I remain silent when I can recognize injustice—regardless of how that injustice may be wrapped in the dirty linen of expediency or necessity."

The next step was marked by the publication of the following article by Eugene Dennis, General Secretary of the National Committee of the CPUSA. It is worth noting that it was the first criticism by a foreign Communist to be acknowledged in the Soviet press prior to the Central Committee resolution of June 30 (Document 11 below). It was likewise carried by the satellite presses. Its publication evoked the first reference in the Soviet press—an editorial note in *Pravda*—to the Khrushchev speech and its public release in Washington.

The Dennis article, as republished by *Pravda* on June 27, omitted from the original text a phrase referring to "snuffing out the lives of more than a score of Jewish cultural figures" under Stalin. This deletion from the writings of the secretary of a leading "fraternal party" prompted the *Daily Worker* to reply with some vehemence. Thus Joseph Clark, the paper's foreign editor, wrote on July 3: "If the charge was untrue, all *Pravda* had to do was to deny it. . . . Deleting the phrase from Dennis' article solved no problems for *Pravda* or for anyone else. It only compounds the wrong that was done in the first place. Candor, not suppression, is called for."

PERHAPS no previous gathering of a political party anywhere has caused as much worldwide interest and provoked such a stir of public opinion as the XXth Congress of the CPSU.

Reactions to and developments since the Congress in the past four months have been varied. In many quarters, including in certain Left circles, there are some for whom the revelations about Stalin have taken up the whole horizon and who seem temporarily to have lost sight of the political significance and far-reaching effect of the XXth Congress as a whole.

But there is also a growing number of non-Communist groups and individuals who see in the XXth Congress, and in the very revelations about Stalin, a completely new possibility for re-evaluating their own views regarding relations with Communists. And these past weeks have seen (not only in New York) an increasing number of important and stimulating informal discussions taking place between Communists and non-Communist liberal and labor leaders.

John Foster Dulles and the State Department recognize that there is a changing political climate abroad and at home, a change sharply away from the atmosphere of the Cold War. They are keenly aware of the fact that the XXth Congress has stimulated this whole trend. The State Department, for instance, is uneasy at the rapprochement between Belgrade and Moscow, the cutting of Soviet armed forces, the Soviet invitation to General Twining, and the fact that a recent Gallup Poll shows a majority of Americans favor that Khrushchev and Bulganin be invited to visit here. It hopes that through its publication and use of its version of the special Khrushchev report, it can disrupt the trend toward peaceful co-existence among Americans and the "neutrals," disorient the Left, and sow disunity among Communists at home and abroad.

But despite all efforts of the State Department, even some conservative spokesmen and many liberals view the XXth Congress as inaugurating a period in which the industrial and technological supremacy of U. S. capitalism will have to meet on an equal level with the historic, peaceful competition of Soviet socialism. And the special report of Khrushchev is viewed in numerous non-Communist as well as in Communist circles as an evidence of that strength and confidence which enables the Soviet Union today to break with some very harmful features of the past, and to pave the way for a vast expansion of democracy in its internal life.

This perspective and these changes must inevitably bring about modifications in the positions of all forward-looking groups, trade unionists, liberals, Socialists, no less than Communists. And it is the recognition of these big changes that has created the growing number of requests for mutual exchanges and deep-going discussions by non-Communist democratic groups in a number of cities in the past weeks.

The Khrushchev report on Stalin tells a tragic story. Shocking and painful as it is, however, it is a part of history. Communists must have the courage to face up to it, analyze it, and draw conclusions from it.

Over the last forty years imperialism exacted a terrible price from the Soviet people and their leaders who dared to storm the heights and build socialism. This we knew. Now belatedly, we see that the heroic path to the most monumental and progressive advance in human history was made all the more difficult at a certain period by shocking crimes and crass violations of socialist law and ethics.

We especially, because we are Communists, understand and share the profound grief and shock of the Soviet people. The crimes and brutalities that sullied the latter period of Stalin's leadership are unforgiveable. Nor did they have any historical or political "necessity." Nothing can justify the use of tortures and rigged trials, large-scale deportations, provocative and chauvinist actions as in the case of Yugoslavia; the persecution of the Jewish doctors* and snuffing out the lives of more than a score of Jewish cultural figures.

Socialism could not continue to allow such terrible injustices to go undisclosed or unremedied. That is the meaning of the morally and politically courageous corrective measures undertaken in the last three years. We can expect to see these measures amplified as Khrushchev's extremely frank report is critically discussed by millions of Soviet citizens.

There are many questions about which all of us are thinking deeply. Many are the honest questions of friends, as well as of those who strongly disagree with us. Some are the loaded questions pressed by the State Department and its various "voices" of radio and press.

Why did these things happen? Were they inevitable? Are they inherent in socialism, in Communist philosophy?

A pet theme of the State Department is that the special Khrushchev report rejects "only" those injustices which were perpetrated against "the wrong people." The claim is made that the rejection of Stalin's methods must be extended to the rejection of Lenin and Leninism and of socialism as a whole.

But not even the brazen advocate of atomic "brink of war" policies can obscure the history of the last four decades. The liberating teachings of Lenin have already

---

* The rest of this sentence was deleted from the translation of this article as published in *Pravda* on June 27, 1956. Instead, there appeared an editorial note stating that "along with Jewish doctors, prominent Russian and Ukrainian physicians were illegally arrested in the so-called 'Doctors' Case.' "—*Editor.*

triumphed in one-third of the globe. The socialist world system has arrived and is irrevocably established. It wants and needs peace. It considers that war is no longer inevitable as it was in Lenin's time, that a thermonuclear war would be a catastrophe, but that it can be prevented. It is confidently competing on a peaceful basis with capitalism in every sphere of human aspiration and endeavor. It recognizes with a new maturity that the paths to socialism are many, and that in today's world more and more peoples and countries will be able to hew a parliamentary and democratic road to socialism in accord with their own national traditions and experience.

As for Lenin's "methods," but two facts need be recalled. Under his leadership the first act of the new Soviet Republic in 1917 was to proclaim peace and bring an end to the massive blood-letting visited on the Russian people during World War I. And in 1921 while foreign armies of intervention were still trying to bring down the Soviet Union, Lenin called for an end to the death penalty and any mass repressive measures.

In this connection it is well to ponder a question that now some would like to conceal:

Who were the real architects of a policy of terror in respect to the Soviet Union? Those who tried to invoke the wrath of heaven and earth to crush the first land of socialism to "strangle it in its cradle," as Winston Churchill put it.

How this new society, built in one of the most backward of nations, was forced to run the gauntlet of every type of attack and suffering! Civil war and military intervention pressed by the strongest governments of Europe, America,

and Asia; merciless blockade and enforced famine; economic and political boycott, devastation by the hordes of
Hitler; and then, with the wounds still gaping, ten years
of bitter cold war—these were the sacrifices and suffering
exacted by reactionary capitalism from those who dared
to build a new world!

It is this grim background that gave a life and death
character to the struggle over policy in the young socialist
state. Industrialize or perish; catch up economically with
the leading capitalist powers or be crushed by them—
these are the conditions that help explain, although they
do not justify, an atmosphere in which, for a period of time
under Stalin's leadership, after the foundations of socialism were established, such gruesome departures from
socialism were possible, as Khrushchev fearlessly disclosed.

As a result of the near miraculous progress of the Soviet
people, the Soviet state and the CPSU over these hard and
turbulent years, the great prestige of Stalin grew. The
USSR became a first rank industrial nation. It wiped out
illiteracy. It developed an unprecedented system of social
ownership of the means of production and full employment, of free medical aid, education and social security
for its people. Workers and farmers achieved a political,
economic and cultural status and dignity undreamed of
under the Czars, and, in many ways, unmatched in the
advanced capitalist countries. Oppression and Czarist
racism gave way to national independence, social development and self-expression for peoples and nations for whom
the ancient Russian empire had been one vast prison.

In the early 1930's when socialism had been built—notwithstanding all external pressures and attacks—Stalin promulgated an analysis and a course of action that undermined the new socialist Constitution and facilitated the grievous violations that are only now being corrected. This was the theory that with the victory of socialism the desperate class enemy would become even more dangerous, would organize increased resistance internally, and would penetrate every echelon of the Soviet state, the country's economy, and even the Party and its leadership.

It would be naive to think that the Soviet Union did not have its Benedict Arnolds. But the search for "enemies of the people" took on hysterical proportions in which virtually all opposition and serious differences of opinion became suspect.

At the same time there developed greater centralization of state power and the cultivation of hero worship of Stalin, especially during and after World War II, and the breakdown of Party and Soviet collectivity, and restrictions in creative intellectual and cultural life. And it was during this period that the security organs of the USSR obtained and wielded abnormal and dangerous powers and criminally violated the Soviet Constitution.

How was it possible for so many Communists in the "West," and so many non-Communist statesmen and political leaders, to accept the idea that treason and treachery had assumed such fantastic proportions in the Soviet Union as were claimed in the series of purges and trials that took place in the 1930's and subsequently?

For one thing, this was the period of the climactic rise of Hitler and his notorious Fifth Column, gathered openly under the "anti-Comintern" banner.

Secondly, especially we here in the strongest imperialist country have always been aware of the vicious anti-Soviet intrigues and espionage sponsored and financed by American Big Business. Moreover, we knew the history of our own labor movement and that the great economic struggles and free speech fights of the past decades are replete with tragic examples of strike-breaking and wreckage caused by labor spies, informers and provocateurs.

The terrible phenomena of false "confessions" and fabricated "evidence"—evil products of a feverishly suspicious and hysterical atmosphere exploited by a Yezhov, a Beria, and other agents of imperialism—have only now been proved by the opening of archives kept secret for many years. Similar to the secret intelligence agencies in our own country, like the FBI and CIA which have dictatorial powers, flaunt the Constitution, and are not accountable even to Congress, Beria and his accomplices obviously were able to perpetuate their crimes against the people under the guise of "national security."

All this was not the "fruit of socialism," but a bitter product of contradictions and abuses alien to socialism which a socialist society could not digest nor tolerate. Certainly we Communists, of all people, cannot ignore nor make light of these facts.

Nonetheless history cannot judge an epic social advance primarily by the evils and mistakes and departures from its principles that may arise in the tumultuous period of its growth and progress. The wise and moving words of one of our own great revolutionary theoreticians, Thomas Jefferson, regarding the French Revolution, are worth remembering today:

In the struggle which was necessary, many guilty persons fell without the form of trial, and with them some innocent. These I deplore as much as anybody and shall deplore some of them to the day of my death.

. . . But time and truth will rescue and embalm their memories, while their posterity will be enjoying that very liberty for which they would never have hesitated to offer up their lives.

(Letter to William Short, Jan. 3, 1793.)

Contrary to the State Department propaganda, the inherent evils of today's world are those of capitalism, not of socialism. Inherent in socialism is the ending of exploitation of man by man; the elimination of the causes of war, depressions, and racism. The inherent spirit of socialism is human, national, and social freedom. Its victory in the USSR, and subsequently in China and the other people's democracies, has broken the back of colonialism, and in the last ten years has inspired a winning upsurge to national liberation and social advance of over a billion colored peoples.

The economic royalists hate socialism—not for its failings, but for its strength, for its inherent social progress and liberating values.

How hypocritical is their effort to sensationalize and make capital of the Soviet Union's determined effort to erase the abuses against socialist justice and democracy! One need only mention that the State Department is not prevented from extolling the "merits" of fascist Spain by Franco's crimes against the people. It is not bothered by the indescribable corruption, degeneracy, and rottenness of the puppet regime of Chiang Kai-shek. Nor is it adverse to the unconstitutional racist rule by force and violence of

Eastland, Talmadge and Shivers, aided and abetted by McCarthy and Walter, Jenner and Nixon—which is sanctioned as an "accepted way of life" for a sizeable part of our own U.S.A.

This, then, is a clue as to which of today's prevailing world social systems harbors the "inherent evil."

In the discussion on the XXth Congress currently being centered around the special Khrushchev report, questions frequently arise about the present Soviet leadership. Did some of them try to bring about changes before the last three years? Could the past evils have been checked earlier? How big and serious are the changes now under way?

Many questions remained unanswered. The Khrushchev report, which was primarily a documented supplement to his main political report to the XXth Congress, reflects only a part of the probing that has gone on, and which may continue for years to come, in the CPSU and among the Soviet people.

There is no mistaking the historic process which is at work today. For example, for years it has been fashionable in Washington to characterize all the peace talk among the Soviet people and the concrete peace proposals of their leaders as a cover for "war-like" or "aggressive" intentions. But when a number of American travelers in the last three years began to visit the USSR, they concluded that no country could organize for war by so completely imbuing all its citizens with the idea of peace. And many conservative statesmen and millions of common folk in the West have concluded also that no "aggressor" could vol-

untarily relinquish all its military bases abroad and uni-
laterally reduce its armed forces, as has been done by the
Soviet Union in the past few years.

In a similar way, along with the elimination of gross
injustices of socialist law and ethics and harmful hero-wor-
ship, the process of mass popularization of the historic
decisions of the XXth Congress seems to be well under way
whereby critical inquiry and expression, and cultural and
scientific interchange are coming into their own, along with
a series of governmental and party measures to ensure the
complete enforcement of the Soviet constitution and the
expansion of democracy in the USSR.

Even a skeptic must admit the fortitude, integrity, confidence and team spirit with which the present Soviet
leadership has moved since 1953 to bring about the present thaw in international affairs, to expand socialist democracy, and effectuate a marked rise in living and cultural
standards. Self-criticism in its highest form and in its
only effective form is being applied in the Soviet Union
today—i.e., actual self-correction. Not least of all, the
steps being taken to restore genuine collective leadership
in the CPSU and the Soviets are providing prerequisites
for overcoming and eliminating all departures and violations of socialist legality and principle.

But this is not just a matter of leaders. The key thing
is the popular character of the process, embracing the
whole Soviet people. It is demonstrated in the sharp discussions among writers and scientists, in the factories and
on collective farms, as reported in the newspapers daily.
The recently announced steps to decentralize the minis-
tries of justice and economic planning seem to be espe-

cially significant. This would mark an historic turnaway from a highly centralized state with certain bureaucratic excesses which inevitably presented a contradiction to the further development of Soviet democracy.

Socialist democracy has broad and strong economic and political foundations for its further development in the USSR. There is no exploiting class that by virtue of its great wealth and corporate power can assume the decisive, commanding positions of the economy and of public expression and political life. There is no material obstacle to democracy's flowering as the abnormal conditions of the struggle for survival fade and the socialist constitution is made inviolable.

Certainly the minds of men and their public institutions are always influenced not only by the historic achievements of the past and present, but by the hangovers of former evils and mistakes. No one can say that new mistakes, of an entirely different type no doubt, may not be made in socialist countries again. To expect infallibility in any group of leaders is to compound the basic error of the past and to have learned nothing from the bitter mistake in elevating a Stalin to the pedestal of a demi-god. One of the key tests of political integrity and socialist strength is the frank recognition of error and, most important, self-correction. And by the record of the last three years and their present public disclosures, discussions and rectifications, it appears as a matter of fact, that the CPSU is meeting this test.

In the currrent worldwide discussions on the special Khrushchev report, we American Communists have much to think over. A myriad of questions have been opened up to which all of us have the responsibility to reflect and seek answers—answers which can come only from a sober re-assessment of facts and a full exchange of views.

We see now that we made some serious mistakes. Based upon mistaken information, as in the case of the rupture with Yugoslavia or the former situation in Soviet agriculture—we defended and accepted the indefensible and unacceptable with uncritical attitudes. We too glibly, or idealistically, assumed that the great job of building socialism could take place without major mistakes. We refused to believe, and regarded as slander, any news that purported to tell of grave injustices in the socialist countries.

While correctly repudiating and counteracting the vile slander and anti-Soviet hostility of the corporate interests and their agents, we were often intolerant of the critical opinions and viewpoints of many labor and liberal spokesmen. We too often treated criticism from sincere trade unionists and liberals as though it came from the professional anti-Communist and anti-Soviet baiters.

For all this we feel profound regret—without reservation or equivocation.

But we also do not detract one iota from the deep pride we feel in the fact that throughout the years we American Communists resolutely championed the cause of socialism, proletarian internationalism and American-Soviet friendship. This we continue to do actively and proudly. For this has always been, and is today, in the best interest of America and of world peace.

FDR, for example, near the end of his life, referred to the establishment of friendly and good neighborly relations with the Soviet Union as "the crowning achievement" of his Administration. The corrections now being made by the USSR, the eradication of all that is alien to socialism, facilitate this goal of amity and peaceful co-existence. And as this process continues, millions of Americans will begin to see socialism in a new light, and with the understanding that socialist society is a changing, evolutionary, and constantly improving system.

In this connection, many socialist-minded Americans will begin to realize that the hard and sacrificial struggles of the pioneers of socialism in the USSR—despite all their errors, malpractices and defects—have made possible the establishment of a worldwide socialist system, and have enormously facilitated the path to socialism everywhere. That road in our own country will be worked out by the American people in accord with our own conditions and traditions.

Certainly we American Communists advocate and strive for a democratic, constitutional and peaceful course of social transformation whereby the majority of the American people ultimately will move forward and establish a new social system on the basis of American needs and experience, traditions and labor-democratic political relationships.

Within the framework of a common concern for peace and the progress and advancement of socialism in all countries, we American Communists—while maintaining at all times our own position as an independent political party with a truly scientific attitude towards all parties and social phenomena—should continue to base our attitude towards the lands of socialism on the principles of international working class solidarity which, as Lincoln noted, is a hallmark of genuine patriotism.

In the past our gaze was often exclusively on the historic gains of socialism against overwhelming odds. And if, in certain respects, our previous vision now appears one-sided in retrospect, how near-sighted to the point of blindness would it be to see today only the grotesque distortions made in the last years of Stalin's leadership, and to lose sight of the historic achievements of socialism and the grand panorama of a new world before us!

It is no surprise that many of us react in different ways to the questions that have erupted with such impact. The *Daily Worker* has opened the way for a democratic discussion and a vigorous clash of opinion. In the process, many invaluable contributions have been made. A number of views and approaches have been put forth. It would be unrealistic to expect all of us to agree with all of them.

As for myself, there are ideas expressed in some of the letters, articles, and editorials appearing in the *Daily Worker* which I cannot agree with. I do not agree with approaches that minimize the errors now revealed. I cannot agree, on the other hand, with sweeping anti-Soviet indictments that fail to take historical fact and perspective into account and that, regardless of intent, foster hostility toward socialist countries. I share the attitude of a frank and honest self-critical apology to honest people we have mistakenly condemned. But I cannot accept the viewpoint that wipes out and undermines pride and confidence in the Socialist countries. Nor do I share the cynical attitudes that would minimize or blot out the historic contributions of us American Communists to the working class and to our nation—contributions past or present, not to speak of the future.

I am confident that our Party—in the process of strengthening its ties with the labor and Negro people's movements and all other democratic forces, and by exercising the greatest independent Marxist judgment—will prove fully capable of helping solve not only the social questions of the future, but also the vital problems now confronting the American people. And parenthetically, let me add, that our "political independence" will not be measured by how much we "criticize" or "pressure" other vanguard parties but, above all, by how we boldly and creatively apply, in accord with American conditions and needs, the principles of scientific socialism to help solve the immediate and fundamental problems of our own, the American people.

This article does not attempt to deal with some of the biggest questions concerning how the American Left, inclusive of the Communists, can move forward and draw the necessary conclusions from the past, effect certain basic and long overdue changes in certain aspects of their programmatic positions, structures, and methods of work, and exert greater political influence on the course of political and social events.

These problems are now being more widely considered not only by us Communists, but by many labor, liberal, left, and socialist-minded people and groups. Opinions need not, and should not, jell prematurely. There is room for much thought and exploration inside and outside our

ranks—for collective thought and action rooted in the
political realities of our country.

Above all, there is the need for greater mass political
and economic activity, such as around the key issues in the
1956 elections, now, even while the current discussions go
on. This, above all else can provide the framework for
new gains and perspectives for a broad, popular realign-
ment, as well as for the eventual emergence of a new mass
party of socialism.

When all has been said and done about the XXth Congress (and that subject won't be exhausted for some time
to come), one thing will remain above all else: the XXth
Congress strengthened world peace and social progress.
It marked a new stage in the advancement of socialism,
and in the struggle for peaceful co-existence that began in
Lenin's day, continued in the following years, and is
becoming ever more effective and successful.

This policy captured the imagination of mankind and
was upheld even in the face of massive hot and cold war
threats, provocations, and the encirclement of the USSR
by A-bomb bases from 1946 on.

The emergence of socialism as a world system, and the
disintegration of the colonial empires has enriched and
given new meaning to many basic Marxist precepts. One
such Leninist proposition that now acquires new social significance is that socialism and capitalism can live and
peacefully compete in the same world, that civilization is
now on the threshold of a lasting peace—because of the
new world relationships, and through the heightened mass
intervention and unity of the peoples.

The peoples and governments of the U.S.A. and the USSR can be friends, can live and let live, as good neighbors. If anything, that is all the more clear after the publication of the State Department's "big scoop" which can no more deter the world-wide trend towards peaceful co-existence and social progress than could King Canute decree a halt to the ocean's waves.

6

Statement of the Political Bureau of the French Communist Party

L'HUMANITÉ, Paris

June 19, 1956

THE PUBLICATION of the Togliatti interview on June 16 (Document 3) prompted a variety of Communist comments. Though not reported in the Soviet Union, the piece appeared in various extracts in Polish, Hungarian, and East German newspapers and broadcasts. On June 19, the Oslo Communist paper, *Friheten*, called Togliatti's criticism of the Soviet Party leadership an "important contribution" to the debate in Communist circles. The same day, the Danish Communist newspaper *Land og Folk* supported Togliatti's demand for more information. The clarification of the questions raised by him, the paper added, would contribute greatly to preventing the recurrence of past errors.

In Belgium, the Communist *Le Drapeau Rouge* of June 19, though concerned about the effect of "reactionary" propaganda on Communist cadres, began republishing Togliatti's interview, adding that it "constitutes a real contribution to an understanding of the problems." On the same date, *Tyokansan Sanomat*, Helsinki Communist daily, wrote that "we have every reason to be grateful that the well-known leader of the Italian Communist party, Palmiro Togliatti, has made an extensive statement on these questions." It urged use of the "right to criticize" in a "discussion on an international scale." (On June 28, the same paper carried an interview with Ville Pessi, Secretary-General of the Finnish Communist Party, in which he declared unequivocally that "the criticism made against Stalin is fully justified," denied that the problem of the "cult of the personality" was applicable to the Finnish Party, and side-stepped the additional queries raised by Togliatti and others.)

Serious differences of opinion apparently occurred within the French Communist leadership with regard to the anti-Stalinist line adopted in Moscow. Stirred by criticism, in the Yugoslav *Borba,* of French Communist failure to endorse the anti-Stalin campaign with sufficient gusto (*The New York Times,* June 23, 1956), the Politburo of the French Communist Party adopted on June 18 the statement published below. The statement, also summarized over the East German radio and reported in the Polish press though not by Moscow, was endorsed by the full Central Committee of the French Communist Party on June 22.

THE bourgeois press has published a report attributed to Comrade Khrushchev. This report, which adds to Stalin's already known errors statements of other grave mistakes committed by him, justifiably provokes high feelings among the members of the French Communist Party.

The French Communists, as do the Communists of all countries, denounce the arbitrary acts of which Stalin is accused and which are contrary to the principles of Marxism-Leninism.

The creditable effort of the leaders of the CPSU to undertake the correction of the errors and faults connected with the cult of the individual emphasizes the strength and unity of the great Party of Lenin, the confidence which it enjoys among the Soviet peoples, and its authority in the international labor movement.

However, the Politburo regrets that because of the conditions under which Comrade Khrushchev's report was presented and divulged, the bourgeois press was in a position to publish facts of which the French Communists had been unaware. Such a situation is not favorable to normal discussion of these problems within the Party. It facilitates, on the contrary, speculations and maneuvers on the part of the enemies of Communism.

The explanations given up to now of Stalin's errors, their origin, and the conditions under which they developed, are not satisfactory. A thorough Marxist analysis to determine all the circumstances under which Stalin was able to exercise his personal power is indispensable.

It was wrong, while Stalin was still living, to shower him with dithyrambic praise and to give him the exclusive credit for all the successes in the Soviet Union which were due to a correct general policy in the construction of Socialism. This attitude contributed to the development of the cult of the individual and negatively influenced the international labor movement. Today, it is wrong to blame Stalin alone for every negative act of the CPSU.

Stalin played a positive role in a whole historic period. With the other leaders of the Party, he took an active part in the October Socialist Revolution, then in the victorious struggle against foreign intervention and counter-revolution. After the death of Lenin, he fought against the adversaries of Marxism-Leninism and for the application of the Leninist plan for the construction of socialism. He contributed in great measure to the formation of all Communist Parties.

Stalin acquired a deserved prestige, which he allowed to be transformed into a cult of the individual. The development of this cult was facilitated by the position of the Soviet Union, for a long time exposed alone to the undertakings of a world of enemies. This necessitated an extreme test of the people's strength, an iron discipline, and strict centralization of power of the proletarian state. These circumstances help to explain the enormous difficulties which the Soviet Union had to face, without justifying Stalin's activities, however. He committed a number of violations of Soviet legality; he carried out arbitrary repressive measures against militant Communists; he transgressed party principles, and, using condemnable methods, he did great harm to the Soviet Union and to the international Communist movement.

The XXth Congress of the CPSU, during which Stalin's errors were justly denounced, was the congress of the brilliant balance sheet of the Soviet Union, which, having achieved the construction of socialism, has started on the road to a Communist society. It was the congress of great victories on the part of the countries in the socialist camp. It emphasized the possibility of avoiding wars in our lifetime and of achieving socialism by new means. It brightened the prospects of the working class's march to unity.

In order that all militants, in preparation for the XIVth Congress of the French Communist Party, can profitably discuss the problems raised by Comrade Khrushchev's report, the Politburo has asked the Central Committee of the CPSU for the text of this report with which the adherents of certain Communist and workers' parties are already familiar.

Faithful to the principles of Marxism-Leninism, aware of the prominent role of the Soviet people, pioneers of socialism, and in close solidarity with the CPSU, the French Communist Party will do everything in its power to make unity of action of the working class a reality, in order to advance toward a new Popular Front and a socialist France.

7

Statement of the Political Committee of the British Communist Party

DAILY WORKER, London

June 22, 1956

THE BRITISH COMMUNIST PARTY, not unlike the French, did not respond promptly to the Soviet criticism of Stalin. Both the party's secretary, Harry Pollitt, and its propaganda leader, Rajani Palme Dutt, maintained what some of their critics were reported to consider an unjustifiably stubborn "pro-Stalinist" position. (See *The New York Times,* March 29 and June 22, 1956, but also the anti-Stalin remarks in Harry Pollitt, "The Role of Stalin," *Daily Worker,* London, March 24, 1956.)

Indeed, in the May 1956 issue of *Labour Monthly* (London), editor Palme Dutt discussed the current "Great Debate" with scant attention to the anti-Stalin drive:

> *What are the essential themes of the Great Debate? Not about Stalin. That there should be spots on any sun would only startle an inveterate Mithra-worshipper. Not about the now recognized abuses of the security organs in a period of heroic ordeal and achievement in the Soviet Union. To imagine that a great revolution can develop without a million cross-currents, hardships, injustices and excesses would be a delusion fit only for ivory-tower dwellers in fairyland. . . .*

(R.P.D., "The Great Debate," *Labour Monthly,* XXXVIII, no. 5, p. 194.) Such was the extent of public criticism.

On May 13, the Executive Committee of the CPGB adopted a resolution on "Lessons of the XXth Congress of the CPSU" (published on May 16), which acknowledged that "a number of serious mistakes and grave abuses" had developed in the Soviet Union between 1934 and 1953. On the same day, Harry Pollitt resigned as General Secretary, allegedly for reasons of health.

Discussion of the Stalin question continued in the London *Daily Worker,* which on June 11 accepted editorially the State Department's version of the secret Khrushchev speech:

The unofficial version fills in the shocking details of the evils which flowed from the cult of Stalin, from the gradual replacement of the leadership of the Party by a "miracle man" and the degeneration of the man as he became increasingly divorced from real life—and from the real day-to-day work of the Party and the People.

On June 21, after the American, Italian, and French parties had pressed Moscow for further clarification, the Political Committee of the British Communist Party issued the following statement, reproduced from the London *Daily Worker.*

The Political Committee of the Communist Party has had under consideration the unofficial published version of Comrade Khrushchev's report to the private session of the XXth Congress of the CPSU, together with the discussion in our party. At the private session of the XXIVth national congress of our party on Apr. 1, a resolution was passed and conveyed to the Communist Party of the Soviet Union, regretting that a public statement on this question had not been made by the Central Committee of the Communist Party of the Soviet Union, which could have enabled the members of all Communist Parties and the staunch friends of the Soviet Union to have understood fully the seriousness of the issues and helped them to a better understanding of everything that is involved. Our Party has not received any official version of the report of Comrade Khrushchev.

The continued absence of an official report has led to the publication of unofficial versions through gradual leakages and by sources hostile to Socialism. This has made many Communists outside the Soviet Union dependent on such enemy sources for information on these vital matters and has thus added unnecessary difficulties to the estimation and discussion of the facts. In the light of the unofficial text now published, which in the absence of official denial may be regarded as more or less authentic, we reaffirm the general lines of the resolution of our executive committee of May 13.

We consider that the XXth Congress of the CPSU was correct in condemning the cult of the individual and in endorsing the return to the Leninist principles of collective leadership and inner party democracy. We consider that the XXth Congress was correct in frankly exposing all the evils which followed from the departure from the Leninist principles, in order to put an end to these evils. All Communists, in common with all democratic and progressive people, are deeply shocked by the injustices and crimes which during the period under review violated the essential principles of socialist democracy and legality and dishonored the noble cause of Communism. We repeat that such evil practices are totally alien to socialism and Communism.

At the same time, we recognize that these evils arose not as a necessary accompaniment of working-class rule and Soviet democracy, as the enemies of socialism pretend, but as a result of the violation of the socialist principles and during a specific period of abnormal strain between 1934 and 1953. This was the period of the rise of fascism abroad, the preparation of war, the Second World War, and the Cold War. The Soviet leaders have exposed the evils and abuses of this period in order to correct them and make a decisive turn to the fulfillment of the principles of Leninism, collective leadership, socialist democracy and creative Marxist work in all fields of science, literature and art.

We recognize that in spite of the grave harm caused by these abuses the Soviet people achieved very great and historic successes. In the face of terrible difficulties, they established socialism, withstood and defeated the Nazi onslaught, and reconstructed their country after the unparalleled devastation of the war. This achievement deserves the admiration of all and shows the superiority of the socialist system over capitalism and the creative possibilities it opens up for the people.

The XXth Congress of the CPSU itself recorded the historic fact that socialism has now become a world system. It made major contributions to Marxist theory, and helped the working-class movement in all countries by its declarations on the possibility of preventing world war, the peaceful transition to socialism, and the new opportunities for developing working-class unity. The discussion arising from the XXth Congress and from the revelations regarding the 1934-1953 period of the Soviet Union is stimulating fresh and fruitful thought and endeavor in every field of Communist work and practice.

It is clear that a further review and discussion of the questions opened up by the report to the private session of the XXth Congress of the CPSU is needed.

We agree with the observations of Comrade Togliatti and the French Communist Party that it will be necessary to make a profound Marxist analysis of the causes of the degeneration in the functioning of Soviet democracy and party democracy; that it is not enough to attribute these developments solely to the character of one individual, and that a more adequate estimate of the role of Stalin, both in its positive and negative aspects, will be necessary.

It is clear that the steps taken for strengthening the operation of socialist legality and safeguarding the rights of citizens will lead to a further examination of all problems of the functioning of socialist democracy and legality. Those responsible for past violations of socialist democracy and for crimes against the people are being punished, and this is just and necessary. At the same time, it is understandable that concern has been expressed at the application of the death penalty in a recent trial in the Soviet Union. We express the view that in the light of the present world situation and the strengthened position of the socialist camp it should now be possible to bring about the abolition of the death penalty in peacetime in all countries, and we recognize that we have a special responsibility to work for the fulfillment of this aim in Britain and in the colonial countries under British rule.

Within our own party, we shall need to carry forward and encourage the widest and most thorough discussion, as already begun, of our political and organizational methods, the functioning of party democracy, and the tackling of the problems before us, our relations with other sections of the labor movement and the aims of unity, as indicated in the executive committee's resolution. We shall also carry forward work on a new edition of "The British Road to Socialism," in which, among the many questions which will come up for review, we shall need to expand that section which shows how the democratic liberties won by the people can be maintained and extended, and how socialist legality will be guaranteed.

The enemies of our party hope that this discussion will weaken the party and open the way for attempts to smuggle anti-Marxist, anti-Communist bourgeois conceptions into the Party, striking at the roots of the Communist principles and organization. On the contrary, our party members and organizations will know how to conduct the discussion so as to strengthen every aspect of our party's work and activity. The democracy of our party is the widest democracy of any party in Britain. The freedom of discussion and democratic functioning which is possible in our party, and which the leaders of other parties fear to permit in theirs, is possible because of the essential unity of our party's Marxist outlook and our determination to reach, in the light of Marxism, unity on the policy which is in the best interests of the British working class.

Let us never forget, throughout this discussion, that the cause of Communism, of national independence, of freedom and peace, is advancing with giant strides throughout the world. All conditions are present here in Britain for a great advance of the labor movement. Given the correct

policy and leadership, the British people will defeat Tory-
ism and move forward to socialism. It is the mission of
our Communist Party to help achieve these aims, and it is
in this spirit that, while discussing the urgent and important issues raised by the XXth Congress of the CPSU, we
work to develop the greatest united movement of the people for the policy put forward by our XXIVth national
congress.

8

Pietro Nenni:
"Il rapporto Krusciov e la polemica
sul Comunismo"

AVANTI!, Rome

June 24, 1956

As HE ANNOUNCED earlier (see Document 4), Nenni planned to give a detailed commentary on the Khrushchev speech. It appeared originally in the next issue of *Mondo Operaio* and is reprinted below in a somewhat abbreviated version, as reported by Reuters, containing all substantively relevant passages but omitting Nenni's recapitulation of some of the charges made by Khrushchev in his speech of February 25, and some remarks on internal Italian affairs not related to the speech.

"Such, Comrades, are the facts. We should rather say, shameful facts." With these words Nikita Khrushchev concluded on the night of February 24-25 the part devoted to "the errors" of Stalin in the secret report presented to the delegates of the XXth Congress of the Communist Party of the Soviet Union. The necessity for the report and for the extraordinary and secret session of the Congress was the consequence of the amazement by which the delegates to the Congress had been seized when they heard in the ten preceding days raining down from the Congress platform a whole series of criticisms of the cult of personality and of the Stalin myth, criticisms which culminated in the drastic affirmation of Mikoyan that for 20 years there had not in fact existed in Russia a collegiate direction of the party and of the state, but instead there had been diffused the cult of the person of Stalin.

It is neither the last nor the least of these surprises of the XXth Congress that the secret report of Khrushchev has been published by the U. S. State Department, which on June 4 put out a version which Moscow has not denied. It is therefore through the medium of the press section of USIS [United States Information Service] that the Communist Parties, themselves represented at the Moscow Congress, have come to know one of the most serious and dramatic documents in Communist international literature. Let us see of what the "shameful facts" revealed by the Secretary of the Communist Party of the Soviet Union consist.

The first part of the report is devoted to the re-evocation of an old polemic—of the antagonism, so to speak, between Lenin and Stalin: an antagonism well known in all its details outside the USSR, but which the official historians of the Soviet Union had passed over for 30 years, as if the testament of Lenin had not even existed.

The report enters its most dramatic phase when it gives details of the purges, trials and executions from 1936 to 1938.

From that tragic period of the Soviet Revolution we already knew the four trials that ended with a series of death sentences: the trial of the "sixteen" ([Grigory E.] Zinoviev, [Lev B.] Kamenev, Smirnov, etc.) in August 1936;

the trial of the "seventeen" (Gregory Piatakov, Karl Radek, Sokolnikov, etc.) in January 1937;

the trial of Marshal Tukhachevsky and of a group of generals and Red Army commanders in June 1937;

the trial of the "twenty-one" (Alexei Rykov, Bukharin, Krestinsky, Henryk G. Yagoda, etc.) in March 1938.

With regard to these trials, with the exception of Tukhachevsky's, which was kept secret for reasons of military security, there exists an abundant literature, including a stenographic summary of the hearings.

It was evident from that time on that Soviet public life had undergone in the previous ten years a double process of degeneration: on the one hand, of the party and state machine toward forms of bureaucratization and terrorism, and on the other hand, of the internal opposition toward forms of conspiracy and palace revolution. I wrote about the weaknesses of the system in 1938 in a series of articles in *Nuovo Avanti* of Paris, reprinted in Number 5 of *Mondo Operaio*.

What was known at that time was only part of the truth. Not even Trotsky in his vehement accusation of Stalin, not even Victor Serge in his "Pamphlets," not even Boris Souvarine in his slashingly critical biography of Stalin were in complete possession of the whole truth, as it is now being revealed by the disciples and successors of Stalin. . . .

Let us ask ourselves for one moment what the XVIIth Congress of the Soviet Communist Party was. It was the

congress of the "victors." It was held in Moscow at the
end of January 1934. It opened with "tempestuous"
applause for the Central Committee and for Stalin.

If one considers that the power of Stalin was not at
that time what it became later, with the war, it is evident
that the massacres disclosed by Khrushchev involve
responsibilities which were not Stalin's alone but those
of the whole directing apparatus. Terror, in conditions
of time and place not justified by necessity, was the price
paid for the suppression of all democratic life inside the
party and the state. . . .

Some of K.'s heavy ironies must have sent a current
of ice [*sic*] through the Congress delegates. For example,
the phrase attributed to Bulganin: "It sometimes happens
that a person is invited by Stalin as a friend, and when
he is before him, he does not know where he will be sent
next, home or to jail." Or, "Stalin toyed also with the
absurd and ridiculous suspicion that Voroshilov was an
English agent. A special tapping device was installed in
Voroshilov's house to hear everything that was said."
Again [a reference to Stalin's alleged criticisms of Molotov
and Mikoyan] "it cannot be excluded that Comrade Molotov and Mikoyan would have not delivered any speeches
at this Congress, if Stalin had remained at the helm a few
months more." At last, the final sally, which was intended
to be a justification for K. and the other members of the
Politburo: "Stalin obviously had a plan to eliminate the
old members of the Politburo." At this point K. answers
the questions that must have been in the air: "Where were
the members of the Politburo of the Central Committee?
Why did they not assert themselves against the cult of the

individual in time? And why is this being done only now?" The answer is: "The members of the Politburo saw these problems in a different way at different times."

This answer may be valid in a strictly personal sense, but it is not valid for the Central Committee of the Bolshevik Party. It is not valid for the Politburo. There is no doubt that the facts cited by Khrushchev, and on which world opinion now awaits proper documentation, must have placed the members of the Political Bureau in a very difficult situation. But they had been placed in posts of responsibility precisely for this purpose, precisely to face difficult situations.

From the revelations of K. we learn that the host of the Kremlin appears to have been practically a maniac who, like the figure of the dictator in which Charlie Chaplin portrayed Hitler, "drew plans on a map of the world." K. cannot contain his laughter at the contempt for Stalin's military genius. Of the historical and military films of Stalin, he says that "they make us sick." The snag is that on those films, on those books, on those poems there was organized the vastest propaganda hoax in the memory of the world.

One of the main results of the K. report is the fact that the polemic on the cult of the individual no longer makes sense, and the fact that it was Stalin who imposed the glorification of his own person becomes entirely secondary, as does the fact that he himself wrote the most laudatory phrases in his biography, on which the Communists of the whole world have fed, and the fact that he was never sated by hyperlaudatory adjectives, anthems, and gifts. . . .

The rapporteur has pointed out the difference between the premise—the criticism of the cult of the myth—and the conclusion—the demolition of the action of a man who for 30 years personified the Communist Revolution. And the question has been asked, at the end of his report: "But how was all this possible? Stalin was at the head of the Party and of the country for 30 years, and in the course of his life many battles have been won. Can we deny it?" K. does not deny it.

He knows, better than we do, the progress that the Soviet Union has made in the past 30 years, winning the battle of industrialization, winning the battle of education, winning the war, becoming the second country in the world in production, and equaling the United States in the field of scientific experimentation and especially nuclear physics. "The Socialist Revolution," he declares, "has been realized by the working class and by the poor peasants with the partial help of the 'middle' peasants. It has been a conquest of the people, guided by the Bolsheviks." After this, evidently, we can return to the original question: Who, then, guided the Bolsheviks in view of the fact that their Congresses, their Central Committee, their Politburo, the soviets, little by little, had allowed themselves to be stripped of their prerogatives of control and their right of initiative over 20 years?

The K. report lacks any kind of Marxist analysis of Soviet society, and historical reconstruction of the moment in which under the influence of determinate objective or subjective relations all power was transferred into the hands of Stalin. There is a list of facts—of "shameful facts," as K. calls them. No attempt is even made to answer the question: "How and why could these things come to pass?" It was known that the dictatorship of the proletariat had been changed to a dictatorship of the Communist Party. We learn that the dictatorship of the Communist Party had become the personal dictatorship of Stalin. We are told neither how or why this could happen. We do not even know how the Soviet ruling group has arrived at its conclusions, whether it is in agreement or divided, and if so on what, and why.

A similar uncertainty manifests itself in the K. report as soon as the rapporteur deals with the questions of remedies. He points out three:

1. Condemn and uproot in the Bolshevik manner the cult of the individual as an element extraneous to Marxism-Leninism. Combat inexorably all attempts to reintroduce this practice under any form whatsoever. Restore and effectively apply the fundamental theses of the Marxist-Leninist doctrine, of the people as the creator of history, and of all the material and spiritual benefits of humanity, the doctrine of the decisive function of the Marxist party in the revolutionary struggle for the transformation of society and of the victory of Communism.

2. Continue systematically and effectively the work carried out by the Central Committee in the last few years.

3. Restore in full the Leninist principles of Socialist Soviet Democracy, with the object of combating the arbitrary conduct of individuals who abuse their power.

Fine declarations which, when Stalin was alive, were made a hundred times by Stalin and other Soviet leaders.

The collective direction of the Politburo or of the Central
Committee would certainly be preferable to the direction
of one man, but if in the collective direction of the Politburo or of the Central Committee there is progress compared to personal direction, enlightened or tyrannical as
it may be, there is nevertheless no guarantee of democratic
life. Now the whole problem of Soviet society, the whole
problem of the People's Democracies which have followed
in the footsteps of Soviet society, is reduced to the necessity for internal democratization, for the circulation of
ideas; in a word, for political liberty, a necessity which
has lain beneath the surface of Soviet society for many
years. It is substantially a question of eliminating in the
state, in the laws, and above all in customs all the surviving
incrustations of War Communism, of creating means and
instruments for the formation of the free political initiative of the citizen, without there hanging over his head the
accusation of being an enemy of the people, a deviationist,
a saboteur every time he tries to give weight, in dealings
with public authority, to his own personal and independent
evaluation of the path to be followed. In this sense, the
Soviet crisis covers not only the so-called "errors" of
Stalin but the Soviet system as it has taken shape under the
influence of factors which are in process of rapid transformation, until they appear completely reversed with
respect to the preceding situation.

After a century has passed, the concept of dictatorship
of the proletariat must be thought out again and recon-
sidered in relation to a society where the influence and
weight of the proletariat and of the workers in general

have become a determinant in public life and where, in countries democratically and socially more advanced, the state reflects the continuous evolution of class positions. With regard to Russian experience in particular, it is a fact that the February Revolution would have disappeared without trace, and the October Revolution would not have gone beyond the phase of civil war and the interference of the imperialist foreigners, if the proletariat had not shown indomitable will and the ability to take control of the apparatus of power of the tsarist state, to smash it, and to provide a substitute. But it would be absurd to close one's eyes to the fact that the dictatorship of the proletariat has resolved itself into a dictatorship of the Bolshevik Party, and this in turn into a personal dictatorship of Stalin, and thus put itself beyond the bounds of the prophecies and concepts of the masters of socialism.

In this Soviet turning-point, two things have a practical and immediate interest for us socialists: (1) repercussions on the foreign policy of the USSR and on the relations between the Soviet workers' movement and the workers' movements in other countries; and (2) the repercussions on the Communist Parties and, in particular, on the Italian Communist Party.

In this sense, the cataclysm of de-Stalinization must be put into relationship with the dissolution of the Cominform, which seems not to have been inspired by the purely tactical reasons which led in 1943 to the dissolution of the Comintern, but to have resulted from the tendency in Moscow to assume toward the other Communist Parties of the world a position of detachment, which would have been inconceivable during the time

in which the Third International was in fact one world
party whose national sections not only accepted but sought
and justified theoretically the guidance of the Soviet state.

It is probable that the way toward an analogous tendency in the relations between the Soviet Union and the
People's Democracies has been opened by the agreements
signed in these last few days at Moscow between Khrushchev and Tito, an agreement that sanctions the principle
of the multiplicity of the socialist experiments and puts
the relations between the two parties and the two states
under the sign of liberty of action on the basis of the
conditions of their respective degrees of development.
Within the framework of such a vast shuffling of the
cards, the claim put forward by Comrade Togliatti in his
replies to the survey promoted by the review, *Nuovi
Argomenti*, to "an ever greater degree of autonomy of
judgment" by Communists of the Soviet experience is a
new fact, indicative of the necessity for Communists to
seek means of a different development, a development of
their own, a development that may be of great importance if not dictated by contingent, tactical considerations.

It is clear that a Communism detached from Moscow,
just like a Communism without the Communist International, would no longer be the Communism of the last
36 years which determined the division of the traditional
Socialist movement. It is difficult to say where a crisis
so profound as that started by the XXth Congress in Moscow may lead, as now we see only its first manifestation.

Meanwhile, as things stand, there is an invitation to the
various workers' movements, to the Socialists, the Social
Democrats, the Communists to get things straight with

themselves, with the new times, with the results of the Moscow process of de-Stalinization. For our part, this means recognizing that a certain tendency toward historical justification, which we applied to what we found wrong and to be condemned in the Communist dictatorships, limited our critical judgment of events, a judgment which a workers' party should never renounce. . . .

9

Palmiro Togliatti's
Report to the Central Committee
of the Italian Communist Party

June 24, 1956

ON JUNE 24, Palmiro Togliatti addressed a plenary session of the
Central Committee of the Italian Communist Party. Addressing
himself to Point 2 of the agenda (preparation of the party's next
congress), he delivered an 11,000-word speech which represents
the most detailed Communist commentary on the Soviet anti-Stalin
campaign. His address published in *L'Unità*, Rome, June 26,
1956, was not reported in the Soviet Union.

COMRADES! Since its founding, our party has met in congress seven times: twice prior to the advent of the Fascist
dictatorship, twice abroad, clandestinely, and three times
after the [party's] return to legality and victory in the
war of liberation. Seven congresses, therefore, the most
important of which were, undoubtedly the first, the third,
and the fifth. The first, the founding congress of our party,
was when the great choice of principle was made by the
vanguard of the working class in a moment of crisis and
shift in international relations, of acute crisis in Italian
society, and of shift in the labor movement. It was the

choice of an ideology, of a policy, of a line of action. That
choice remains completely valid. It is to that choice that,
in the subsequent life of the party, we have continually
referred and will continue to refer. The third congress
took place clandestinely and abroad, in 1926. It caused
the party to take a big step forward from the standpoint
of quality which was decisive with regard to all subsequent
developments, although not in the sense that all the positions taken at that congress were correct. Some of those
positions today appear censurable, on the basis of the
more thorough examination of our doctrine made by us,
of our knowledge of the facts, and of our capacity to be
flexible. That congress, however, caused the entire party
to take a decisive step forward inasmuch as it worked out
the concept of the party itself, of its nature, of its function,
of its strategy and of its tactics, according to the principles
of Marxism and Leninism. This was, I repeat, a decisive
conquest of the working method of the party. Subsequently it was to undergo a series of vast developments and
remained as the base on which we have been able to build.
The fifth congress, in 1946, was held at the beginning of
a new period of our national life. It summed up what
had been done in the past, the struggles fought and the
great victories won, and laid the foundations of a vast
new action of our party, of the working class, and of all
the Italian popular forces which was to be carried out on
the solid ground of the democratic victories won by striking down fascism. In this new situation, from 1946 to
1956, over a period of nearly 11 years, there have taken
place seven party national assemblies, namely, three con-

gresses, two national conferences, and two national councils. It is clear that the tasks of a national council are not those of a congress, and the tasks of a congress are not those of a conference. The very nature of these meetings differs, and the difference is obvious to everyone. I believe, however, that over a period of such duration, save for exceptional circumstances, and for a numerous, large, and well developed party such as ours, it would be difficult to do more.

Despite this, there has been criticism of the delay in convoking the eighth congress of the party. This criticism is in part justified and, I believe, should be accepted. I do not believe, however, that it should be accepted in the sense in which it is being advanced by our adversary, who uses the fact that the 1955 meeting was a conference and not a congress to accuse us of not being a democratic party, of not knowing and of not following the correct rules of internal operation of a large, modern political organization, and so on. These charges, in my opinion, have no validity, because in reality the 1955 conference, although it was a conference and not a congress, was preceded within the party by such a wide consultation of the entire base—from cells to federal organizations—as, thus far, I do not believe has taken place in any other Italian party. But there is no doubt that there was an error at that time. Being engrossed in the material organization of this great work which was being carried on even by the lowest peripheral units, we partly lost sight of the political objective and, therefore, found at a certain point that we were not in a position to qualify the assembly as a congress, i.e., to give a democratic name to what in reality had been prepared in the most democratic possible manner. Moreover, the preparation of the congress, which dragged on for too long a time, could not be tied in with those two or three fundamental questions which would have made it possible to give to the party's consultation itself that emphasis and that substance which it should always have.

Where lies the importance of the congress which we are now about to convoke? It lies in the fact that we are confronted by a complex of new facts and elements, both in the international situation and in the situation of our country and of the party. These new facts and elements must be correctly evaluated, in order to be able to draw from them all the conclusions necessary for our further development, for the struggles which we will have to carry on, for the orientation of the revolutionary movement of the working class and of the Italian people.

The work necessary for this purpose must be commenced at this session of the Central Committee. It will not end with this session of ours. It will only begin with it, and I am issuing this warning so that all comrades will be clear, from the start, on the nature of my report, as well as on what, in my opinion, should be the nature of the discussion which will follow the report. Today it is a question of stating the problems, of expressing their scope, of attempting to delimit them and indicate their content, i.e., of giving the general outline of the discussion which is to take place within the party, but not of solving these problems as yet. It is a question of making an effort to evaluate correctly, from the start, the importance of the questions which we are to examine and the validity of the solutions which we are to give. It is a question of underscoring, from the start, this importance and of setting down a general line, but not of giving, as of today, definitive solutions. The solutions must be given by the entire party through the debate in which it is called upon to participate and for which the congress will tally up the score.

Actually, the pre-congress debate has already begun. Various comrades have reported on the discussions which took place before and after the election struggle in connection with some aspects of the XXth Congress of the CPSU. All of us consider as positive the fact that this discussion has begun, even though it has begun without prior definition on the part of the party. In fact, this was a very difficult thing to do under the conditions in which we found ourselves, and the fact that the debate has been opened anyhow is, at any rate, proof of the party's vitality and liveliness, of the existence in it of comrades who reason, think, have political and moral sensibility, have a critical spirit and express it freely. In fact, it is to be regretted that in the past, a few times, when we carried out political actions of great importance to define the line of our party and its activity, but difficult to understand, the same thing did not happen, i.e., that the party did not engage more in those discussions which we urged several times but which did not take place. This time things have gone this way because the criticisms leveled against Comrade Stalin at the CPSU Congress contained elements which have caused a sentimental, as well as a political reaction. Even this, however, is a positive fact, and the whole thing is a sign of the maturity of our party, it is in no way a sign of internal crisis, even though a certain amount of perturbation on the part of our militants has come to light in the discussion itself, as has already been pointed out, because of the way in which things have been presented and because of the very seriousness of the facts discussed.

The debate which has already begun has had two phases: one before and one after the elections. I shall not now embark on a discussion of the fact that some of the organizations engaged in the discussion before the election results. In general, when there is in the party increased activity on the part of the militants brought about by discussion of any problem, progress is always noted throughout the sphere of its activity. On the other hand, it must be recognized that we could not prevent things from going as they have.

Criticisms of the Manner in Which Was Set Up
the Discussion at the Last National Council

I know that some reservations have been expressed, for example, concerning the manner in which I, in agreement with the Party Directorate, set up the discussion at the National Council, emphasizing problems pertaining to the election struggle with which we were about to come to grips, and not, instead, problems resulting from the criticisms leveled against Stalin at the XXth Congress. Those who know what our party is, how great is the task of mobilizing it, and how little time we have, will have to admit that that way of setting up [the discussion] was correct. This also means, comrades—and I say it in a completely open manner—that in the report which I made to the party Central Committee immediately after the XXth

Congress of the CPSU, I deliberately did not face and deal thoroughly with all the questions which could and had to be faced and dealt with, because I was acutely aware that those questions, once faced, had to be dealt with thoroughly, and this could not be done except in a party congress and in a debate preceding it. And a congress could not be called at that time.

There have also been some weaknesses in the discussions held thus far in the federations. But I wish to say clearly that we do not consider as a weakness or error the fact that the party leaders are being criticized, even though they are the leaders who carry on their shoulders the heaviest burden of responsibility and experience. All the leaders of the party have a need for their activity pertaining to political and practical leadership to be verified and stimulated, and it is a very good thing for the verification and critical stimulus to come from the whole party. Naturally, this does not mean that all the criticisms which are expressed are correct, but all the criticisms certainly present problems which are to be faced, debated, and solved.

We do not consider as a weakness or error the fact that in the debate which is already under way we are faced with questions of principle, even though, sometimes, in reading reports of meetings and resolutions passed by cell and section meetings, we find that on certain questions of principle the things stated and the conclusions formulated are not acceptable, or are acceptable only in part, while they are deficient in other aspects. We are glad that problems of principle are discussed, because this will contribute to our freeing ourselves, once and for all, from a certain atmosphere of duplicity. The party leaders are invited today to state clearly, without implied meanings hidden in the creases, what they think and what the party should do. Actually, this has always been done, and with the greatest possible clarity. Those who imagined who knows what implied meanings were concealed in the [party] ranks, those are in reality the ones who did not feel that they were in agreement with the very clearly formulated judgments and tasks.

What the Debate Must Be: Exchange of Opinions in Order to Arrive at Definite Conclusions, Not a Vague Outlet

We do not consider as a weakness or error of the debates which are now under way the fact that there come to the surface mistaken attitudes due to lack of factual knowledge, errors in the evaluation of episodes in the life of the party, of the international Communist movement or of the situation of these last years. We shall be more informative, we shall state things precisely, clarity shall be practiced.

What is, instead, to be considered as an element of weakness in the discussions which are going on today is the fact that often we are faced not merely with a debate, i.e., with an exchange of opinions to arrive at definite conclusions, but with a sort of vague outlet. Everyone says what is on his mind, without arriving at any conclusion and, in the criticisms of, as well as in the attitude toward new problems, no connection is established with the concrete element of the party's activity, with the questions by which we are confronted today, in order to examine them with serious-mindedness and derive from them conclusions of principle as well as practical conclusions. That type of generalized revisionism which reveals itself here and there and has no precise substance, the ineffective desire to criticize which leads to no practical conclusion, and even the lack of proper direction of the debate itself, which is such as to manifest itself in the very course of the discussions, are negative phenomena. Our party is a great democratic organism. Our concept of the party's internal life, however, is inspired by the rules of democratic centralism, i.e., of an intense, active democratic life which, however, must proceed along the great track of our doctrine and of our practice, cannot descend to the level of tittle-tattle or recriminations devoid of any validity, in order to determine the line along which the activity of the party is to be carried out.

How to discuss, then? It is necesary first of all to refer to our doctrine, to the Marxist and Leninist doctrine, to what our classical authors have written, to what the party itself has elaborated in this field in the course of its existence. My opinion is that in this field the balance sheet which we can present to the working class and to the Italian people is substantially a positive balance sheet. Suffice it to think of what was the so-called ideological baggage of the Socialist Party when we left it, to recall the void against which Gramsci so fiercely raised his protest, the lack of any knowledge of our doctrine, the total incapacity to refer to principles in order to conduct a correct analysis of objective situations and derive from them precise political indications, suffice it to do this to understand how we have gone forward. Suffice it to recall the position in Italian cultural life, when we rose and for decades afterwards, to which was relegated Marxism, considered as a cadaver which was rotting and which could be looked upon only with pity and almost with derision.

The Two Points of Reference: Our Doctrine and the Reality of International and National Life in Its Political, Economic, Cultural, and Social Aspects

This situation no longer exists. Today Marxist doctrine, through our work, through the work of our party, of its militants, of its leaders, of its intellectuals and of its friends, has been brought back to being one of the pillars of the organization, development, and guidance of national [Italian] culture. Marxism is again to be reckoned with, and this result has been obtained because we Marxists have given proof of reckoning not only with political reality, but also with the traditional currents of Italian thinking.

We know that in this field, too, there are gaps and deficiencies which will have to be filled, but it is not true that the balance sheet is negative. Our party had the good fortune of having been founded by Antonio Gramsci, the thinker who, I believe, in Western Europe contributed greatly, in the last 50 years, to the thorough examination and to the development of Marxist doctrine on the basis of a vast knowledge of intellectual developments in the entire West and of a profound knowledge of conditions in our country. It is necessary to refer to Gramsci and our entire doctrine. It is necessary to remember that this doctrine is the most advanced and effective among doctrines which help to understand the economic, political and social world, and correctly to evaluate the currents of thought and action which move through history, to face and solve the questions of national and international life. We must know how to draw from this doctrine. A Marxist cannot be like the donkey who carried on his back barrels containing wine but he, himself, drinks water. The Marxist must always drink of the wine of the doctrine which he possesses. He can drink neither the tasteless broth of the slogans stated and wearily repeated, nor the dirty water of the refusals of doctrines of different origin, or of tittle-tattle which may be placed under his nose by the adversary and by the enemy. Let our doctrine, then, be the first point of reference of our discussions.

The second great point of reference must be the reality of international and national life in its political, economic, cultural, and social aspects. It is inevitable that some of the questions discussed at the XXth Congress prevail, initially at least. They are, in fact, the questions which have aroused and are arousing more interest, and debating them it is possible to discover fundamental questions pertaining to our movement. However, I believe it to be equally inevitable that little by little, in the course of the debate, will prevail our questions pertaining to our [own] policy, the development of our party, the analysis of the situation in our country, and the determination of the tasks before us.

Where, then, lies the importance of our next congress? It lies in the political weight which our party carries in the

Italian situation and which the results of the last elections confirmed. But it lies first of all in the new elements, which have partly matured and are partly coming to maturity, in the international situation, and in the situation of individual countries, including our own.

The Great New Fact: Socialism Presents Itself to Mankind as an Imposing, Real, Growing, Advancing Force Which Tends to Extend More and More the Sphere of Its Domain.

We can say that in the world today we find ourselves faced with a shift or, if you wish to put it more prudently, with the beginning of a shift in the international situation, as well as in the development of the labor movement and of the popular movement which is oriented toward socialism. What this shift or this beginning of a shift means is what we must be able to understand from the start, in order to be able to arrange with precision our thoughts and the conclusions which we will be able to draw from them. Undoubtedly, thus far the greatest contribution toward determining what this shift is has been made by the XXth Congress of the Communist Party of the Soviet Union. That congress started—and actually it is necessary to start —from certain realizations. First of all from the realization that a system of socialist states has been established in the world. There is no longer only one state where the working class is in power, but a vast system of socialist states. If you look at the area which these states occupy and at the populations which belong to it, you will have a picture of enormous dimensions, known to all. At the same time, you must realize the collapse of colonialism as a system of world domination by the small minority of imperialistic states. As a result of these two facts, we find ourselves before a change of the objective structures of the entire world, and it is as a result of this change of objective structures that we are witnessing profound changes, some already completed and others still under way, in the ideological and practical orientation of mankind. Such is, for example, the tendency of the new peoples and states, which have freed themselves from imperialistic domination and no longer follow the capitalist line in their economic, political, and social development. From none of these new states—be it Indonesia, India, Egypt, or Indochina, for example—is heard a [single] voice proclaiming the necessity of instituting the "American way of life." Instead, there are heard from them ever more authoritative voices which proclaim the necessity of taking the road of socialism, i.e., to change the economic, political, and social relationships in the great direction indicated by socialism. From this comes also the tendency on the part of these countries to draw near to the countries which are already socialist, as comes the growth not only of the material strength, of the economic and political strength, but also of the prestige of the socialist countries, and of the Soviet Union first of all. The fact that for some years the initiative in international life has belonged to the socialist countries and no longer to the old capitalist and imperialist states is not without significance in or without profound repercussions on the spirit of all peoples. The last initiatives of the capitalist countries have been the cold war, the hot wars interspread with it, the war blocs, the atomic threat, and the rearmament race. Socialist states or new states arisen out of the collapse of the colonial system are responsible for all the initiatives capable of changing the course of international relations, of putting an end to the hot wars and of terminating the cold war, of bringing about the conditions for a durable peace and for mutual understanding, active co-existence, and collaboration among all peoples.

What conclusions should be drawn from this new world picture which is before us? Can we draw the conclusion that capitalism is finished? No. That would be a serious error. Capitalism is still in existence; in fact, in certain countries and for certain periods of time, it can still develop. The solid power of the capitalists still exists in an entire part of the world. Can we draw the conclusion that imperialism is finished? No, we cannot draw this conclusion. This would also be a serious error. Imperialism still exists. It maintains sway over at least one third of the world. The capitalist economy, in a whole series of large and highly developed countries, retains its characteristics of imperialistic economy, which are those known to you. There also remain and are developed, therefore, the internal conflicts of the capitalist world, just as there remain the tendencies which are congenital to imperialism itself. However, the profound change of structure which has already occurred leads to evident and ever more extensive conclusions, both in the field of relations between states and between organized mass movements, and as regards the development of the awareness of the masses and of ideas, and, therefore, as regards the advance of all of mankind along the road to progress.

The XXth Congress particularly emphasized one of these conclusions when it asserted that today wars are no longer inevitable. But it is possible and necessary to draw also other conclusions which, in equally direct fashion, affect us, who live in the capitalistic world and are fighting for peace and for socialism. Socialism—and this is the great new thing—presents itself to mankind as an imposing, growing, real, advancing force which tends to extend more and more the sphere of its domain. The productive forces are growing in the capitalistic world as well as in the socialist states. In the socialist countries, however, the development of the productive forces is not in conflict but in harmony with the organizational forms of economic life. In fact, it is accompanied at least by the beginnings of a unitary process, a process of coordination of economic developments in different parts of the world. It is the socialist countries that today proclaim the necessity, I do not yet say of uniting the world, but at least of establishing among the various peoples a higher degree of cooperation in order to solve the great problem with which mankind is faced. The march toward socialism thus takes on wider forms and poses new problems, includes diverse peoples and countries, and therefore becomes even more certain [of success]. The confidence which in 1917 was kindled for the first time in the hearts of the workers and of the popular masses of the vanguard, when they saw that at last in one country the working class had been able to seize power and use it to build a new economy and a new society, [that confidence] today has not only increased, but is already qualitatively a different thing because in every country, both in those which are highly advanced and in those which are not as yet, there present themselves real and new possibilities for gathering ever greater forces in order to push these countries along the road of socialist development. From this comes the assertion that the democratic method, in the struggle for and in the advance toward socialism, today is taking on an importance which in the past it could not always have. It is possible, therefore, to obtain specific and great results in the march toward socialism, without abandoning this democratic method, by taking roads different from those which have been followed and which were almost compulsory in the past, avoiding the breaks and the asperities which were then necessary.

The Question of the Different Roads to Socialism and the Popular Front Policy

Is this new situation, from which stem such important consequences, stable, will it remain, or must it be considered transitory? We are not prophets. We see, however, that this situation is the expression of transformations, of which some are definitive, and we work and call upon all peoples to fight so that what today is new and worthwhile may become permanent and never disappear.

From this situation stems a greater clarity and a new way of considering the question of the different paths to reach socialism and to build a socialist economy and society. Not that this question has not been noted previously. It was noted and treated by the Marxist classical authors. It was noted and treated by Lenin in the early period of the revolution. Afterwards, the statements which emphasized the possibility of different paths of political development toward socialism were forgotten, at least partially. Perhaps this happened because the Soviet example exercised such a strong attraction on the entire labor world, especially on the vanguards of the working class, as to contribute to their forgetting. I would like to stress, however, and this point must be brought home if only to the "young" comrades (as we say today), whose historical experience is more limited—that the search for paths of development different from that followed in the Soviet Union has never been abandoned. A search for new roads to the working classes' and the popular forces' advent to power, to governmental organization, and, therefore, to a march toward socialism, with new methods, was made not without originality and courage, when the capitalistic world, after the terrible crisis of 1929, brought forth new fascist forms of outright reactionary dictatorship and deep political crises appeared throughout Europe.

Stable, permanent achievements were not attained, but attempts were made. The best known attempt was made at the time of the popular front policy, when, jettisoning numerous old positions, we succeeded in affirming that the Communist parties could and should enter governments under specific circumstances. Especially in the case of Spain we succeeded in defining the character of a new democratic state in which the working class and its parties participated in the government, but which was not similar in any way to the state organized when the working class seized power in Russia in 1917.

*The Thesis of Lenin on the Possibility for the
Overthrow of Specified Developmental Phases of
Capitalism by Original Forms of Evolution,
Aided by Assistance from Socialist Countries*

The doctrine of the diversity of paths of development
toward socialism, however, today calls for a more thorough
elaboration, precisely in keeping with the changes in the
objective structures of society and the lines of the movement
which tends to change it.

Here, too, it is necessary to commence with an examination of the development of the productive forces, from
which stems an objective impetus toward socialism. This
impetus manifests itself in a specific manner in countries
with a highly developed economy, and manifests itself in
another way in countries whose economy is not fully
developed. Previously Lenin had corrected the thesis
enunciated by Marx according to which it is possible to
proceed toward socialism only in those countries which
have attained the highest degree of capitalist development.
Today it is evident that corrections made by Lenin must be
further defined, at a time when we see new peoples and
states, after breaking the colonial yoke, assert their intention to proceed toward socialism and ask for help from
countries which are already socialist so that they can take
at least some steps in a direction which is no longer the
traditional one of capitalist development. This was foreseen, at least in part, by Lenin when he stated that in specific circumstances certain developmental phases of
capitalism can be overthrown by original forms of evolution, helped by assistance from countries where a socialist
society already exists. This prediction by Lenin acquires

today a concrete substance which it did not have before. Thus, great new problems are arising, and they have to be dealt with in a new manner. For example, the problem of eliminating from the world hunger areas, areas of despair, endemic diseases, areas where there do not exist even the elementary forms of the development of a civilization capable of satisfying the basic needs of human life and of guaranteeing to men the required degree of well being.

I believe that in the political field we can assert that the subjective development has not yet been reached, and that it does not correspond at all to the objective development. In general the conscious action of the vanguard parties of the working class has not kept pace and is not in step with the structural changes which have taken place and with the new states of mind arising among the masses. There has not been a uniform and general development of the Communist parties throughout the world, i.e., of the working-class vanguard organized within these parties.

The Diversity of Situations in the Field of Socialism Itself and in General in the International Workers' Movement

Political factors also intervened to block this uniformity of development: the force, at time the violence, of ruling classes. There have been errors, apparent inability of the Communist vanguards and of their leadership to enter into the national historical processes, to understand the historical tradition of individual countries and exploit them [the traditions] to give impetus to the advance of the Communist vanguards, gaining control of large popular move-

ments. All of these factors have held up—and here and
there even prevented—the development of the Communist
parties. Moreover, the field of socialism itself has internal
differences which cannot be ignored. It would be odd if
someone thought that the problems which arise in the
organization of a socialist economy and society in China
can be regarded as being the same as those which arose
after the seizure of power in the Soviet Union. The same
also can be said for countries where there are regimes of
People's Democracy. Among these countries, and between
one another, there are marked differences of economic
structure, political traditions, and organizational setups.
The progress made to date in the building of a socialist
economy and society also has varied. It would be a serious
error if these differences were not duly considered in the
establishment of tasks, objectives, and the pacing of the
action.

If we turn our glance outside the field of the countries
which are already socialist, the differences are even more
pronounced. In fact, we can find even in those countries
where the Communist parties not only do not participate
in the government, but at times are not even great forces,
a drive toward socialism and an orientation, more or less
apparent, toward economic reforms and changes of a
socialist type. What is the function facing the Communist
parties in these cases is a problem for study, and it is not
primarily up to us to study the problem. It is up to the
worker vanguards, to the Communists who are active in
these countries. But it is certain that here we find ourselves facing a new aspect of the relationship between the
Communist parties and the government, between the Com-

munist parties and the working masses, between the tasks of the Communist parties and the progress of entire countries toward socialism. This situation presents itself today, and takes on special significance in areas of the world recently freed from colonialism. Also in countries with highly advanced capitalism, however, it may happen that the majority of the working class follows a non-Communist party, and we cannot rule out that even in these countries, parties which are not Communist but are founded in the working class can express the drive provided by the working class in the march to socialism. Moreover, even where strong Communist parties exist, there can exist at their side other parties which have some roots in the working class and a socialist program. The effort to carry out radical economic changes in the capitalist system, along lines which in general are those of socialism, can also originate, lastly, from movements which are not considered as socialist.

The Great Soviet Experience Remains an Invaluable Lesson, but It Cannot Contain Instructions for Solving All Questions

Naturally, in these cases there arises the question of how to reach among various organizations, some Communist or socialist, clearly oriented toward the building of socialism, others non-Communist and non-socialist but oriented toward social reforms of a socialist type, a normal relationship which, commencing with mutual understanding, might arrive at agreement and eventual collaboration. Presented in a new manner is also the problem of how to achieve unity among the various organized forces

which today tend to move, in different ways, toward a
socialist society.

As you see, in this way a multiform, complex movement is coming about. We face a greatly different picture from that which we encountered in the past decades,
and in this picture, the problem of leadership of the movements toward socialism and of the Communist movements
and parties themselves, inevitably also must be viewed
differently than in the past. For us there is no doubt that
the Soviet Union remains the first great historical model
of conquest of power by the working class, and of utilization of this power in the most energetic and effective manner in order to succeed, once the resistence of the bourgeois and other reactionary classes was swept away and
foreign attempts to intervene repelled, in readying itself
for the task of constructing a new economy and society
and in carrying out this task.

The experience which thus has been accomplished is
an enormous experience which has its great, prevailing
positive aspects and also its negative aspects. The study
of this experience has been, and will continue to be, invaluable instruction not only for the Communist parties, which
must always refer to it, but also for all those who wish to
understand today's conditions, who aspire to economic and
social changes of a radical nature, and who want to proceed toward these changes. But this experience cannot
include either the ready-made solution of all the problems which today present themselves in those countries
which are already ruled by the working class and by the
Communist parties, or much less, the ready-made answer

to the questions which arise where, instead, the Communist parties or the parties oriented toward socialism are opposition parties which move in an environment completely different from that in which moved the vanguard of the working class in Russia during and after the seizure of power. The experience accomplished in the building of a socialist society in the Soviet Union cannot contain instructions for resolving all the questions which may present themselves today to us and to the Communists of other countries, whether in power or not, and to all the vanguard parties of the working class and of the people.

The "Polycentric System": Full Autonomy to
the Individal Communist Movements and Parties,
and Bilateral Relations between Them. Need for
Intensifying the International Proletarian Spirit

Thus various points or centers of development and orientation are established. There is established what I called in the interview which you have read, a polycentric system, corresponding to the new situation, to the alteration in the world make-up and in the very structure of the workers' movements, and to this system correspond also new types of relations among the Communist parties themselves. The solution which today probably most nearly corresponds to this new situation, may be that of the full autonomy of the individual Communist parties and of bilateral relations between them to establish complete, mutual understanding and complete, mutual trust, conditions necessary for collaboration and to give unity to

the Communist movement itself and to the entire progressive movement of the working class. Such a system is probably also one which can make possible
a better expansion of relations between the Communist
movements and the non-Communist, socialist-oriented
movements (socialists, social democrats who favor national
liberation, etc.); which can make it possible to face and
resolve in a new way the questions of bringing together
different sectors of the workers' movement, of understanding, of mutual trust, and eventually, tomorrow, of agreement among all the parties working for socialist changes
in the world. Unity of action, such as we have attained
in Italy with the Socialist Party and such as has been
attained in other countries at other times, is one of
the means by which is solved the problem of this agreement, but it is not the only possible one, even though it is
among the most widely proposed.

It is evident that in this new situation, while we are
working in a new way to establish contact with the other
parts of the international Communist movement and with
the other sectors of the socialist-oriented workers and
popular movements, we are reaffirming with energy, and
must struggle to intensify in our own ranks, in the working class and among the people, the spirit of proletarian
internationalism. However, the more we shall succeed in
achieving this aim, the more we shall succeed in giving
our proletarian internationalism a precise, solid-tone substance which corresponds to the situation facing us, which
does not fall into a repetition of formulas of the past, but
which faces with spirit and new initiative all the prob-

lems which today may present themselves to the vanguard parties of the working class.

Our Relations with the League of Yugoslav Communists. Tito's Trip to Moscow

Faithful to this orientation, we have worked to solve and we have solved the question of our relations with the League of Yugoslav Communists. You remember the past, the errors which have been committed, the way in which these errors have been corrected, and you recall the steps which we have recently taken to re-establish normal relations with the Yugoslav Communists. My trip to Belgrade, which took place in a slightly hasty manner because on both sides it was necessary to take into account prior commitments, had been preceded by contacts between other leaders of the party and leaders of the League of Yugoslav Communists and has come to an excellent result. We have established with the League of Yugoslav Communists bilateral relations of solidarity and trust, relations which we shall develop so as to succeed in understanding even more what our Yugoslav comrades are doing, to have them understand better what we are doing, and to lend our hand, at this time and in this field, to the solution of the great problem of establishing new relations among all the sectors of the workers' movement which are marching toward socialism, each following its own path.

We especially hail the agreement recently reached between the Communist Party of the Soviet Union and the leaders of the League of Yugoslav Communists during Tito's recent trip to Moscow. I invite our comrades to read and study the text of this agreement because it seems to me

that it could constitute a model for the new relations which
are being set up among the different sectors of the Communist movement.

In this new situation, the relations with the Communist
Party of the Soviet Union and with the great movement of
the Soviet Communists appear in a new light. The treatment of this question has been partly complicated by the
interference of the revelations contained in the report made
by Comrade Khrushchev in a secret session of the XXth
Congress.

Relations between the Various Communist Parties and the Communist Party of the Soviet Union: The October Revolution

These revelations have aroused surprise and commotion,
have caused the perturbation which you know, and have
given rise in our party, and I believe also in other Communist parties, to a vast debate which is still under way.
Aside from this fact, the question of relations between the
Communist Party of the Soviet Union and the Communist
movement of other countries was making itself felt in any
case. It was an objectively mature question, because the
situation itself required that these relations be examined
and clearly placed on a new basis. Without a doubt, the
events which have occurred have speeded up the process:
these events have given impetus toward its [the process?]
best solution and have clarified it to the large masses of
Communists and workers with progressive views, and this
is a positive thing.

You know how the enemy and his lackeys treat this question. With the greatest vulgarity and stupidity, by assert-

ing that the Communists in all the world always have been, and always will be the servants of Moscow, obedient to the orders which come from the Communist Party of the Soviet Union and from the state which this Party administers. We can ignore this way of presenting the question, which corresponds to a complete inability to understand reality, to understand what the development of the Communist movement between the first and second world wars and, subsequently, during and after the [second] war, meant to the history of the world and Europe.

When the working class seized power in Russia in 1917, they held it in their hands, they victoriously repulsed the attacks of every type of enemy, they united in the building of a socialist society, and for the first time they gave to the world a clear, living example of a socialist society built under the direction of a great Communist party; when this happened, the vanguards of the working class throughout the world could not help but orient themselves with this great example and see in it a center of guidance and orientation for the entire advance toward socialism in a world fiercely hostile to socialism and completely dominated by capitalism. And it is this orientation which has enabled the Communist movement to rise, to develop, to assert itself, to go forward, to make its own decisive contribution to the development of the great democratic and social struggles which fill the last decades of European history. Naturally, this contribution has been all the greater, all the more efficient, and all the better, the more the Communist movement, following the guidance and examples which have been given, has been able to maintain, strengthen, and develop its own roots among the working class, among the people, in the historical environment and in the traditions of its own country, thereby becoming a permanent factor in the development of the political struggle and of society.

The Correct Teaching and the Guidance Function of the CPSU in the Period from the October Revolution to the Outbreak of the World War and Thereafter

It is not necessary to repeat that during the entire period of history following the October Revolution, and until the outbreak of the world war and even afterwards, the political positions affirmed and defended against every sort of enemy by the Communist Party of the Soviet Union have correctly oriented in essential matters the vanguards of the working class of Europe and of the entire world. During this period of history, there was not forthcoming from any other place a teaching and a guidance which could correctly orient the vanguards of the working class and the democratic vanguards, as they were oriented first by Lenin, and then by the accomplishments of the party of the Russian Bolsheviks. From Lenin and the Russian revolution came the necessary impetus for the radical break with the ideology and the practical aspects of reformism, which [the break] was indispensable in providing a solid basis for development of the workers' movement and for advancement towards socialism. From the same source came the required inspirations for the establishment of those revolutionary workers' parties without which a progressive assertion of the working class as leader of the large popular masses and of national life is not possible. And subsequently, when Europe and the world underwent for several decades a period of such serious crises, the positions taken by the comrades at the head of the Communist Party of the Soviet Union correctly oriented not only the vanguards of the working class, but also the entire progressive and democratic movement in Europe and the world.

Let us examine, for example, the decade between 1930 and 1940. It was a period of tragic break-up and almost of the ruin of Europe. This period was highlighted on the one hand by the destruction of democratic liberties in the greater portion of the European continent, outside the Soviet Union, and on the other hand by the outbreak of the Second World War. Fascism ruled and was in power in Italy from 1922. It came to power in Germany. It was dominant in all the Balkan countries. A fascist-type regime existed in Poland. Fascism unleashed a civil war and a real war to destroy the democratic and republican regime in Spain. It succeeded by intimidation and with arms in conquering Austria and Czechoslovakia. In the countries of so-called Western democracy a tendency prevailed among the ruling class to compromise with fascism, to come to agreement with the Hitlerites and Fascists, so as to liquidate in one way or another all the democratic achievements made by the people, and to install outright dictatorial regimes of the most reactionary classes. It is back to this period that date the correct and efficacious actions of the Soviet Union and the Party which led it, which served to inspire and guide not only the working class, but all the democratic forces and all the peoples of Europe to conduct a successful defense of democracy, to unite [in order] to defeat fascism, and to ward off the

danger of a new world conflict. The leaders of the Soviet
Union conducted a stubborn, long and patient struggle to
bring about the prevalence of that line of collaboration of
democratic forces which could have saved the world from
the horrors of the Second World War.

The Struggle of the Soviet Union for Democracy, Liberty, and Peace and against Fascism

Today it is easy to forget these things, and to picture
reality as though there were only assassins in the Soviet
Union and, here, lambs standing in adoration before the
ideals of democracy! This picture has nothing to do with
reality. In that terrible decade of European history, the
Soviet Union was the strongest bulwark, the most consistent defender of the principles of democracy, of liberty,
and of peace. That is why, with a policy of justice, it led
the vast masses of the people of the entire West. It is easy
today to deny this, as it is always easy to tell lies. We
knew, and everyone else knew very well what were then
the intentions of the ruling classes of the so-called democratic European West, of France and also, in particular,
of England. Predominant in them were those who
intended, with the aid of fascism, to prepare for the throt-
tling of the democratic regimes and to launch the attack
of fascist barbarism against the country of socialism. If
there had not been that non-aggression pact between the
Soviet Union and Germany in 1939, the only prospect
that in all probability would have remained open was
that of a new compromise among the great Western powers
and fascist Germany, at the expense, perhaps of the Polish
people, but with the principal aim of pushing Hitler into
attacking the country of socialism and into destroying all

the revolutionary conquests of the working class. If there were aspects of that pact which might at the time have appeared to be negative, they were due to those who had rejected that policy of democratic unity and of unity for the defense of peace which had been proclaimed and defended for years and years by the Soviet Union, in the face of the resistance, the intrigues, the slanders of the rulers of the Western democracies, as well as of fascism.

What policy did we follow then? We followed, according to the inspiration which we received from the Soviet Communists, a great democratic, socialist, and peaceful policy. This was and continues to be our principal historic merit, in addition to the undeniable heroism of our militants of the resistance and in the war, which some people now would like to have us believe was our only one. We corrected errors of evaluation and errors of strategy and tactics which we had made in the preceding period, particularly on the eve of fascism's advent to power in Germany; we placed at the heart of our work and struggle the action of the working masses of all Europe to hinder the advance of fascism and to prevent the outbreak of the Second World War. The Popular Front, which it is fashionable to speak of today as though it were something rotten, was the greatest attempt made in the last few decades to give a new direction to democratic policy in Europe and, I would say in the whole world, to prevent fascism from being liquidated through the horrors of a new war. The failure of this attempt was the basis for the collapse of democracy and was the basis of that desperate attempt which the fascists made to gain mastery of the world with their arms and their barbarity.

The Great and Serious Political Disputes Which
Took Place within the Communist International

And I do not recall these things today in order to
emphasize the particular services of our party and of its
leaders in the preparation and implementation of that
policy. I recall them, instead, in order to recall the part
which the Soviet Union and that Communist Party had
in instilling that great democratic policy in all the Communists and in the working class of all Europe. It is
true that this was happening while in the Soviet Union,
they now tell us, a wave of lawless activities, of violence,
of violations of revolutionary legality was taking place
to the detriment even of Party leaders. We could neither
know about nor imagine it. Our confidence and working
solidarity with the Communist Party of the Soviet Union
derived specifically from the fact that we developed that
great policy under the inspiration and guidance of that
Party, and for that very reason we could not entertain
any doubt about the forms of the development and attain-
ment of democracy in the Soviet Union. Was not the
approval of that Soviet constitution which abrogated the
restrictions on democracy which had existed under the preceding constitutions, characteristic of those years?

It was precisely then that the Communist movement was
beginning to have its own autonomy of development, if
not in all countries, at least in several, and that those
conditions were developing which later forced the dissolution of the Communist International. It is a lie that
the Communist International contained only a group which
gave orders and non-Russian Communists who obeyed.

We shall have to recall these things also to the minds of comrades who do not know them because they have not lived them. Great disputes took place within the Communist International for years and years, accompanied, to be sure, by great discipline. One great dispute accompanied the liquidation of the groups of Trotskyites and of the right, which denied even the possibility of building a socialist society. Serious disputes took place when, between 1928 and 1931, extreme judgments and directives which we considered mistaken were frequent. A great dispute took place before the Seventh Congress forum of the Communist International. Errors were made also. There were mutual misunderstandings. I can remember, for example, that the judgment which was given at the XVIIIth Congress of the Bolshevik Party concerning our party, in the report which was made to that Congress on the status of the world Communist movement, was a thoroughly wrong judgment, as well as a bad one. Our party was spoken of as though it did not exist, whereas our party was living and fighting, in conditions entirely different from those in which any party had ever worked and developed. But that judgment was swept away, and there was no more talk of it when the war began and our party began to show openly what it was and what it was capable of doing, at the head of the workers and of the people.

The Autonomous Development of the Various
Communist Parties During and After the War
Later, during and after the war, and especially where the Communist parties had grown, as parties which had

deep roots in their respective countries, the autonomy of
these parties became greater, even though—and I must say
this, I cannot possibly allow this to be forgotten—even
though in this period a decisive inspiration came once
more from the Soviet Union, for the resistance and the
struggle against the policy which the American imperialists
had initiated a couple of years after the end of the war, in
order to try to impose their domination on the entire world.

The most important thing, however, is that in this last
period the Communist movement has developed with broad
autonomy. And the parties which have known how to work
by themselves and well have progressed along in their own
path.

I understand that a comrade said in a cell meeting that
he was amazed to read that from 1947 on we had never
discussed our political problems and our work in an international assembly. Yet this is the exact truth. It is certain, however, that the comrades who have followed the
developments of our policy and of our activity in all fields
with any degree of acuteness would have had to realize
that such was and had to be the case, because the developments in our policy have been so closely bound up with
the affairs of our country that these developments could
not have been dictated from outside, and outsiders could
not have exercised any sort of control over us. We have
grown and have established ourselves as Italian Communists, whose political conduct was dictated by the conditions
of our own country and by the vital necessities of our
people, and by nothing else.

When the Information Bureau [the Cominform] was
formed, I do not deny that there was some doubt among

us, as we warned that the action was substantially contrary
to the line of development of the Communist movement
which had been adopted when the Communist International
was dissolved. However, we felt the need, in that situation,
for renewing contacts among the different sectors of the
Communist movement, precisely because that was the very
time when the great cold war offensive was launched
against the Communist forces, against socialism, against
democracy and peace.

In 1951 Togliatti Rejected Stalin's Proposal That He Become Secretary-General of the Cominform

I do not hesitate to recall to the memory of my comrades
that in several cases there were differences between what
the Soviet Communists said on certain matters and what we
maintained, but this never broke our mutual solidarity and
understanding.

The most obvious and perhaps the most serious conflict
—I recall it because it has a certain degree of importance
in relation to matters which are being discussed today—
took place as recently as January 1951. At that time I had
gone to Moscow for a period of convalescence, after the
serious accident which had happened to me and the subsequent surgery, and I found myself faced with Comrade
Stalin's proposal that I should abandon the post of secretary of the Italian Communist Party to assume that of
Secretary-General of the Information Bureau. I immediately opposed it, for many reasons. I considered that
such an action could not fail to have serious and unfavorable repercussions on the development of the international
situation, at a time which was already of extreme gravity,

as it could not fail to indicate, in the eyes of public opinion, a return to the organization of the Communist International. In the second place, I considered that it was not right to take that course regarding the organization of the international Communist movement. Finally, there were personal reasons against it. There were heated arguments, but the matter was resolved satisfactorily, as Comrade Stalin withdrew his proposal.

Today the criticisms which have been made concerning the activity of Comrade Stalin and the denunciation of the terrible errors committed by him have impelled and continue to impel the re-examination of a whole series of questions, including the question of relations between the Communists of the Soviet Union and the Communist movement of the other countries. I do not know whether this re-examination will include the problem, which has been raised in a number of cell and section discussions, of the manner in which our party was informed of these criticisms, and in particular of the report made by Comrade Khrushchev. We recognize that the method was bad, but on the other hand we ask you to recognize that our responsibility is not involved in any way. For obvious reasons of courtesy toward our Soviet comrades, we could not have acted otherwise than as we did. A certain amount of critical dissatisfaction also has been expressed in our party concerning certain aspects and concerning the form of the report. I wish to remind the comrades that the report cannot be considered as something isolated. It must be related to everything that was said at the Congress, which provides its background. Aside from the fact that the report, as a document isolated from everything else, might appear to be unfortunate in certain respects, there remain several fundamental points on which we ought to be in agreement, on which, moreover, we cannot but be in agreement. The first is the fact that the report relates facts, and we cannot dispute these facts. We cannot fail to believe those who relate these facts, although in the past we were not aware of these facts and could not even imagine them. The denunciation of these facts had to be made before the Party. As to the manner of making it, it is not for us to express an opinion, as every party has its own rules and its own internal practices. We may not be satisfied with the manner in which the denunciation was brought to the attention of the Communist movement in the capitalist countries, but this is another problem. We should recognize that the denunciation of the errors and the action which has been initiated and energetically carried out to correct them are highly positive acts. The correction had to be made and ought to be hailed. It constitutes a reaffirmation and will result in a reinforcement of the democratic character of socialist society. It is restoring the principles and the practice of democracy in the internal life of the Communist Party of the Soviet Union, where this democratic character had failed. This had to be done and cannot fail to have favorable results on the development of the Communist Party and of socialist society in the Soviet Union, on the development of the Communist movement in the countries where the Communists are already in power, on the development of the Communist movement in the capitalist countries, and on the development of the entire workers' and socialist movement throughout the world.

It is evident that the personality of Stalin emerges from

the present grave denunciations and criticisms as very
different from that which we had pictured to ourselves.
However, it does not emerge as destroyed. It will have to
be viewed on a new scale. It appears to be thoroughly
contradictory intrinsically and in its development. A great
many bad qualities were coupled in it with a great many
good qualities. But this problem now is a problem of
history. Our Soviet comrades, who know the facts as we
cannot know them, will have to help us to understand and
solve this problem better and better.

Stalin's Errors, the Cult of the Individual, and
Our "Co-Responsibility"

As regards our "co-responsibility," of which so much is
being said today by our adversaries and which has been
one of their warhorses in the election struggle, it has a
political substance. It exists because we have accepted,
without criticism, a fundamentally false position in regard
to the inevitable exacerbation of the class struggle along
with the progress of socialist society, a theory which was
enunciated by Stalin and from which stemmed terrible violations of socialist legality. We also have a responsibility
for having accepted, and for introducing into our propaganda, the cult of the person of Stalin, although it should
be recognized that in this we have refrained from transferring that approach into the internal life of our party.
Considering the way in which we have striven to organize
our party, to orient it and to direct it as regards its problems and its internal life, it can also be asserted that there
has been an attempt actually to overcome many of the
defects which the criticisms of Stalin are laying bare.

Having granted all these things, many problems nevertheless remain unsolved. The report itself does not give an exhaustive and satisfactory answer to all the questions which arise in the mind of anyone who examines it. However, the debate and criticism on this point should be transferred to the political arena, in which the Marxists operate when they want to analyze specific situations and draw specific conclusions. The question arises as to what made such serious errors possible, and above all the fact that around these errors there arose an atmosphere of consent and connivance reaching as far as the co-responsibility of those who today denounce those errors. From this follows the question not only of the necessary corrections, but also of guarantees against a repetition of similar errors.

Correction of Errors and Guarantees against Their Repetition

The answers which I have given to the questions that have been put to me are a first attempt at dealing with a few of the questions which arise in regard to these problems. My written report, with which you are acquainted, was seen before publication by the comrades of the party secretariat. However, it bears my signature and involves essentially my own responsibility, for I recognize that the subjects discussed are of such scope that a single comrade cannot claim that his own opinion can be at once and forever right. At present the debate is open in the international Communist movement and in the entire socialist and democratic movement. Our party too should make its own further contribution to this, in preparation for its next congress.

You have read how I treated the question of the so-called institutional reforms which some people say should be carried out in the Soviet Union, as they are indispensable for preventing the repetition of acts as serious as those denounced in Comrade Khrushchev's report. The answer which I gave tends to emphasize what I still regard as a basic fact, i.e., that the October Revolution created a new type of political society, entirely different from the democratic societies of the capitalist West. Corrections will have to be made, measures will have to be taken, guarantees will have to be given, but in my opinion the originality of this society, as it has emerged from the Revolution and from the work of economic and political construction of a new socialist society, cannot fail to last. This originality lies in the Soviet system and in the political guidance of the Communist Party.

In regard to this question, the problem of the dictatorship of the proletariat is being raised. We are asked whether such reprehensible acts as those denounced by Khrushchev's report, for which the primary responsibility falls upon Comrade Stalin and certain of his collaborators, are not due to the form of social organization which the dictatorship of the proletariat represents. This question also is worth facing, and we should not be afraid to face it, provided that we are careful not to oversimplify matters and not to fall into social-democratic banality and vulgarity.

Sometimes, when doctrinal problems like this are faced, one observes a mistaken tendency to seize upon only one aspect of our doctrines, for example, certain opinions held by Lenin and developed by the Marxist classical authors and by the Soviet leaders as regards the very concept and the forms of the dictatorship of the proletariat. One must always be able to see the sum-total of these opinions. In the elaboration of the concept of the dictatorship of the proletariat, which is an essential concept of Marxist doctrine, various points have been brought out.

Theory of the Dictatorship of the Proletariat and the Thesis According to Which the Bourgeois Governmental Apparatus Cannot Be Used for Building a Socialist Society

First of all, the affirmation of the class nature of the state and of all states, both of the state directed by the bourgeoisie and of the state directed by the working class, is a part of the doctrine of the dictatorship of the proletariat. "Every state is a dictatorship," said Gramsci. This statement is true and remains valid. The building of the socialist society constitutes a period of transition between the revolution which demolishes capitalism and the triumph of socialism and the transition to Communism. In this period of transition, the leadership of society belongs to the working class and to its allies, and the democratic nature of the dictatorship of the proletariat results from the fact that this leadership is effected in the interest of the overwhelming majority of the people, against the remnants of the old exploiting classes. It is debatable how long this period of transition should and could last, and it is equally evident that in the course of this period various phases can exist, and consequently various forms of democratic development. Various phases have occurred in the Soviet Union. The Constitution of 1924 was one thing; the Constitution of 1936 was a different matter. On the basis of this example, we cannot rule out the possibility, nay, we consider it entirely probable, that democracy in the Soviet Union can and should develop in a new way, but retain its original characteristics, even though the leadership remains in the hands of the working class and of its allies.

But this is not all that there is in the doctrine of the dictatorship of the proletariat. First Marx and Engels and later Lenin stated, in developing this theory, that the bourgeois state apparatus could not be used in the building of a socialist society. This apparatus must be broken up and destroyed by the working class, and replaced by the apparatus of the proletarian state, that is, of the state directed by the working class itself. This was not the original position of Marx and Engels; it was the position which they arrived at after the experience of the Paris Commune and which was developed in particular by Lenin. Is this position still entirely valid today? Here is a subject for discussion. When, in fact, we state that it is possible to proceed toward socialism not only through democracy but also by using parliamentary forms, it is evident that we are correcting something in this position, taking into consideration the changes which have taken place and which are still taking place in the world.

*The Organizational Forms of the Dictatorship of
the Proletariat in Russia Are Not Compulsory in
All Countries. Possibility of Co-existence of Various Parties in a Society Which Is Building
Socialism*

The third point on which attention may be concentrated
is that concerning the forms of exercising power in the
regime of the dictatorship of the proletariat. Lenin said
clearly, in the beginning, that the organizational forms
which the dictatorship of the proletariat took in Russia
would not be compulsory in all other countries. Can
we, giving particular emphasis to this statement, expand
it somewhat today, so as to arrive at the conclusion that,
also as regards the exercise of power, Lenin's statements
made in the first few years of the existence of the Soviet
Republic applied to that situation, to a situation of revolutionary breakup, of civil war, of development of a
power which had to be defended by all means and at any
cost against the attackers who came from all sides, but
cannot apply to different situations? It seems obvious
to me that in different situations, those statements are
not valid. Here too arises the question of the existence
of different parties in a socialist society and of the contribution which different parties can make to the advance
toward socialism. It is useless and even silly to go on
repeating that our exaltation of the victory of the October
Revolution and our decades-old solidarity with the Communist Party of the Soviet Union mean that we maintain
that the same things which were done in Russia must
necessarily be done everywhere in the world and in any

situation. What has been done in the Soviet Union is not the model—especially not in this field—for what can and should be done in other countries, according to the conditions existing there. We admit without hesitation that in a society where socialism is being built there can exist different parties, some of which co-operate in this building activity. We admit that the impetus toward profound changes of a socialist nature can come from different parties, which come to an understanding in order to be able to effect these changes. The prospects which open up in this connection are undoubtedly manifold. It is possible (and, if I am not mistaken, this is being discussed among the leaders of a great country which is today directed by the Communists) to consider the very extinction of the parties as the result of the establishment of a unitary socialist society, as the result of a process which equally affects the Communist Party and the other parties which cooperate with it. Thus would be achieved, through a process of a new type, the establishment of a new type of society, having a political structure of its own corresponding to the advance and ultimately to the final victory of socialism.

In taking up these questions we have gradually approached the questions which should and undoubtedly will stand at the heart of our pre-congress debate, the questions pertaining to our party's political line and to its application, and to the way in which we believe should be raised in Italy the questions pertaining to changing the economic structures through the building of a socialist society.

The Basic Elements of the Political Line of the PCI

I do not believe that it is the task of the Central Committee, at the beginning of a pre-congress debate, to state outright that the line followed by the party has been or has not been right. This is the problem which we are to place before the party today and to the discussion of which the party must contribute. It is of interest to us that the discussion be carried on in the freest possible manner. However, it is our duty to highlight the elements of the political line which we have followed, so that the judgment which can be made concerning its correctness will be well grounded and will tackle seriously the questions which must be discussed.

What, then, have been the basic elements of our political line? We started out with an analysis of the economic and political structure of Italian society. This analysis led us to pin-point the motive forces of a democratic and socialist revolution (and I am using these terms because both of these elements have characterized our movement) in the working class and in the peasant masses, between which a class and political alliance should be established for the struggle against the old capitalist ruling classes. In particular, we pin-pointed, in the backward conditions of the south, objective conditions brought about by the historical development of our country, which give a special substance to this class alliance and which extend its scope to the point of embracing also large groups of the petty and middle urban bourgeoisie in these more backward regions. The greatest contribution to

this analysis has been made by Comrade Gramsci, and
you are familiar with it.

> *The National Function of the Working Class. The*
> *Problem of Building a New Society. The Struggle*
> *for the Application of the Constitution*

After the Resistance, after the war, and after the
collapse of fascism, new conditions arose. A great new
experiment has been undertaken; new laws have been
passed; the class forces have been aroused in a different
way; and special conclusions have been derived from
all these factors; accordingly, we have endeavored, in connection with the development of the facts, to enrich our
analysis both of the structure of our society and of the
tasks of the working class. The first and the most important conclusion which we have drawn from all that
happened under fascism and during the war has been
the reaffirmation of the national function of the working
class and of the working masses closest to it, at the time
when the capitalist ruling classes were giving up their position of leadership and when they were bringing the nation
to disaster with their policy. Our entire policy, in all its
manifestations, has always been inspired by the purpose
of achieving this national function of the working class,
of making it clear, of giving national coherence to the
political actions carried out by the party in all the fields
of its activity.

After the fall of fascism, the problem arose of building a new society, and, in view of the part which the
working class and the forces of democracy had in that
fall, certain positions of essential value could be seized,

positions which represented points of arrival of a great process of renovation which was arrested at a certain time, but points of departure for our subsequent activity. These positions are, fundamentally, the democratic and republican State Constitution, the principles affirmed in it, and accordingly the organization of a democracy which, if it were actually to correspond to what the Constitution states, would already be a democracy of a new type, different not only from everything that had ever existed in Italy before fascism, but also different from the capitalistic democracies of the traditional type. From here we have derived the general orientation of our political struggle, which has been a democratic struggle for the application of the republican Constitution in its political principles and in its economic principles, for the achievement, that is, of those reforms which it indicates, more or less explicitly. The political line, then, of consistent democratic development and of development in the direction of socialism, through the achievement of the structural reforms envisaged by the Constitution itself.

Of course, following a democratic line of development could not mean and never was intended to mean, for us, the empty affirmation of the necessity for specific reforms. It meant the struggle of the masses for their immediate demands and for great social reforms; it meant the struggle for the unity of the working masses and, first of all, of the working class; it meant a great and continuous effort on the part of the working class to make broader and broader alliances with all those strata of the working population which can and should be interested in a thorough alteration of the structure of society.

New Aspects of Our Policy and of Our Organization

It is from this that the positive and constructive nature of our policy has derived. Hence, the fact that the activity of our party has sought always to formulate the objectives, near or distant, which were to be achieved through the movement and the struggle of the masses on democratic grounds, utilizing all the institutions of our democracy. This we have sought to do in regard to the interests, the claims, and the tasks of the working class, of the peasant classes, and of certain categories of the middle class. This we have tried to do by stating in a new way—even though the party has not always clearly understood everything that it has been asked to do—specific problems, such as, for example, that of the emancipation of the masses of women, an important instrument for a consistent democratic alteration of Italian society. The same applies as regards the problems of youth, of culture, and so forth.

If we approach the specific field of party organization, has there been anything new in our activity? I believe that there have been new developments, at least as regards the directing organs of the party. First of all, there was the matter of building a party which, because of its composition, of the number of its adherents, of its internal structure, and of its method of operation, would be in a position to fulfill a positive and constructive function; it was capable not only of propaganda activity, of agitation, of proclaiming great principles, but also of leading day after day the working class, the workers' masses, and the majority of the population in the understanding and

defense of their interests, and particularly in the defense
and consolidation of the democratic regime, and in developing it in the direction of thorough social reforms.

To these novelties in the party organization, upon which
I do not dwell but which could be amply illustrated,
should be added an internal regime which also has a
special nature, markedly democratic, for a party which
is shut up in itself, which has become bureaucratic, in
which prevails the tendency not to think but only to command or to obey, is not in a position to establish a broad
connection with the masses, that connection which we have
always wanted the party to establish and which ought to
be the essential characteristic of our party. Hence, a
continual struggle for internal democracy within the party,
for strong activity and internal alertness on the part of
our organizations, which cannot and should not interfere
with political and work discipline or with the method of
democratic centralism.

Lack of Understanding and Resistance in the Implementation of the Party's Political Line

At this point, however, it must be said that the constructive elements of a policy in those who established and
directed it are not yet the policy of a party. It is necessary to see how these things were achieved, how they
were put into effect, how the party was guided in carrying them out. Has the line, of which I have given the
main points, the line which has been established and confirmed repeatedly in the national congresses, been understood and implemented as it should have been? Has the
party mastered it fully, properly, and promptly? I believe

that it has mastered it gradually and only in part. There
have been, over long periods, considerable lack of understanding, reservations, gaps in our activity. There has
been resistance to the implementation of the instructions
which have been issued. The most serious of these misunderstandings and reservations, in my opinion, was that
which consisted—I do not know whether it still consists—
in considering that our affirmation of the democratic nature
of our struggle for the alteration of Italian society, was
a sort of trick, something which we made use of in order
to deceive the enemy or to overcome difficulties, in order
not to expose ourselves to specific attacks, and that it was
not, instead, the true heart of a policy which derived
from the great victories which the working class had
already won and which, going beyond those victories,
desired and continues to desire to push all society forward.

From this resulted a number of impediments to the
development of our party, besides, of course, the resistance
and the attacks of our political adversaries and the actual
development of events. It must be said that our party
has acquired a great capacity for overcoming these impediments through a vast practical program of organization.
This practical program of organization must not be dis-
regarded or underestimated. It is an essential element
of the activity of a great Communist party. Let us
remember what Lenin said, that organization is the "sole"
weapon which the working class has in its hands with
which to strike at the adversary. However, it is impossible
for a practical program of organization to take the place
of a policy. In the last analysis, if one is reduced to an
organizational program detached from ever new and sub-

stantial political undertakings, one is faced with deficiencies and failures, and it is impossible to achieve the advances which objective conditions would render possible.

Two Different Attitudes toward the Pella Government. The Victorious Resistance to Scelba's McCarthyist Government

In the debate on the first item of the agenda, attention has been concentrated particularly on the shortcomings of the policy and activity of the party in the most recent period, since the elections of 1953. This is partly true. Undoubtedly there was some political uncertainty in the beginning, at the time of the Pella government. At that time two different attitudes emerged: on the one hand the attitude of those who said it was a case of a crude attempt made by the party in power to seek a new path; on the other hand, the attitude of those who said that there was nothing new except the fact that our enemies were greasing the rope with which they wanted to hang us. These two positions, however, were not faced openly: this was unfortunate. But let us not forget that after that brief period there was a year and a half of the Scelba government, which was the most reactionary government in Italy since the liberation. That government unleashed a ruthless offensive against us, an offensive which reached the point of open McCarthyism, of proclaiming in a communiqué of the Council of Ministers, as the principal line for all government activity, discrimination among the citizens according to whether or not they belonged to the progressive working-class movement. We had to face this offensive and resist. Our capacity for organization and for practical work made a decisive contribution to that resistance and to its success. If that resistance had not been made, no use talking about an opening to the left! None of the conditions would have been provided for that new political development, of which something, though not much, is taking shape today. I recognize that subsequently there may have been some timidity and weakness. It will be necessary to see to what extent these also are to be ascribed to what I said above, that is, to the difficulty which our party still finds in passing from resistance and from self-assertion, achieved by the method of organization and of immediate struggle, to constructive activity, to proposals with a new and broader substance, to the organization of a permanent impetus which would emanate from the masses of the people, and succeed in pushing forward the entire movement by plucking one victory after another. In this field our party does not yet have a capacity equal to the situation. After the great success achieved in 1953—which marked, in substance, the failure of the line followed until then by DeGasperi—and after the victorious resistance to Scelba's McCarthyist government, these shortcomings became more apparent, and I do not rule out that they may have manifested themselves even in the activity of the directing organs.

> *Criticisms of Bureaucracy and Corporal's Pettiness in the Party. The "Italian Road" May Not Be Summarily Identified with the "Parliamentary Road"*

As regards internal administration, we are now receiving good deliberations from our organizations which criticize bureaucratic defects, corporal's pettiness, lack of democratic life on the primary level, and so on. However, the clearest affirmations in this connection, of party criticism and of indication of its tasks, have been found up to the present in documents of the directing organs of the party. Read the reports and documents of the last Congress and of the National Conference held last year, and you will find these things better expressed than they were in the letter by Comrade Durante to *Rinascità*, with which certainly everyone is acquainted. But we cannot be satisfied with this. Even here we are faced with a separation between general assertions, indications, advice, directives, and the reality of party life. We are faced with the great defect that requests for development of internal democracy and therefore of more liveliness in the party are not always connected with the struggle for specific political objectives and for acquainting the party with the need for working in the necessary manner to attain them. The struggle for a proper internal administration was not connected to a debate on present and urgent political questions. From this came the limited effectiveness of this struggle, the limitations on internal democracy of the party, the tendency to restrict this democracy, corporal's pettiness, and lastly the failure to develop our political action.

It is now for the entire party to judge this complex of things, the major aspects of our political line and how it was understood and applied, to arrive at the necessary conclusions, indicate the corrections which must be made, and commit the entire party to this course.

How should we further develop our party line? We must continue the search for and actuation of a road of our own way, of an Italian road of development toward socialism. But I would like to correct those comrades who said—as though it were something quite pacific— that an Italian road of development toward socialism is nothing more than a parliamentary road. This is not true. Who said that "Italian road" means parliamentary road? The Italian road is a road of development toward socialism which takes into account conditions already attained and victories already won. Since these victories have established a broad base for democratic develop- ment, the Italian road is a road which foresees a devel- opment on democratic grounds, the strengthening of democracy, and its evolution toward specific, thorough social reforms. If the problem is not posed in this man- ner, if a summary unrelated identification is made between "Italian road" and "parliamentary road," dangerous illu- sions may arise on the one hand, and even serious delu- sions on the other. The comrade who works in a factory, who knows the weight of the owner's power, the citizen who has come to know the nature and the weight of the capitalistic directing classes in present-day society, and on the other hand sees what our parliament is today, can arrive at the conclusion that this road will never lead to a radical change. Therefore, the question must be stated properly.

*A Hard Struggle by the Masses, a Widespread
Action in the Country to Prepare Really Democratic Grounds for the Successful Development of
the Struggle for Socialism*

The road followed by us so far has been a consistently
democratic road; however, in working and struggling
along this road we have met with bitter resistance. We
have had to fight with clenched teeth to protect the interests of the workers, their freedom, and their life, to make
some improvements and some small reforms. At certain
times there has even been the problem of fighting to save
the legality of our great movement, which some persons
believed they could threaten. We knew that those were
the vain illusions of reactionaries, but they were vain
illusions because we were strong and resisted, and the
great mass of workers were gathering around us in the
struggle and even in sacrifice. The utilization of parliament is one of the possibilities of developing a consistently democratic action to obtain thorough structural
reforms. Before this possibility can materialize, however,
specific conditions must occur. A truly representative
parliament is necessary, it is necessary that it function,
and there must be a great popular movement to bring
out the country's demands which then can be satisfied
by a parliament in which the people's forces have obtained
a sufficiently strong representation. Nor is it enough for
the parliament to be truly representative, that there be
proportional representation. It is necessary to shatter,
to shatter to a great extent the entire system of constric-
tions, of coercions, of intimidations, and of spiritual

terrorism which is resorted to in Italy increasingly to prevent the parliamentary vote from coinciding with the conscience and the needs of the working masses which vote. We must bear in mind what Lenin said about the deceptive nature of bourgeois democracy. We can now put an end partly and even in great measure, to this deceptive nature, i.e., we can prepare a truly democratic ground on which the struggle for socialism can be victoriously waged, as the classical authors of Marxism foresaw. But in order to establish this ground, to bring it into being and to make it broad, a hard struggle by the masses and a widespread action in the country are equally necessary.

The Problem of the Functioning of Parliament, Which Is Today Deficient and Limited

We must also realize that the functioning of the Italian Parliament, especially in the last year or so, is deficient and limited, so that it prevents parliament from carrying out its functions. Parliament today exercises almost no function of control over the activities of the executive branch. This means that this problem of the functioning of parliament must also be made by us the subject of debate, action, and struggle in the country. In sum, the effective utilization of parliamentary possibilities for purposes of a democratic and socialist rebirth requires a great popular mass movement from which might come large parliamentary groups bound to the working masses and capable of causing Parliament to satisfy the people's requests and demands.

I should also like to remind you that when the question of an Italian road toward socialism is broached, it is necessary to avoid thinking that it is a question which can be solved at a desk, through the drafting of more or less new formulas supplied by the shrewdness and originality of some [party] leader. What progress we have made thus far along the "Italian road" is first of all due to the struggle of the popular masses, and what we shall be able to gain in the future will be the result of other struggles and the experience gained through them. The democratic commitment of the party is a premise, just as is an irrevocable premise its commitment to be more and more closely bound to the conditions and traditions of the country and of our workers' movement.

But what is especially important today for the determination of our political line? The search for new things, for what has changed, for the way it has changed, and for the situation resulting from these changes. We hail all search for the new, although we caution against oversimplifications and abstractions which are sometimes encountered in this field. It is not enough to say, for example, to a group of comrades that an election was lost in such-and-such a factory because they do not understand that the second industrial revolution is in progress. This type of general statement does not help the comrade to understand. When confronted with it he withdraws into a shell, sometimes does not even understand what is being talked about, and above all does not know what he should do.

Need for a More Thorough Study of the Economic Structure of Our Country

The search for new things must always be connected to an examination of the concrete and practical aspects

of the class movement, of the workers' movement, and of
our work. I realize that for the past few years the study
of economic problems has been neglected by the party
center as well as throughout the party. It is necessary to
recover what has been lost. In the past, when, for example, it was a matter of fully analyzing the objective,
economic bases of the fascist regime and the influence of
economic developments on the changes of its fascist policy,
we succeeded in making vitally important contributions.
Today we must better study the economic structure of the
country. It is still a capitalistic structure, but of a particular kind. There are on the one hand areas of great
development and rise, not always independently of the
aid given by the state, that is, by customs protection which
is a burden on the entire country. Alongside this there
are areas of non-development and decadence, as proved
by sweeping investigations into unemployment and poverty.
Economic development has moved in the direction favoring the monopolistic structures, both in the city and rural
areas, and the prevalence of these structures has brought
about contradictions of a new kind, has given rise to
growing imbalances, has not led the country to a harmoni-
ous development of its resources and possibilities, has not
allowed it to advance toward the solution of essential
problems, which are those pertaining to the work and
welfare of its citizens, to the historic imbalances between
north and south, and so on. We must therefore not close
our eyes to the progress which is taking place, but woe if
we should at the same time close our eyes to the backwardness of entire regions which continues to be the sorriest
characteristic of our country.

Regarding the political structures, we cannot say that they fit the framework traced in the Constitution, and for two reasons. First of all because of persistent failure to implement the Constitution. The constitutional political principles are still being largely violated. The reforms of the political structure provided for by the Constitution— such as the establishment of regions and the affirmation of local government—have not been carried out. Discrimination among citizens, which is a degeneration of the democratic regime, continues to be the standard behavior of the ruling classes and also of the government authorities.

Relations between Church and State Should Be Brought Back to the Limits Fixed by the Constitution

In addition to this, it must be openly stated that we are witnessing today another kind of degeneration in our democratic regime, specifically as regards the new relations being established between the state and the church. We have been criticized for approving Article 7; but relations between the state and the church, as stipulated by Article 7, are much more progressive than those which now exist and which were instituted by the more than five years of the DeGasperi government and the subsequent years of church-inspired governments. In this field, relations have been established for which reciprocal responsibilities and spheres of power are no longer clearly definable. The ecclesiastical organizations intervene in a gross manner, violating specific articles of law to bring about the prevalence of the Catholic party in elections.

Naturally, the Catholic party, having arrived at the control of power through this intervention, is paying its debt
by ceding to the church authority a part of those prerogatives which belong to the State. This is happening in
the fields of social welfare, education, job placement, etc.,
that is, in fields which are essential to the construction
of a democratic society. We would be committing a
serious error if we did not mention these things, if we
did not place before the working class and all Italian
democrats the need to fight to check and terminate this
degeneration, to return to a true and solidly democratic
regime by bringing the relations between state and church
back to the bounds fixed by the Constitution.

What are the objectives we must propose for ourselves
today? We intend to develop on democratic grounds the
action and struggle of the laboring and working masses
to change thoroughly the economic structure of Italian
society. We intend, that is, to orient Italian society
towards an economy based on the guarantee of the greatest possible well-being for workers, on the elimination of
unemployment, on the struggle against poverty, in order
to abolish historic and regional imbalances, etc. Great
technological progress and the progress of the entire
national economy are necessary to obtain this. We want
this progress and we denounce monopolistic capitalism
because, while it does guarantee some small island of
progress here and there and draws the resulting advantages
therefrom, it does not guarantee the general progress of
the entire nation, technical as well as economic and social.
Tied in with the struggle for new courses in the national
economy are economic demands, labor union problems,

and those demands which we formerly referred to as
transitional but which are now given the general name of
structural reforms.

The Objectives of Our Struggle in the Agricultural
Field and in the Industrial Field. The Vanoni
Plan

Regarding the rural areas, I believe that there is no
debate; we realize that a general agrarian reform is indispensable, based on the principles sanctioned by the Constitution, that is, through a general limitation on property
in order to give the land to whoever works it.

In the field of industry, that is, as regards the principal
aspects of the capitalistic economy, there are questions
which must be discussed. They are the problems of
nationalization, of the intervention of the state to regulate economic life, of the struggle against the monopolies.
There is a tendency to reject and criticize any positive
position of the Communist Party with respect to anything
that can be done along these lines, with the statement
that only [legal] power can decide. Nationalization
would be effective only if carried out by a socialist
workers' power, and the same goes for the intervention
of the state in the economy, the struggle against the monopolies through legislative measures, etc. These statements are true, but only as abstractions because, in
practice, under today's existing conditions around the
world and even in our country, concrete power is something which can change and which can be made to change
by efficacious movements and struggles of the working
class and of the laboring masses. Therefore, the prob-

lems of nationalization, of intervention by the state in our economic life, etc., must be posed and solved in relation to the development of the entire movement and, in particular, of the struggle of the masses in these fields. If these problems are thus posed, we cannot but conclude that an *a priori* denial of the possibility that the vanguard of the working class have or support demands and positive measures in this field is a mistaken denial. In Italy today there is the big problem of the Vanoni Plan which undoubtedly has been and is for most people an expedient capable of giving the illusion of a new economic policy, but at the same time it can serve as a point of reference and as a foothold for an efficacious struggle to really begin an alteration of the Italian economic structure.

"Human Relations" and Respect for the Democratic Rights of Workers

Other questions which for us have very great importance are those pertaining to the introduction of a general system of social security to overcome the backwardness of our country, even as compared to other capitalistic countries, and to the status of the workers in places of production.

There is more and more talk today of introducing human relations into the factories. It is thought and said that it is a form of the struggle against us. Perhaps it is thus in the intention of someone; however, it is up to us to say openly that the introduction of human relations into the factories is our byword and our objective of struggle. We desire human relations in the factories and in all work places, but we say that human relations begin with respect for the democratic rights of the workers and for their union rights, that is, with the elimination of any discrimination and with the recognition of the right of the workers to discuss with the owner or with management all their remunerations, and not, instead, to be subject to the system of bonuses given at the will of the owner. Even here we are in danger of a degeneration of relations between management, especially between a big industrialist and his workers, precisely because of the extended system of bonuses given at will and arbitrarily by the owners on the basis of a criterion of discrimination.

It can also be understood that it is useful to determine a part of the pay on the basis of over-all work productivity, but that leads to another question, foreseen by our Constitution, and it is that of the management boards; the problem of the powers of the shop-steward committees and of the labor unions to regulate the pace of work, the intensity of exploitation and, in relation to this, the entire question of salary, piece work, and bonuses.

A movement which we succeed in orienting and steering in the direction of these demands and these reforms is undoubtedly a movement toward socialism. But can we move successfully in this direction in our country today? We believe so because there exist favorable objective and subjective conditions. They stem from the complex of things that are happening in the world as well as in our country, from the manner in which the consciousness of the Italian workers and working masses is maturing. However, it is insufficient to note these favorable objective and subjective conditions and lightheartedly draw the con-

clusion that we will surely forge ahead by approving a
little law now and then, by signing some little agreement
and then another, until we have changed the structure of
our society. This manner of considering matters dis-
regards the evaluation of the obstacles and difficulties.
It is the result of a unilateral historic and political view,
and therefore mistaken and dangerous. As regards the
protection and consolidation of our democracy, the democratic consciousness existing among the Italian working
masses, and the popularity of the idea of socialism among
the Italian masses, there are still limitations which must be
overcome. We have not yet won the majority of the
Italian people to socialism.

There Is Still the Question of Preventing a Return to Serious Forms of Reaction

Moreover, let us remember that there still remain the
class enemy, the capitalists and large landowners, the big
monopolists who are in power today, who make use of it
and make use of it well. Fascism once grew out of Italian
society, and certainly it did not rise from either the madness of one man or the inertia of others, but from the
economic development of Italian society, from contradictions and struggles which were rooted in the economy of
the country. We note today that the parties of the right
suffered a defeat in the last elections. Fine, but let us
remember that Scelba's McCarthyism is lurking under
the ashes. The question of preventing a return to those
or to other even worse forms of reaction is definitely not
yet solved. To become aware of this, suffice it to leaf
through the pages of the large dailies which the upper
middle class orients in a more direct manner.

Democratic development must therefore be carried out, and the ground for the democratic struggle is guaranteed only by continuous vigilance, action, and struggle which, through continuous reinforcement of the democratic forces and socialist forces and their unity, succeed in containing, restricting, limiting, and preventing the action of class enemies. The forms of the advance toward socialism do not depend only on us: they depend on us and on what the adversary does. Up to the present, in Italy, only the ruling classes have stooped to violence to prevent the political and economic changes demanded by the popular masses. They did so during the first post-war period and tried to do so also at other times. This stems from the very nature of these class forces and of Italian capitalism, to which even the concessions of a reformist type made in other countries are repugnant. Big monopolistic capital holds tightly in its grasp a network of interests, of economic and political positions through which it exercises its power and dominates the situation. At one of the recent meetings of the Socialist Party Central Committee, Comrade Riccardo Lombardi broached the problem of what forms of democratic action can shatter this power of big monopolistic capital. It is a question which really exists, and we must state it, because we would otherwise deceive the working and laboring masses, if we did not say that there must be a great struggle on democratic grounds to succeed in going forward, in exacting those structural changes which are necessary in the course toward socialism. It is necessary that the front of the working and laboring forces expand, organize itself, be united internally, be strong, and have very clearly before it the objectives which it wishes to attain.

The Social-Democratic Reform Doctrine and the
Catholic Social Reform Doctrine

Social reform doctrine today is quite widespread and
occurs in two different forms. There is the traditional
social-democratic reform doctrine and there is the Catholic
social reform doctrine. They have points of contact and
differences. The traditional social-democratic reform doctrine tends to take as its basis a workers' aristocracy, to
detach it from the remainder of the class, and to make
use of the bourgeois State apparatus not, to be sure, for
the purpose of structural alteration, but to make this
schism permanent, thus making fools of the ruling classes.
In this way it goes so far as to collaborate with the most
reactionary forces. In Italy it collaborated first with
DeGasperi and later with Scelba, in a policy of capitalist
restoration and of open reaction. The Catholic reform
doctrine has various characteristics. It does not reject
the support of specific groups of the workers' aristocracy,
but at the same time it tends to establish a basis for itself
among the masses who live in more miserable conditions,
using for its own purposes paternalism on the one hand
and clericalism on the other; that is, using ideological
pressure and spiritual intimidation to keep the working
masses in bondage and to prevent their unity and their
movement.

In this situation we should see clearly that it is not a
question only of proclaiming that by moving on democratic ground we can advance toward socialism, but it
is also a question of seeing the things we should do in
order to succeed in advancing towards socialism. It is
necessary that the economic, political, and social changes

which we demand always to be translated for the masses into something clear, simple, and precise. It is necessary that we demand, using all forms of expression, those changes of political orientation that are indispensable for opening the way for the alteration of the economic structure. It is not sufficient to speak of an opening to the left. It is necessary that we match this watchword with a concrete substance. We must make it understood that an opening to the left does not mean that votes are to be cast in favor of this or that minister, followed by rejoicing over this fact as though it were a great event. An opening to the left should mean at least the beginning of a change in the political orientation which prevails today. It should mean at least the beginning of a change in the orientation of the economic course of the country. This enables us to develop a mass struggle unitary in character; and we must work to see that it [this struggle] will have a unitary character, both in the trade-union field and in other fields.

Besides this first and fundamental requirement, I believe it necessary that the working class and the parties which lead it know how to approach new working masses. Accordingly, we should have to discuss whether something should not be modified in our concept of the allies of the working class in Italy, whether we should not extend this concept not only to the peasant masses of the South and of the rest of Italy, but also to the working and producing middle-class masses in the cities. In this connection it is not a question of talking, but of conducting careful research and of presenting solutions in the form of programs capable of dispelling the fear

which these masses may have toward an alliance with
the party which demands socialism, in order to make
them understand that in our country, considering its structure, the working middle class in the cities can and must
make its contribution to the building of socialist society,
that it will not in any way be the victim of the building
of that socialist society, but will cooperate in its leadership.

The struggles of the masses must also be accompanied
by a development of socialist consciousness, and this does
not develop spontaneously, it does not take shape by
itself.   Lenin taught us this, and that doctrine is still
true.   Socialist consciousness develops in the masses
through the experience of the struggles conducted by
and through the activity of the vanguard party.   This
party must know how to arouse and to cultivate socialist
consciousness among the masses; it must be capable of
drawing the necessary conclusions from every struggle
fought, from every victory and from every defeat, and
thus cause all the workers to acquire a new capacity for
understanding facts and, consequently, for acting, for
uniting themselves, for going forward.

In a word, it is necessary, in order to carry out its
own tasks, that the working class have at its head a revolutionary party, a party inspired by a revolutionary doctrine, a party which knows the scope of the task with
which it is faced and knows how to act in order to carry
it out.   Granted the same historical conditions in which
the movement has developed, it is possible for parties
different from ours to exist which appeal, as we do, to
the working class, which affirm, as we do, the ideals of
socialism, and which claim to be, as we do, a revolution-

ary party. Even the Social Democratic Party has specific bases among the working class and claims to appeal to the ideals of socialism. Thus arises the problem of unity, which must be faced and solved, as I have already mentioned, on the basis of mutual understanding in order to arrive at mutual confidence, at harmony, and at working agreements.

The Pact for Unity of Action with Our Socialist Comrades

We have achieved a very high degree of unity with the Socialist Party, establishing, in agreement with it, that unity of action which represents a fundamental achievement of the working class and of the Italian laboring masses. We ascribe an essential value to this achievement. We are in agreement with Comrade Nenni in saying that this value does not lie so much in written documents as in activity, in general orientation, and in effective cooperation to achieve specific objectives. The entire movement toward socialism, however, would suffer profoundly if this unity of action were to be, I shall not say lost, but attenuated or weakened. Let us work to see to it that this does not happen.

How can the party be capable of applying a policy like the one whose principles I have tried very broadly to outline? During the discussion which is beginning, it will be necessary to develop, to define, if necessary to correct, the statements that have already been made, from 1946 to the present, to define the character of our party, the form of its organization and the forms of its work. The goal which the organization is to achieve is to give the party the greatest possible capacity for connection with all strata of the working population. Therefore, the organization must be such as to make possible and to stimulate the activity of all the members of the party, in order to establish ever new bonds with the most diverse groups of the population. However, in order that this be possible, a renewed study of the structure of the party is necessary, as well as a better definition and management of its internal regime, as a regime characterized by democracy and by constant active participation of all our comrades in the solution of all questions.

As regards structure, I believe that in preparing the congress it will be necessary to examine seriously the question of our contacts and bonds with the working class in the factories, in order to maintain these bonds, without remaining anchored of necessity to old organizational forms, but correcting them, if necessary, by taking into consideration the way in which the life of the workers is organized today, both inside and outside the factory. The essential thing is that a flow of new forces should come constantly from the working class, and that we should be able to give the working class that ideological and political guidance and that direction which it needs.

Greater Democracy and Greater Liberty in the Party Mean Greater Activity on the Part of Our Comrades

As regards the internal regime, I repeat that many true statements are being made in the debates which are already going on, but there are also some statements which are completely exaggerated insofar as judgments of the past are concerned. We should emphasize the true statements above all because both the leaders of the party and all our comrades should always be glad that greater democracy in the party and greater freedom of criticism and discussion are being demanded. Greater democracy and liberty mean and must always mean greater activity of the party membership not only in obeying and not only in discussion, but also in working seriously, with enthusiasm and initiative, for the implementation of the party's policy in all fields.

I have read the minutes of the meeting of intellectuals which was held in Rome, of which I spoke above. I did not find anything terrible or shocking there. Here and there, there is an atmosphere of outlet rather than of orderly discussion, but nevertheless this episode of our party life should be considered desirable and hailed, especially as I hope this means that this group of comrades from now on will devote more activity to the party and participate more in the life of its organizations, as this is the only way in which it is possible to contribute to increasing democratic life in the party, to combating bureaucracy, corporal's pettiness, and stagnation.

Let there be among the questions being discussed in preparation for the congress the problem of the formation of the local and central directing offices and of their staffs, whether they should be numerous, composed only of comrades who devote themselves exclusively to party work, whether they are well utilized, and how it is possible to combine the utilization of the comrades who devote all their efforts to the party with the utilization of comrades who remain in jobs. Probably there are many things here

which should be reviewed and changed in order to advance
the party's interests better. Let there be discussions of
the way in which the central staffs should be made to
operate. Let it be considered whether changes should be
introduced in the actual composition and in the functioning of the central offices, of the Central Committee, of
the Directorate, of the Secretariat.

Let all these questions be examined and discussed seriously, with a feeling of responsibility and in a manner
which helps the party to solve them properly.

*A Committee to Prepare the Thesis to Be Pre-
sented to the Congress and One to Work Out a
Statement of Program*

The practical proposals which I am making are: that
the debate on the questions brought up here and on others
which may be brought up begin immediately in the peripheral organizations, and that the leaders of these organizations make the necessary effort to see the greatest
possible number of comrades take part in the discussions.
Let the party's daily press and periodicals devote a part
of their space to the progress of the debate.

This Central Committee should decide on the appoint-
ment of two committees (if it is not possible to select
them in the present session or in tomorrow's, we can
instruct the Directorate to choose the members, inform-
ing all the members of the Central Committee, however,
and taking into consideration their objections and sug-
gestions). The first committee should have as its objective the study of the party's activity as it has developed,
and the conclusions which can be drawn from it in order

to determine the new tasks which lie before us. This committee should prepare, in this connection, a draft of the proposals to be presented to the congress.

The second committee should work out a statement of the party's program. These two committees, to be set up at the beginning of July, should, about the middle of September, present their conclusions and the documents they have prepared to the Central Committee, which should then make its own changes in these documents and present them to the party for the consideration of whatever amendments might be proposed. The Central Committee can also, if it sees fit, present these documents to the party before working out its own version, in which it might commit itself too much and which might put too much pressure on the party to approve the texts which are presented to it.

The preparation for the congress through cell, section, and federation meetings should be very rapid. We should not fall again into the error which we made in connection with the conference of 1955, from the consequences of which we are still suffering. The general debate being open from now on, once the two principal documents have been presented, about the middle of September, in a couple of months we should have completed all the congresses and should be able to call the National Congress. It will not be necessary that a member of the directorate or of the secretariat participate in every congress, nor will it be necessary in each congress that the local party leaders be required to make a thorough examination of the local objectives of their activity. It will

be necessary that the congresses discuss the texts that
will be presented, the questions which will be debated
publicly, the proposals, and the draft of the program
statement that will be made public.

How to Work and Struggle to Achieve the Objectives Which the Party Faces Today

Comrades, I have finished. In my report I have raised
a number of questions. I do not believe I have examined
all the topics that could be presented in the pre-Congress
debate. This is, however, a beginning. It is now up to
the party to go ahead. Are we capable of going ahead?
I am deeply convinced that we are. The same debate
which took place in this Central Committee on the first
item of the agenda proves this. It was a serious debate,
lively, thorough, and on the proper level, which abandoned the usual procedure of coming here to deliver only
descriptive reports on peripheral matters, in order to give
instead, effective assistance in examining thoroughly all
the questions which are being raised today. It is evident that the result of the elections and the debate on
these results also should be inserted in the general debate
preparatory to the congress, for, in substance, the party
has undergone a great experience in working and struggling. I am profoundly convinced that our party is
capable of formulating positions which fit the situation
which faces us, of establishing proper and specific objectives, of criticizing itself seriously and effectively, utilizing both the international experience of the Communist
movement and our own experience. Let us remember,

however, that mere clarity of objectives is not sufficient. In order to reach the objectives which are placed before us and in order to go forward, it is necessary to know how to work, to struggle, to combat. It is necessary, accordingly, that we carry on discussions in a manner that will contribute toward increasing this ability of the party, which will make the mind clearer, the will more certain, the unity and compactness of the party even greater than before. If we carry on discussions and work in this way, I am certain that the next congress will constitute a new and great forward step for the party.

10

Statement of the National Committee of the Communist Party of the United States, DAILY WORKER, New York

June 25, 1956

THE New York *Daily Worker*, in an editorial of June 20 entitled "A Welcome Development," stated: "Today the solidarity of labor is being enhanced by the frank and critical relationship among Marxists. It was in this spirit that the two biggest Communist Parties in the capitalist world—the Italian and French —this week demanded from the Soviet leaders more fundamental and more logical explanations of how violations of law and democracy became so widespread under the Stalin regime." The organ continued:

We have called upon Communist leaders in socialist countries to explain the real origins of injustices that arose and threatened the existence of socialism there. We have differed in this regard with some readers and prominent contributors to our paper. We are strengthened in our conviction that only such an independent position helps the cause of labor and socialism. . . .

On June 24, Steve Nelson in a *Daily Worker* article captioned "Upholds Duty to Criticize Fraternal Parties" appealed: "Let us tell our Russian comrades that certain of their deeds do not square with the demands of the hour. At this juncture, the most important evidence of the old weakness seems to rest in the lack of self-criticism by the leadership of the CPSU. To keep silent

on such matters does not help the world struggle for socialism."
As for relations between the Soviet and the other Communist
parties, they must be kept "on the basis of equality." The same
day, the National Committee of the Communist Party of the
United States issued the following statement on the new policy
toward Stalin.

Editorially, the *Daily Worker* acclaimed this "historic statement," pointing out that Marxists had begun to outline just such a
critical approach as far back as mid-March.

THE publication of the State Department's text of Khrushchev's speech to a closed session of the Twentieth Congress
of the CPSU has given a fresh impetus to the already widespread discussions in our country about the changes taking
place in the Soviet Union.

The State Department would like Americans to believe
that nothing has changed in the Soviet Union. It hopes
to cancel out the positive impact of the XXth Congress,
which registered, among other things, a new relationship
of world forces, opening up for the first time in history
the real prospect for a lasting peace. It hopes in this
way to keep alive the disintegrating remnants of the cold
war.

However, the people of our country who desire peaceful
co-existence cannot but welcome the actions taken by the
Soviet government since Stalin's death as well as the
determination expressed in Khrushchev's speech to end
the brutalities and injustices which marred a period of
Soviet life.

The State Department wants the American people to
believe that the tragedies, crimes and injustices which
took place during the Stalin era are evils which are inherent in socialism.

But the crimes against innocent people perpetrated under Stalin's leadership are, in fact, alien to socialism. They were an intolerable hindrance to the advance of socialism. Socialism is dedicated to the liberation of mankind from social injustice and to releasing the full capacities for the flowering of humanity. It requires an ever expanding democracy, the growth of human freedom and personal liberties, the development of conditions which will ultimately eliminate altogether the use of force in the relations between people.

We have been and will continue to be the proud supporters of socialism everywhere. We have fought and will continue to fight against the efforts of big business to calumniate and villify the Soviet Union and other socialist countries.

We Communists know that socialism must eradicate the inhumanity of capitalist society. That is why we, above all, are deeply shocked by the revelations contained in Khrushchev's speech.

In our opinion this speech should have been made public by the CPSU itself. We do not share the view that the questions dealt with, no matter how painful and abhorrent, are exclusively the internal affair of the CPSU. The role which the Soviet Union has played in world affairs for the last forty years, and the defense of its socialist achievements by workers in the U. S. and other countries have made these matters public issues everywhere.

A basic analysis of how such perversions of socialist democracy, justice and internationalism were permitted to develop and continue unchecked for twenty years must still be made by the leadership of the CPSU. It needs also

to be made by Marxists everywhere. Khrushchev's contribution to the exposure of mistakes and to the process of
correction now going on, makes only a beginning in this
direction.

We cannot accept an analysis of such profound mistakes
which attributes them solely to the capricious aberrations
of a single individual, no matter how much arbitrary
power he was wrongly permitted to usurp. It is just as
wrong to ascribe all the mistakes and violations of socialist
principles to a single individual as it was to ascribe to
him all the achievements and grandeur of socialist progress
in the USSR.

In our opinion the mistakes made were primarily a
result of wrong policies and concepts arising, in part, out
of the fact that the Soviet Union was the pioneering land
of socialism and was surrounded for decades by a hostile
capitalist world. Some of these policies and concepts
have already been repudiated. But the historic objective
factors associated with these errors need to be more fully
assessed. Also required is a further and deeper examination of such questions as the structure and operation of
socialist democracy in the Soviet Union and other socialist
countries as well as of the new problems and perspectives
arising as the workers of other lands move toward socialism. This will illuminate the source of past errors and
help avoid future ones.

We are deeply disturbed by facts revealed in information coming from Poland that organs and media of Jewish
culture were summarily dissolved and a number of their
leaders executed. This is contrary to the Soviet Union's
historic contributions on the Jewish question. Khrush-

chev's failures to deal with these outrages, and the continuing silence of Soviet leaders, requires an explanation.

The Communist Party of the U. S. has some serious conclusions to draw from all this. For we are responsible to the working class and people of our own country. And to them we admit frankly that we uncritically justified many foreign and domestic policies of the Soviet Union which are now shown to be wrong.

We have begun to re-examine our previously over-simplified and wrong concept of the relations which should exist between the Marxists of various countries, including the socialist countries. These relations must be based on the principles of serving the best national interests of each people and the common interests of all progressive humanity; of the equality of parties; of the right and duty of the Marxists of all countries to engage in friendly criticism of the theory or practice of the Marxists of any country, whenever they feel this is necessary. Far from weakening, this will strengthen international working-class solidarity. This new approach was reflected in the *Daily Worker* as early as last March, as well as in the position adopted by the National Committee at the end of April.

Our stand is rooted in the primary concern of our Party for the present and future welfare of the American people. As an independent Marxist Party of American workers dedicated to socialism, we seek to add our influence to ensuring friendship of peoples and world peace. We shall continue to work for greater economic security, democracy, and civil rights in our own country, and for unity with all socialist-minded groups to attain socialism by constitutional, peaceful means, expressing the free choice of the majority of the American people.

11

Resolution of the Central Committee of the Communist Party of the Soviet Union, June 30, 1956

PRAVDA, Moscow

July 2, 1956

REACTION OF other European Communist parties to the demands of Italian, French, British, and American Communists for further Soviet clarification of the Stalin question was varied. Speaking on the Amsterdam radio on June 26, Paul de Groot, leader of the Dutch Communist Party, appealed to foreign Communists to be "discreet" in their comments and leave the Soviet CP to wash its dirty linen in private; the Dutch Party, he declared, was in no position to judge the abuses denounced by Khrushchev. On the same day the Belgian Communist Party's Central Committee, in a four-point resolution (*Le Drapeau Rouge*, June 27), both praised Togliatti's statements as an "important contribution" and "rejoiced at the frank recognition of errors by the Soviet Communists."

The Communist Party of Austria joined the other Western parties in welcoming the "wide, useful, and creative discussion being held in the Communist Parties of all countries." In its midst, too, the discussions had provoked "the use, sometimes, of harsh language, and not everything said is quite correct, but this could not be otherwise and is not harmful so long as the criticism is guided by the will to help the party." Like other Western Communist parties, the Austrian Central Committee "sometime ago requested the CC/CPSU to place at its disposal" the Khrushchev speech. (*Volksstimme*, June 26, 1956.)

The secretariat of the West German Communist Party (KPD) executive issued a lengthy statement "in answer to frank questions" (published in *Freies Volk*, Düsseldorf, July 2, 1956). Endorsing the Moscow attack on the abuses perpetrated under Stalin, the statement acclaimed "the uncovering of the causes for the mistakes which occurred in the Soviet Union." Echoing the Togliatti text, it described the present development as the abolition of "illegalities and symptoms of degeneration alien to socialism," but did not otherwise refer to or support additional requests for clarification by the CPSU: "To uncover the causes which led to the mistakes committed is a task which . . . can be solved only by the CPSU." Meanwhile "the open criticism at the XXth Party Congress, which at the same time represented the severest self-criticism, as well as the changes already made, guarantee that a repetition of similar mistakes will be impossible." The total effect of the questions raised by the leading Western European parties was such as to lead observers to predict, in late June, that Moscow would soon issue a statement by way of reply and explanation. On June 30, the Central Committee of the Communist Party of the Soviet Union adopted the following Resolution, which was published in *Pravda* on July 2, 1956. Its publication marked the first official and open statement of the CPSU leadership for domestic as well as foreign consumption in response to the questions raised by Communists abroad.

On Overcoming the Personality Cult and Its Consequences

THE CENTRAL COMMITTEE of the CPSU notes with satisfaction that the decisions of the historic XXth Congress of the Communist Party of the Soviet Union have met with full approval and ardent support from our entire Party, the entire Soviet people, the fraternal Communist and Workers' Parties, the working people of the great commonwealth of socialist countries, and millions of people in capitalist and colonial countries. This is understandable since the XXth Party Congress, which marks a new stage in the creative development of Marxism-Leninism, gave a profound analysis of the present international and internal situation, armed the Communist Party and all the Soviet people with a majestic plan for a further struggle in the building of Communism, and opened up new prospects for joint action by all parties of the working class in warding off the threat of another war and for the interests of the working people.

Implementing the decisions of the XXth Congress of the CPSU, the Soviet people under the leadership of the Communist Party are attaining new and outstanding successes in all spheres of the political, economic, and cultural life of the country. The Soviet people have rallied still closer around the Communist Party and are displaying high creative activity in the struggle for the implementation of the tasks set by the XXth Congress.

The period since the Congress has at the same time revealed the great vital force of its decisions for the international Communist and workers' movement, for the struggle of all progressive forces for the strengthening of world peace. Important, fundamental theoretical theses on peaceful co-existence of states with different social systems, on the possibility of preventing war during the present epoch, and on the variety of forms of transition of countries to socialism set forth by the Congress are having a beneficial influence on the international situation, are helping to ease tension and strengthen the unity of action of all forces fighting for peace and democracy, for a further consolidation of the positions of the world system of socialism.

While among the Soviet people, among the working people in the countries of People's Democracy and of the whole world, the historic decisions of the XXth CPSU Congress have aroused great enthusism and a new upsurge of creative initiative and revolutionary energy, in the camp of the enemies of the working class they have given rise to alarm and rancor. Reactionary circles of the U. S. A. and several other capitalist countries are clearly perturbed by the great program of struggle for strengthening peace mapped out by the XXth CPSU Congress. Their anxiety grows as this program is actively and consistently put into effect.

Why is it that the enemies of Communism and socialism are concentrating their attacks on the shortcomings about which the Central Committee of our Party spoke at the XXth CPSU Congress? They are doing so in order to distract the attention of the working class and its parties from the *main* topics advanced by the XXth Party Congress that are clearing the way to further successes for the cause of peace, socialism, and unity of the working class.

The decisions of the XXth Party Congress and the domestic and foreign policy of the Soviet government have caused confusion in the imperialist circles of the U. S. A. and other states.

The bold and consistent foreign policy of the USSR in ensuring peace and co-operation among states, irrespective of their social systems, finds support among the broadest masses of the peoples of all countries of the world, broadening the front of peace-loving states and causing a profound crisis for the Cold War policy—the policy of setting up military blocs and of the arms race. It is no accident that the loudest hue and cry about the struggle against the personality cult in the USSR has been raised by U. S. imperialist circles. The presence of negative factors associated with the personality cult suited them, as they could use these facts to fight socialism. Now that our Party is boldly overcoming the consequences of the personality cult, the imperialists see in this a factor that is accelerating the progress of our country to Communism and weakening the positions of capitalism.

Striving to lessen the great attraction of the decisions of the XXth CPSU Congress and their effect upon the broadest masses of people, the ideologists of capitalism are resorting to all sorts of tricks and artifices to distract the attention of the working people from the advanced and inspiring ideas put before mankind by the socialist world.

Lately the bourgeois press has launched an extensive, slanderous anti-Soviet campaign which reactionary circles are trying to base on certain facts connected with the condemnation by the Communist Party of the Soviet Union of the cult of the person of J. V. Stalin. The organizers of this campaign are exerting every effort to confuse the issue and conceal the fact that this is a stage in the life of the land of the Soviets that is past; they also want to pass over in silence or distort the fact that during the years since Stalin's death the Communist Party of the Soviet Union and the Soviet government have been exceptionally persistent and resolute in liquidating the consequences of the personality cult and are successfully carrying out the news tasks in the interest of strengthening peace, of building Communism, in the interest of the broad masses of people.

Launching a slanderous campaign, the ideologists of the bourgeoisie are again attempting, though unsuccessfully, to cast aspersions on the great ideas of Marxism-Leninism, to undermine the trust of the working people in the first socialist country in the world, the USSR, and to sow confusion in the ranks of the international Communist and workers' movement.

The experience of history teaches that the enemies of international proletarian unity have in the past repeatedly tried to make use of what in their opinion have been favorable opportunities for undermining the international unity of the Communist and Workers' Parties, for splitting the international workers' movement, for weakening the forces of the socialist camp. But the Communist and Workers' Parties have discerned the maneuvers of the enemies of socialism each time and have drawn their ranks still closer, demonstrating their indestructible political unity, their unswerving loyalty to the ideas of Marxism-Leninism.

The fraternal Communist and Workers' Parties have also discerned this maneuver of the enemies of socialism in time and are duly rebuffing it. Yet it would be wrong to close our eyes to the fact that certain of our friends abroad are not completely clear on the question of the personality cult and its consequences and sometimes give incorrect interpretations of certain points connected with the personality cult.

In its criticism of the personality cult the Party proceeds from the principles of Marxism-Leninism. For more than three years now our Party has been waging a consistent struggle against the cult of the person of J. V. Stalin, persistently overcoming its harmful consequences. Naturally this question occupied an important place in the work of the XXth Congress of the CPSU and in its decisions. The Congress noted that the Central Committee quite correctly and in good time came out against the personality cult, the spread of which belittled the role of the Party and the masses of the people, lowered the role of collective leadership in the Party, and frequently resulted in grave omissions in work and gross violations of socialist law. The Congress charged the Central Committee with consistently carrying out measures to ensure the full overcoming of the personality cult, alien to Marxism-Leninism, the elimination of its consequences in all areas of Party, state, and ideological work, and strict adherence to the norms of Party life and the principles of the collectivity of Party leadership worked out by the great Lenin.

In the struggle against the personality cult the Party leadership is guided by the known tenets of Marxism-Leninism on the role of the masses of the people, the Party, and specific individuals in history, on the inadmissibility of the cult of a political leader, however great his merits. The founder of scientific Communism, K. Marx, stressing his dislike of "any personality cult," stated that his and F. Engels' entry into the society of Communists "was conditional upon removing from the statutes everything that contributes to the superstitious worship of authorities" (K. Marx and F. Engels, *Works*, Volume 26, first Russian edition, pages 487 and 488). In creating our Communist Party, V. I. Lenin fought implacably against the anti-Marxist concept of "hero" and "the crowd" and resolutely condemned the juxtaposition of the individual hero against the masses of the people. "The minds of tens of millions of creators," V. I. Lenin said, "create something immeasurably higher than the greatest foresight of genius" (*Works*, Volume 26, page 431).

In putting forward the question of combating the cult of the person of J. V. Stalin, the Central Committee of the CPSU proceeded from the fact that the personality cult contradicts the nature of the socialist system, and became a brake on the path of the development of Soviet democracy and the advance of socialist society toward Communism.

The XXth Party Congress, on the initiative of the Central Committee, deemed it necessary to speak boldly and frankly about the grave consequences of the personality cult and the serious errors made during the latter period of Stalin's life, and to call upon the entire Party to end through joint efforts everything that resulted from the personality cult. At the same time the Central Committee was aware that the frank admission of errors made would be linked to certain shortcomings and losses which might be exploited by enemies. The courageous and relentless self-criticism in the matter of the personality cult was a new and brilliant proof of the power and strength of our Party and the Soviet socialist system. It can be stated with assurance that none of the ruling parties in the capitalist countries would ever have risked taking a similar step. On the contrary, they would have tried to conceal matters from the people and pass over such unpleasant facts in silence.

But the Communist Party of the Soviet Union, brought up on the revolutionary principles of Marxism-Leninism, told the whole truth, no matter how bitter. The Party took this step strictly on its own initiative, guided by considerations of principle. It believed that even if the stand taken against the cult of Stalin caused some temporary difficulties, in the long run, from the point of view of the vital interests and ultimate aims of the working class, it would have a tremendous positive result. This creates firm guarantees that such phenomena as the personality cult will never again develop in our country, that in the future the leadership of the Party and country will be collective and based on a Marxist-Leninist policy under conditions of broad intra-Party democracy, with the active, creative participation of the millions of working people, the comprehensive development of Soviet democracy.

Having taken a resolute stand against the personality cult and its consequences, having openly subjected to criticism the mistakes to which it gave rise, the Party has demonstrated once more its devotion to the immortal principles of Marxism-Leninism, its devotion to the interests of the people, its solicitude for creating the best conditions for the development of Party and Soviet democracy in the interests of successfully building Communism in our country.

The Central Committee of the CPSU notes that discussion in Party organizations and at general meetings of working people on the question of the personality cult and its consequences has been participated in actively by members of the Party and by non-Party people, and that the line of the Central Committee of the CPSU has met with the complete approval and support of the Party and people.

The violations of socialist legality and other errors connected with the cult of the person of J. V. Stalin, now made public by the Party, cause feelings of bitterness and profound regret. But Soviet people understand that the condemnation of the personality cult was necessary in the interests of building Communism, in which they are active participants. The Soviet people see that the Party has during recent years persistently carried out practical measures aimed at removing the consequences of the personality cult in all spheres of Party, state, economic, and cultural construction. As a result of this work, the Party, whose internal forces are no longer fettered by anything, has drawn still closer to the people and is now in a state of unprecedented creative activity.

II

How could the cult of the person of J. V. Stalin, with all its negative consequences, have arisen and become widespread under conditions of the Soviet socialist system?

When examining this question it is necessary to keep in mind both the objective, concrete historical conditions in which socialism has been built in the USSR and certain subjective factors connected with Stalin's personal qualities.

The October Socialist Revolution has gone down in history as a classical example of the revolutionary transformation of a capitalist society carried out under the leadership of the working class. From the example of the heroic struggle of the Bolshevik Party of the world's first socialist state, the USSR, Communist Parties of other countries, and all progressive and democratic forces are learning to solve the basic social questions arising from present-day social development. In the course of almost 40 years of building a socialist society, the working people of our country have amassed vast experience which is being studied and creatively assimilated by workers of other socialist countries, as it applies to their specific conditions.

This was the first experience in history of building a socialist society, molded in the course of searchings, of testing in practice many truths known hitherto to socialists only in general outline, in theory. For over a quarter of a century, the Soviet country was the only country paving the way to socialism for mankind. It was similar to a besieged fortress encircled by capitalism. After the intervention of fourteen states in 1918-1920 failed, enemies of the Soviet country in the west and east continued to prepare new "crusades" against the USSR.

Enemies sent into the USSR a large number of spies, and diversionists, trying in every way to undermine the world's first socialist state. The threat of a new imperialist aggression against the USSR became particularly acute after the advent to power in Germany, in 1933, of fascism, with its announced aim of destroying Communism, destroying the Soviet Union, the world's first state of the working people. Everybody remembers the formation of the so-called "Anti-Comintern Pact" and the "Berlin-Rome-Tokyo Axis," which were actively supported by all the forces of international reaction. In an atmosphere of a growing threat of a new war and the rejection by the Western powers of measures to bridle fascism and to organize collective security, repeatedly proposed by the Soviet Union, the Soviet country was compelled to harness all

its efforts to strengthen defense, to struggle against the
intrigues of the enemy capitalist encirclement. The Party
had to train the whole people in a spirit of constant vigilance and mobilized readiness in the face of foreign
enemies.

The intrigues of international reaction were all the more
dangerous because an embittered class struggle had been
going on in the country for a long time; the question,
"Who will gain the upper hand?" was being decided.
After Lenin's death, hostile elements became active in the
Party—Trotskyites, right-wing opportunists and bourgeois
nationalists—whose position was a rejection of Lenin's
theory that socialism can triumph in one country; this in
point of fact would have led to the restoration of capitalism
in the USSR.   The Party waged a merciless struggle
against these enemies of Leninism.

Fulfilling Lenin's behests, the Communist Party struck
a course toward the socialist industrialization of the country, the collectivization of agriculture, and the realization
of a cultural revolution.

In the course of solving these majestic tasks of building
a socialist society in a single specific country, the Soviet
people and the Communist Party had to overcome incred-
ible difficulties and obstacles. Our country, in the shortest
period of time from a historical point of view, without any
economic help whatsoever from abroad, had to erase its
centuries-old backwardness and rebuild its entire national
economy on new socialist principles.

This complicated international and internal situation
demanded an iron discipline, a continuously growing vigilance, and the strictest centralization of leadership, which

could not help but have a negative effect on the development of certain democratic forms. In the course of a fierce struggle against the whole world of imperialism, our country had to submit to certain restrictions of democracy, justified by the logic of our people's struggle for socialism under circumstances of capitalist encirclement. But these restrictions were at that time regarded by the Party and the people as temporary, subject to removal as the Soviet state grew stronger and the forces of democracy and socialism developed the world over. The people consciously assumed these temporary sacrifices, seeing as they did new successes of the Soviet social system every day.

All these difficulties on the part of building socialism were overcome by the Soviet people under the leadership of the Communist Party and its Central Committee, which consistently carried out Lenin's general line.

The victory of socialism in our country, under conditions of enemy encirclement and a constant threat of attack from the outside, was a world-historic exploit performed by the Soviet people. During the initial five-year plans the economically backward country made, as a result of the intense heroic efforts of the people and the Party, a gigantic leap in its economic and cultural development. On the basis of successes of socialist construction, the working people's living standard was raised and unemployment ended for all time. A most profound cultural revolution took place in the country. Within a short period of time the Soviet people trained numerous cadres of the technical intelligentsia, who took their place on the level of world technical progress and raised Soviet science and technology to one

of the first places in the world. The inspirer and organizer
of these victories was the great party of Communists. On
the example of the USSR, the working people of the world
became clearly convinced that workers and peasants, having taken power into their hands, could, without capitalists
and landowners, build and develop successfully their own
socialist state, expressing and defending the interests of the
broad masses of the people. All this played a tremendous,
inspiring role in the growth and influence of Communist
and Workers' Parties in all countries of the world.

Holding the position of General Secretary of the Central
Committee of the Party for a lengthy period, J. V. Stalin,
together with other leaders, actively struggled for the realization of Lenin's behests. He was devoted to Marxism-
Leninism and, as a theoretician and a good organizer,
headed the struggle of the party against the Trotskyites,
right-wing opportunists, bourgeois nationalists, and against
the intrigues of the capitalist encirclement. In this political and ideological struggle Stalin acquired great authority
and popularity. However, all our great victories began to
be incorrectly connected with his name. The successes
attained by the Communist Party and the Soviet country
and the adulation of Stalin went to his head. In this atmosphere the cult of Stalin's person began gradually to take
shape.

The development of the personality cult was to an enormous extent contributed to by some individual traits of
J. V. Stalin, the negative character of which was already
pointed out by V. I. Lenin. At the end of 1922, Lenin sent
a letter to the current Party Congress, in which he said:

"Comrade Stalin, by becoming General Secretary, has accumulated immeasurable power in his hands, and I am not certain whether he will always be able to use this power with the required care." In a postscript to this letter, written at the beginning of January 1923, V. I. Lenin again returns to the question of some personal traits of Stalin which are intolerable in a leader. "Stalin is too rude," wrote Lenin, "and this shortcoming, which is quite tolerable among us Communists, becomes intolerable in the office of the General Secretary. Therefore I advise the Comrades to think of a way of removing Stalin from this post and appointing to the post another person who in all other respects differs from Comrade Stalin in only one quality, to wit, is more tolerant, more loyal, more polite, more attentive toward Comrades, less capricious, etc."

At the XIIIth Party Congress, which was held soon after V. I. Lenin's death, his letters were made known to the delegations. As a result of the discussion of these documents, it was recognized as expedient to leave Stalin in the post of General Secretary, on the condition, however, that he should take into consideration Lenin's criticism and draw all the necessary conclusions.

Having remained at the post of General Secretary of the Central Committee, Stalin, in the first period after Vladimir Ilyich's death, took into account his critical remarks. Later on, however, Stalin, having excessively overrated his merits, came to believe in his own infallibility. He began making some of the limitations on Party and Soviet democracy—unavoidable in conditions of a bitter struggle against the class enemy and its agents and, subsequently, during the war against the German fascist invaders—the norm of

intra-Party and state life, riding roughshod over the Leninist principles of leadership. The plenary sessions of the
Central Committee and congresses of the Party were held
irregularly, and later they were not convened at all for
many years. In fact, Stalin became above criticism.

Great harm to the cause of socialist construction, the
development of democracy inside the Party and the state,
was inflicted by Stalin's erroneous formula that, allegedly,
with the moving of the Soviet Union toward socialism, the
class struggle would become more and more acute. This
formula—which is only correct for certain stages of the
transition period, when the question of "who will beat
whom" was being solved, when a persistent class struggle
for the building of the foundations of socialism was in
progress—was put to the fore in 1937, at a moment when
socialism had already become victorious in our country,
when the exploiting classes and their economic base had
been liquidated. In practice, this erroneous theoretical
formula was the basis for the grossest violations of socialist law and for mass repressions.

It was in these conditions, in particular, that a special
position was created for organs of state security. Enormous confidence was placed in them because of their
unquestionable service to the people and country in the
defense of the conquests of the revolution. For a considerable period of time the state security organs justified this
confidence, and their special position did not cause any
danger. The situation changed when the control over them
by the Party and government was gradually replaced by the
personal control of Stalin, and the normal administration
of justice was often superseded by his unilateral personal

decisions. The situation became even more complicated when the criminal band of the agent of international imperialism, Beria, was at the head of the state security organs. Serious violations of Soviet law and mass repressions occurred. As a result of enemy machinations, many honest Communists and Soviet non-Party people were slandered and suffered innocently.

The XXth Party Congress and the entire policy of the Central Committee after the death of Stalin bear vivid testimony to the fact that there was within the Central Committee of the Party a Leninist core of leaders, who correctly understood pressing requirements in both domestic and foreign policy. It cannot be said that there was no counter-action against the negative manifestations which were connected with the personality cult and which put a brake on the forward movement of socialism. There were certain periods, for instance during the war years, when the unilateral acts of Stalin were sharply restricted, when the negative consequences of lawlessness, arbitrariness, and so forth were substantially diminished.

It is known that precisely during the war period members of the Central Committee as well as outstanding Soviet military leaders took over certain sectors of activity in the rear and at the front, made independent decisions, and through their organizational, political, economic, and military work, together with local Party and Soviet organizations, ensured the victory of the Soviet people in the war. After victory the negative consequences of the personality cult re-emerged with great force.

Immediately after the death of Stalin, the Leninist core of the Central Committee set a course of resolute struggle against the personality cult and its grave consequences.

One might ask why, then, did these people not take an open stand against Stalin and remove him from leadership? This could not be done under the circumstances which had developed. The facts show clearly that Stalin was guilty of many lawless deeds, committed particularly in the later period of his life. However, at the same time, we should not forget that the Soviet people knew Stalin as a person who always acted in the defense of the USSR against the intrigues of the enemies, and that he fought for the cause of socialism. At times he applied unworthy methods in this struggle and violated the Leninist principles and norms of Party life. This was the tragedy of Stalin. But at the same time all this made more difficult the struggle against the lawless deeds perpetrated, because the successes of the construction of socialism and the consolidation of the USSR were ascribed to Stalin as long as the personality cult prevailed. Any action against him under these conditions would not have been understood by the people. It is in no way a question of a lack of personal courage. It is obvious that if anyone in this situation had acted against Stalin he would not have received support from the people. Moreover, such a stand under these conditions would have been regarded as a stand against the cause of socialist construction, as a blow against the unity of the Party and the entire state, which would have been extremely dangerous in the situation of capitalist encirclement. In addition, the successes which the working people of the Soviet Union attained under the leadership of their Communist Party had aroused justifiable pride in the heart of every Soviet person and created an atmosphere in which individual mistakes and shortcomings seemed less important against the background of such enormous successes, while the negative consequences of these mistakes were quickly made good by the colossal growth of the vital forces of the Party and the Soviet society.

One should also bear in mind that many facts about wrong actions of Stalin, especially in the sphere of the violation of Soviet law, became known only during recent times—after the death of Stalin, mainly in connection with the exposure of the Beria gang and the establishment of Party control over the organs of state security.

Such are the main conditions and causes which resulted in the rise and spread of the personality cult of J. V. Stalin. Obviously everything that has been said explains, but in no way justifies, the personality cult of J. V. Stalin and its consequences, which have been so sharply and justly condemned by our Party.

III

Indisputably the personality cult has seriously harmed the cause of the Communist Party and Soviet society. It would, however, be a serious mistake to deduce from the fact of the existence in the past of the personality cult some kind of changes in the social system in the USSR, or to look for the source of this cult in the nature of the Soviet social system. Both alternatives are absolutely wrong, as they are not in accord with reality and contradict the facts.

In spite of all the evil which the personality cult of Stalin brought to the Party and the people, it could not change and has not changed the nature of our social system. No personality cult could change the nature of the socialist state, based on public ownership of the means of production, the

alliance of working class and the peasantry, and the friendship of peoples, even though this cult did inflict serious
damage on the development of socialist democracy and
the upsurge of the creative initiative of millions.

To imagine that an individual, even such a major one
as Stalin, could change our social-political system is to
enter into profound contradiction with the facts, with
Marxism, with truth, and to sink into idealism. This would
be attributing to an individual such excessive and supernatural powers as the ability to change the system of a
society, even a social system in which many millions of
working people are the decisive force.

As is known, the nature of the social-political system is
determined by the nature of the means of production, to
whom in society the means of production belong, and what
class holds the political power. The entire world knows
that in our country, as a result of the October Revolution
and the victory of socialism, the socialist method of production was established, and that for nearly 40 years power has
been in the hands of the working class and peasantry.
Thanks to this, the Soviet social system is gaining in
strength from year to year, and its production forces are
growing. This is a fact even those who wish us ill must
admit.

The consequences of the personality cult were, as is
known, certain serious mistakes in the leadership of various branches of the activity of the Party and Soviet state,
both in the internal life of the Soviet country and in its
foreign policy. One can, in particular, point to serious
mistakes made by Stalin in guiding agriculture, in organizing the country's preparation to rebuff the fascist invaders,

in gross arbitrariness which led to a conflict in relations with Yugoslavia in the postwar period. These mistakes harmed the development of individual aspects of the Soviet state's life and impeded the development of Soviet society, particularly in the last years of J. V. Stalin's life. But it goes without saying that they did not divert it from the correct path of development toward Communism.

Our enemies assert that the personality cult of Stalin was not engendered by definite historical conditions which have already passed but by the Soviet system itself, by what they consider its lack of democracy, and so on. Such slanderous assertions are refuted by the entire history of the development of the Soviet state. The Soviets as a new democratic form of state rule arose as a result of the revolutionary creative activity of the broadest popular masses who had risen to the struggle for freedom. They were and remain organs of genuine people's rule. It is precisely the Soviet system which created the possibility of bringing out the immense creative energies of the people. It put into motion inexhaustible forces inherent in the popular masses, drew millions of people into conscious direction of the state, into active creative participation in the building of socialism. In a brief historical period, the Soviet state came out victorious from the most difficult tests and survived a baptism of fire in World War II.

When the last exploiting classes were liquidated in our country, when socialism became the dominant system in the entire national economy, while the international situation of our country had radically changed, the framework of Soviet democracy immeasurably extended and is continuing to do so. Contrary to any kind of bourgeois democracy, Soviet democracy not only proclaims but also materially assures the right to labor, education and leisure, participation in state affairs, freedom of speech and of the press, freedom of conscience and also a real opportunity for the free development of personal abilities, and other democratic rights and freedoms for all members of society without exception. The essence of democracy is not in formal appearances but in whether political power really serves and reflects the will and interests of the majority of the people, the interests of the working people. The entire internal and foreign policy of the Soviet state shows that our system is truly democratic, a truly popular system. The highest aim and constant concern of the Soviet state is the raising in every respect of the people's living standards, the securing of a peaceful existence for its people.

A testimony to the further development of Soviet democracy are the measures which are being put through by the Party and government for extending the rights and competence of the Union republics, the strict adherence to law and the reorganization of the system of planning with the aim of releasing local initiative, activating the work of local Soviets, and developing criticism and self-criticism.

In spite of the personality cult and contrary to it, the mighty initiative of the people's masses led by the Communist Party, which is engendered by our system, has performed its great historical task, overcoming all barriers on the path to the building of socialism. And in this the democratic nature of the Soviet socialist system finds its highest expression. The outstanding victories of socialism in our country did not come about by themselves. They were gained thanks to the tremendous organizational and educational work of the Party and its local organizations, thanks to the fact that the Party always trained its cadres and all Communists in a spirit of loyalty to Marxism-Leninism, in a spirit of devotion to the cause of Communism. Soviet society is strong through the awareness of the masses. Its historic destinies have been and are determined by the creative labor of our heroic working class, our glorious collective farm peasantry and people's intelligentsia.

By liquidating the consequences of the personality cult, restoring Bolshevik norms of Party life, and by developing socialist democracy, our Party has achieved a further strengthening of ties with the broad masses, and rallied them still closer under the great Leninist banner.

The fact that the Party itself boldly and openly posed the question of the liquidation of the personality cult, the question of inadmissible mistakes made by Stalin, is a convincing testimony that our Party firmly guards Leninism, the cause of socialism and communism, the observance of socialist law and the interests of peoples, and the guaranteeing of the rights of Soviet citizens. This is the best proof of the strength and vitality of the Soviet socialist system. It speaks at the same time of the determination to overcome completely the consequences of the personality cult and not to allow mistakes of such a nature to be repeated in the future.

Condemnation by our Party of the personality cult of J. V. Stalin, and of its consequences, brought approval and wide response in all fraternal Communist and Workers' Parties. Noting the tremendous significance of the XXth

CPSU Congress for the entire international communist and workers' movement, Communists of foreign countries consider the struggle against the personality cult and its consequences as a struggle for the purity of the principles of Marxism-Leninism, for a creative approach to the solution of contemporary problems of the international workers' movement, for the affirmation and further development of the principles of proletarian internationalism.

In statements of a number of fraternal Communist Parties, approval and support is expressed of the measures against the personality cult and its consequences carried through by our Party. The organ of the Central Committee of the Chinese Communist Party, the newspaper *Jen Min Jih Pao*, in presenting the conclusions from a discussion of the decisions of the XXth CPSU Congress at a meeting of the Politburo of the Central Committee of the Chinese Communist Party, states in an editorial article, "On the Historic Experience of the Dictatorship of the Proletariat": "The CPSU, following Lenin's behests, treats seriously some of the grave errors made by Stalin in directing socialist construction and the consequences they have provoked. Because of the gravity of these consequences the Communist Party of the Soviet Union, while admitting the great services of J. V. Stalin, is faced with the necessity to reveal with all sharpness the essence of the mistakes Stalin made and to urge the entire Party to beware of a repetition of this, and to urge it to a determined eradication of the unhealthy consequences of these shortcomings. We Communists of China profoundly believe that after the sharp criticism which developed at the XXth Communist Party of the Soviet Union Congress all those active factors which were strongly restrained in the past because of certain political mistakes undoubtedly will be set in motion everywhere, that the Communist Party of the Soviet Union and the Soviet people will be united and made one as never before in the struggle for the building of a great Communist society never yet seen in history, in the struggle for a stable peace in the entire world."

"The merit of the leaders of the Communist Party of the Soviet Union," says the statement of the Politburo of the French Communist Party, "is contained in the fact that they undertook to correct mistakes and shortcomings connected with the personality cult. This testifies to the strength and unity of the great party of Lenin, to the confidence which it enjoys among the Soviet people, as well as to its authority in the international workers' movement." The General Secretary of the National Committee of the Communist Party of the U. S. A., Comrade Eugene Dennis, noting the tremendous significance of the XXth Communist Party of the Soviet Union Congress, states in his well-known article: "The XXth Communist Party of the Soviet Union Congress strengthened universal peace and social progress. It marked a new stage in the development of socialism and in the struggle for peaceful co-existence which started in the time of Lenin, was pursued in subsequent years, and is becoming more and more effective and successful."*

At the same time it should be noted that in discussing the question of the personality cult a correct interpretation of the reasons which engendered the personality cult and of the consequences of this cult for our social system has not always been given. Thus, for instance, a detailed and interesting interview given by Comrade Togliatti

* See pp. 164 and 168 above.—*Editor.*

to the magazine *Nuovi Argomenti* contains, along with many most important and correct deductions, incorrect tenets. In particular, one cannot agree with the question posed by Comrade Togliatti as to whether Soviet society may have reached "certain forms of degeneration." There is no foundation for posing such a question. This is all the more incomprehensible because in another part of his interview Togliatti says quite correctly: "It is essential to deduce that the essence of the socialist system has not been lost, just as none of the preceding gains, primarily the support of the system by the masses of workers, peasants, and intelligentsia who form Soviet society, has been lost. This support proves in itself that, in spite of everything, this society has retained its basic democratic character."*

Indeed, without the support by the broadest popular masses of the Soviet regime of the policy of the Communist Party, our country would not have been able to create, in an unprecedentedly short space of time, a powerful socialist industry and to carry out the collectivization of agriculture and it would not have been able to gain a victory in the Second World War, on the issue of which the destinies of all mankind depended. As a result of the complete rout of Hitlerism, Italian Fascism, and Japanese militarism, the forces of the Communist movement received extensive development. The Communist Parties in Italy, France, and other capitalist countries grew and became mass parties, the system of People's Democracy was established in a number of countries of Europe and Asia, a world system of socialism arose and was consolidated, and the national-liberation movement which led to the disintegra-

* For Togliatti's text see p. 127 above.—*Editor.*

tion of the colonial system of imperialism attained unprecedented successes.

IV

Unanimously approving the decisions of the XXth Communist Party of the Soviet Union Congress, which condemned the cult of personality, Communists and all Soviet
people see in them a proof of the increased strength of our
party, its Leninist adherence to principles, its unity, and
solidarity. "A party of the revolutionary proletariat,"
V. I. Lenin pointed out, "is sufficiently strong to openly
criticize itself, to call unambiguously a mistake a mistake
and a weakness a weakness." (*Works*, Volume 21, page
150.) Guided by this principle of Lenin, our Party will
continue to boldly disclose, openly criticize, and resolutely
remove mistakes and omissions in its work.

The Central Committee of the Communist Party of the
Soviet Union considers that the work accomplished up to
now by the Party in overcoming the cult of personality and
its consequences has already given positive results.

Proceeding from the decisions of the XXth Party Congress, the Central Committee of the Communist Party of
the Soviet Union urges all Party organizations:

Consistently to observe in all our work the major
tenets of Marxism-Leninism on the people as the creators
of history, the creators of all the material and spiritual
riches of mankind, on the deciding role of the Marxist
party in the revolutionary struggle for the transformation
of society, for the triumph of Communism;

Persistently to continue the work done in recent years
by the Party Central Committee for strictest adherence in
all Party organizations from top to bottom to the Leninist

principles of Party leadership, above all to the highest
principle, that of collective leadership, for observance of
the norms of Party life affirmed by the Statutes of our
Party, for the development of criticism and self-criticism;

Fully to restore the principles of Soviet socialist
democracy expressed in the Constitution of the Soviet
Union, completely to correct violations of revolutionary
socialist legality;

To mobilize our cadres, all Communists and the broadest masses of the working people in the struggle for practical realization of the tasks of the Sixth Five-Year Plan,
developing in every way for this the creative initiative and
energy of the masses, the true creators of history.

The XXth Communist Party of the Soviet Union Congress pointed out that the most important trait of our era
is the conversion of socialism into a world system. The
most difficult period in the development and establishment
of socialism is past. Our socialist country has ceased
to be an isolated island in an ocean of capitalist states. At
present, more than one third of all mankind is building a
new life under the banner of socialism. The ideas of
socialism have captured the imagination of many millions
of people in capitalist countries. Immense is the influence
of the ideas of socialism upon the people of Asia, Africa,
and Latin America, who are opposing all forms of colonialism.

The decisions of the XXth Communist Party of the Soviet
Union Congress are received by all the advocates of peace
and socialism, by all democratic and progressive circles,
as an inspiring program for the struggle for consolidating
world peace, for the interests of the working classes, for
the triumph of the cause of socialism.

Under present conditions, broad, inspiring prospects open up before Communist Parties and the entire international workers' movement—to achieve together with all peace-loving forces the prevention of a new world war, to restrain the monopolies and ensure lasting peace and the security of peoples, to stop the arms race and to relieve the working people of the heavy burden of taxation engendered by it, and to defend the democratic rights and freedoms which ensure for the working people the struggle for a better life and happy future. It is precisely in this that millions of common people, in all countries of the world, are vitally interested. The peace-loving policy and the ever new successes of the Soviet Union, the Chinese People's Republic and all other countries following the road of socialism contribute to a tremendous degree to a peaceful solution of these problems.

Under the new historical conditions such international working class organizations as the Comintern and Cominform have ceased their activities. It does not follow from this, however, that international solidarity and the need for contacts among revolutionary fraternal parties adhering to positions of Marxism-Leninism have lost their significance. At present, when the forces of socialism and the influence of the ideas of socialism have grown immeasurably throughout the world, when the difference in paths to socialism in various countries is becoming apparent, the Marxist parties of the working class, naturally, must retain and strengthen their ideological unity and international fraternal solidarity in the struggle against the threat of a new war, in the struggle against the anti-people's forces of monopolistic capital striving to suppress all revolutionary and progressive movements. Communist Parties are united by the great aim of liberating the working class from the oppression of capital. They are united by loyalty to the scientific ideology of Marxism-Leninism, to the spirit of proletarian internationalism, by selfless devotion to the interests of the popular masses.

In their activity under present conditions all Communist Parties proceed from the national peculiarities and the conditions of each country, expressing with the greatest completeness the national interests of their peoples, realizing at the same time that the struggle for the interests of the working class, for peace and the national independence of their countries, is at the same time the cause of the entire international proletariat, they are rallying together and strengthen their ties and cooperation among themselves. The ideological unanimity and fraternal solidarity of Marxist parties of the working class of various countries is all the more necessary because capitalist monopolies are creating their own international aggressive unions and blocs, such as NATO, SEATO, and the Baghdad Pact, aimed against peace-loving peoples, against the national liberation movement, against the working class and the vital interests of the working people.

While the Soviet Union has done much and is doing much for a reduction of international tension—and this is acknowledged now by all—American monopolistic capital continues appropriating large amounts for intensifying subversive activities in the socialist countries. At the height of the "cold war," it is known, the U. S. Congress officially (in addition to the funds that are being spent unofficially) appropriated $100,000,000 for subversive activities in the People's Democracies and the Soviet Union.

Now, when the Soviet Union and other socialist countries are doing everything possible for a reduction of international tension, the adherents of the "cold war" are trying to increase the activity of the "cold war," which is condemned by the peoples of the entire world. This is shown by the decision of the United States Senate on the additional appropriation of $25,000,000 for subversive activities, which is cynically being called "an encouragement for freedom" behind the "iron curtain."

We must soberly appraise this fact and make corresponding deductions. It is clear, for instance, that the anti-people's demonstrations in Poznan were financed from this source. However, the provocateurs and the diversionists, who were paid from the overseas funds, had sufficient courage only for a few hours. Working people of Poznan gave a rebuff to the enemies' sallies and provocations. The plans of the knights of the "cloak and dagger" have failed, their foul provocation against the people's rule in Poland have failed. The subversive activities in the People's Democracies will continue to fail in the future as well, even if such actions are lavishly financed by the money appropriated by American monopolists. One can say that this money is spent for nothing.

All this demonstrates that one must not show carelessness in relation to new machinations of the imperialist agents who are trying to penetrate into socialist countries for the purpose of harming and undermining the working people's achievements.

The forces of imperialist reaction are attempting to drive the working people from the correct path of the struggle for their interests, to poison their souls with the poison of mistrust in the success of the cause of peace and socialism. Despite all the machinations of the ideologists of the capitalist monopolies, the working class led by the experienced Communist vanguard will march on its road, which has led to the historic achievements of socialism and will lead to new victories of the cause of peace, democracy, and socialism. One can be confident that the Communist and Workers' Parties of all countries will raise even higher the glorious Marxist banner of proletarian internationalism.

The Soviet people are justly proud of the fact that our Motherland was the first to lay the path to socialism. Now, when socialism has become a world system, when among socialist countries fraternal cooperation and mutual assistance are established, new favorable conditions have developed for the flourishing of socialist democracy, for further strengthening of the material production base of Communism, the steadfast upsurge of the living standard of the working people, for all-sided development of the personality of a new man, builder of a Communist society. Let the bourgeois ideologists concoct fables about the "crises" of communism, about "confusion" in the ranks of the Communist Party. We are accustomed to hearing such invocations from the enemies. Their forecasts always burst like soap bubbles. These luckless predictors have come and gone but the Communist movement, the immortal and life-giving ideas of Marxism-Leninism have triumphed and are continuing to triumph. This also will be the case in the future. No malicious, slanderous attacks by our enemies can stop the irresistible cause of the historical development of mankind toward Communism.

12

Togliatti Statement on Soviet Party Resolution,

PAESE SERA, Rome

July 3, 1956

THE DAY following *Pravda's* publication of the CPSU resolution, Togliatti issued a statement carried by the left-wing newspaper, *Paese Sera,* reprinted in the Communist *L'Unità* on July 4 (and rebroadcast in full by Moscow radio). According to *The New York Times'* Rome correspondent, "some of his lieutenants seem to have pressed him to talk back to the Soviet reprimand. But the majority of the leading Italian Communists backed him in his determination to accept the Soviet explanation" (July 4, 1956).

I HAVE not yet read the full text of the CPSU Central Committee final resolution on the origin and consequences of the personality cult. Judging by what I know of the resolution, it seems to me that that document provides a contribution of extreme importance for the clarification of the questions aroused among the international workers and Communist world by the criticism of Stalin's work made by the XXth CPSU Congress.

As for my attitude at my well-known interview, perhaps the best thing to do now is to read carefully what I have written. In my opinion, and I have said so openly, the line followed by the Soviet comrades in the construction of a Communist society was undoubtedly right; but within the general framework of this acknowledgment, there may be differing opinions on the value and importance of the errors committed under Stalin's leadership, the violations of legality, the restrictions on democracy, and so on, over the economic and political development of the Soviet Union.

I repeat that such differing opinions are possible and a frank discussion on the matter cannot but prove useful for the development of our movement, because it corresponds to a higher degree of maturity and of mutual understanding and confidence.

This is all the more true since such differences of opinion do not diminish, but, in fact, as far as myself and the leading organs of the Italian Communist Party are concerned, perhaps they enhance our unreserved approval of action taken by the CPSU leaders to overcome completely the consequences to which the cult of Stalin's person has led in the USSR and in the international workers' movement.

13

Editorial: "Le ombre rimangono"
AVANTI!, Rome

July 3, 1956

PIETRO NENNI responded to the CPSU resolution with the following unsigned editorial on the front page of *Avanti!* After a two-day policy meeting, the directorate of his party endorsed on July 5 Nenni's criticism of the treatment of Stalin. However, (according to *The New York Times*, July 6, 1956), the declaration also said that, apart from current ideological discussions, "the new course of Soviet policy represents an increasingly effective contribution toward the peaceful coexistence of the world's peoples."

Avanti! and the next number of *Mondo Operaio* (issued on July 29) continued to expound Nenni's views in a similar vein and, as a result, drew criticism from his political allies, the Italian Communist Party. *L'Unità* described Nenni's criticism of the Communists as "hasty" and excessively "journalistic," rather than a sound Marxist analysis. The anti-Stalin campaign had apparently subjected the "alliance" of the two left-wing movements to a substantial strain.

The Shadows Remain

THE DOCUMENT of the Central Committee of the CPSU on overcoming the cult of the individual and its consequences, explains several things in the famous secret report of Khrushchev which up to now remained obscure or unknown. It illustrates with the greatest Marxist coherence the causes of the formation of the cult and of the personal dictatorship of Stalin, but it still does not answer the fundamental questions which the Khrushchev report has raised so dramatically with its revelations of the illegalities and the atrocities of Stalin.

The summary that we have of the resolution of the Central Committee confirms, for example, with the greatest clarity the secret report of how Stalin's personal dictatorship evolved, how difficult it was to combat Stalin during the last twenty years, because his guilt was unknown to almost all of the Soviet people while all the successes of the USSR were attributed to his personal merit.

We know better why the abnormal situation of the last twenty years developed. Thus we know that certain circumstances contributed to the personal dictatorship of Stalin, among which, as the document of the Central Committee states, was the capitalist encirclement of the USSR, which Stalin used to justify a temporary restriction of democracy which he later rendered permanent. From the resolution of the Central Committee emerges the principle of the necessity of "War Communism" which Stalin exploited for his dictatorial ends.

But all this is still not sufficient. The phases of passing from the dictatorship of the proletariat to that of the Party, and from the latter to that of Stalin, are not described in the document; nor is there any treatment of how and why Stalin succeeded in carrying out his plans. The practical impossibility of overthrowing Stalin or seriously resisting him after he had gained control of the Party, his seizure of absolute power, the substituting of himself for the Party and for the constitutional organs of the state, which the Khrushchev report describes, is comprehensible. But why was Stalin able to succeed in ridding himself with relative ease of all his adversaries, in depriving the directing organs of the Party of authority, in substituting himself for justice and government from local soviets all the way up to the Supreme Soviet? Why did the Party, the soviets, the proletariat not resist before Stalin triumphed, and why were those who did resist isolated and defeated?

The document of the Central Committee does not answer all this; it does not explain why Stalin's power was such that he could exploit a fundamental error which prevailed in the Bolshevik Party after the death of Lenin. Having suppressed the other parties—and thereby democracy based on the plurality of parties—democracy within the party was also suppressed. Having eliminated the other parties, from the Mensheviks to the Socialist Revolutionaries, from competition with the Bolshevik Party, having eliminated the internal factions of the Bolshevik Party, utilizing the rivalry of his followers and oftentimes that of his adversaries whom he succeeded in pitting one against the other, it was easy for Stalin, who in the course of this operation had accumulated immense personal power, also to eliminate democracy from within his own faction, remaining the only legal force in the Party and in the state.

This is why we believe that the process of democratization in the USSR will be complete and efficacious only if it is accompanied by a return to legality and to the constitution, a return to freedom of expression.

In what manner this must express itself and by which institutions it must be guaranteed—that is a problem for the Soviets. There is no democratic formula which in itself guarantees democracy. It must be above all a matter of conscience and of custom: a good which both the rulers and the ruled must sincerely accept.

14

Editorial: "A Fraternal Discussion"

DAILY WORKER, New York

July 3, 1956

IN CONJUNCTION with the publication of the CPSU resolution
of June 30, the New York *Daily Worker* printed the following
editorial.

THIS discussion, now going on among the various Communist Parties, is something new in the history of the
Communist movements.

It is a fraternal, critical discussion, conducted on an
equal basis among Marxists who are seeking the scientific
answers to profound questions of importance to themselves,
to the working class and to the general cause of democracy
and socialism.

This discussion confounds the foes of socialism who
insist that there is nothing new in the Communist movements and that the unmistakable evidence of independence
and equality is all a "plot."

The recent declaration of the Communist Parties of the
Soviet Union and of Yugoslavia stated that the "delega-
tions have agreed, guided by the principles of Marxism-
Leninism, to a prompt mutual cooperation and exchange

of views in the field of socialist scientific thought both in their mutual relations and in the international workers' movement in general."

It is in this spirit that various Communist Parties, including the American, raised questions regarding the speech of Nikita Khrushchev on Stalin—particularly with regard to the need for a deeper explanation of the errors and crimes ascribed to Stalin.

In the latest chapter in this discussion, the Central Committee of the Communist Party of the Soviet Union has now given its reply to some of these questions. Many Marxists will feel satisfied with the answers which the Soviet Communist Party now presents. Many will feel that the final answers still need to be found and that the discussion must continue.

The Daily Worker will have more to say on the Soviet Communist Party's statement in the future and we will keep our readers informed, as the discussion goes on, of the views of Marxists here and throughout the world.

A deeper probing of the errors in the Soviet Union can only result in speeding the profound changes already getting under way in that country. It can be of invaluable help to the Communist movements elsewhere, and to the cause of co-existence and world peace.

15

"Dennis Comments on Soviet CP Statement"

DAILY WORKER, New York

July 4, 1956

FOLLOWING the publication of the CPSU resolution, Eugene Dennis, as General Secretary of the CPUSA, issued the comment reprinted below. As if to underscore that the discussion was not closed, the *Daily Worker* now published a statement adopted by the National Committee of the Canadian Labor Progressive Party on June 28 ("Canada Party Calls Khrushchev Statement Inadequate," *Daily Worker*, July 3); and began (on July 5) to publish "the greater part of the questions and answers" contained in the Togliatti interview with *Nuovi Argomenti* (Document 3 above).

A few days later, the *Canadian Tribune*, organ of the Labor Progressive Party, devoted a lengthy editorial to the Central Committee resolution. It found that on balance it served to "clear the air" and "restore confidence" in the CPSU leadership. On the other hand, the editorial continued (as cited in the New York *Daily Worker*, July 13, 1956):

We believe, however, that there remain some still unanswered questions, such as the demand for more light on the excesses against certain nationalities or against Jewish cultural life and the Jewish writers. These are not mentioned [by Moscow]. All that is said is that Stalin was "guilty of many lawless deeds."

Nor does it answer the criticism of the way in which the Khrushchev report on Stalin was handled. The Tribune *has de-*

clared it should have been made available to the Press as soon as it was delivered and not allowed to "leak" out through the U. S. State Department.

While it offers further clarification, it does not acknowledge that the present leaders of the Central Committee of the CPSU accepted the erroneous theory originated by Stalin, from which so many crimes ensued, that the class struggle must be intensified following the victory of socialism. This "theory" is attributed solely to Stalin and not to the Central Committee or the Party Congress that also accepted it.

Frank criticism of the CPSU resolution of June 30 came from the Communist Party of Trieste. Its organ, *Il Lavoratore* (July 6), editorially called Moscow's failure to publish the Khrushchev speech "deplorable" and attacked those "who with speeches and writings actively collaborated in the creation of this [Stalin] cult, and especially those who were near him. . . . There exists an enormous difference, an absolute contrast between what they were saying of Stalin yesterday and what they say today."

The Danish *Land og Folk* (which earlier had endorsed Togliatti's queries) stated on July 8 that there was considerable "confusion" in Communist ranks. It hailed the CPSU resolution for its "sober, profound self-criticism," but (again, not unlike the Italian Party) concluded: "The Soviet declaration is a valuable contribution to the discussion which is taking place in the international labor movement. This discussion will of course continue."

An editorial in the Stockholm Communist daily, *Ny Dag*, of July 12, likewise insisted:

On many points the declaration [of June 30] is very illuminating and important, but there are reasons for placing several question marks in the margin. These apply to those sections of the declaration which deal with the origin of the cult of the personality and the breaches of Soviet democracy and socialist justice. . . . A thorough study of the whole development of Soviet society is necessary. . . . The declaration of the Central Committee leaves the impression that an attempt is being made to circumvent the core of the problem [the role under Stalin of the present leadership].

The Dennis statement which follows was broadcast by Moscow on July 6.

THE Soviet Communist Party's resolution is a most welcome development in the friendly interchange of opinion among Marxists of the world. It correctly turns attention to the profound significance of its XXth Congress, with its historic decisions paving the way for new socialist advances and its far-reaching conclusions on the non-inevitability of war and the possibility for peaceful paths to Socialism in democratic countries.

The resolution correctly estimates the sinister aims of those reactionary circles who would bury the tremendous achievements of the XXth Congress under an avalanche of speculation about the re-evaluation of Stalin. It coincides with our estimate that reactionary circles here and elsewhere are trying to distort and utilize Khrushchev's special report on Stalin to disrupt the solidarity of the international working class movement. These "cold war" forces are not interested in making peaceful co-existence a settled national policy: they seek to prolong world tensions and maintain a suicidal arms race. They vainly seek to frustrate the will of the peoples for world peace which was reflected at Bandung and Geneva and continues to grow.

In my opinion the resolution of the CPSU goes a long way in explaining—while clearly not justifying—what has become known as the growth of the cult of the individual and the unforgivable violations of socialist legality and principles that took place in the latter period of Stalin's leadership. The substance of this matter will be discussed shortly by our National Committee which will then collectively express its views.

16

Statement of the Central Committee
of the French Communist Party
L'HUMANITÉ, Paris

July 7, 1956

ANDRÉ STIL, editorial writer of *L'Humanité*, commented on the CPSU resolution in an article ("Un texte capital," July 4) reprinted by the Moscow *Pravda* on July 6. It concluded: "The French Communists, in their struggle against the diversionary attempts and libelous campaigns in connection ·with the XXth Congress, are grateful to the fraternal Party of the Soviet Union for this resolution of its Central Committee, a new capital contribution to the effort of the international workers' movement for peace, for socialism."

On July 7, *L'Humanité* reported that, after a report by Etienne Fajon on the recent visit of a French Communist delegation to Moscow, the Central Committee of the French Communist Party unanimously passed the following statement (which was reprinted by *Pravda* on July 8 as well as the Polish and Rumanian press). It set the tone for the XIVth Congress of the French Communist Party, which opened in Le Havre on July 18. The Congress witnessed no unusual revelations and bared no internal differences. It voiced "warm approval" of the Soviet stand on "the cult of the individual," and it proclaimed "complete unanimity of views" between the French and Soviet Communist Parties.

THE Central Committee of the French Communist Party has heard the report of the Party's delegation which visited

Moscow in order to discuss with the representatives of the
CPSU problems which interest both parties and the entire
international workers' movement. It approves the work
of the delegation and expresses satisfaction at the talks,
in the course of which it became clear that there was complete unanimity of views between the two parties concerning all the questions raised by the XXth Congress, among
them the necessity to make every effort to achieve unity
of action of the working class in its struggle for peace,
democracy, and socialism.

The Central Committee warmly approves the decision of
the Central Committee of the CPSU which shows how the
cult of Stalin's person was overcome in the USSR. The
decision rightly recalls that the most important questions
raised by the XXth Congress, which open the way toward
new successes in the cause of peace, socialism, and unity of
the working class, must especially win the attention of the
working class and Communist parties.

Having stressed the new outstanding successes which
have been achieved in the economic, political, and cultural
life of the USSR and having armed the Soviet people with
a grandiose plan for building Communism, having shown
that the courageous and consistent foreign policy of the
Soviet Union, which is aimed at strengthening peace, is
acquiring ever-increasing support of broad popular masses
in every country, and having revealed possibilities for
doing away with wars in our time and for proceeding to
socialism along new paths, the XXth Congress of the CPSU
considerably facilitated a relaxation of international tension, the strengthening of the unity of action of all the
forces fighting for peace and democracy and the consolidation of the positions of the camp of world socialism.

Having recalled the objective and concrete historical conditions under which the building of socialism was taking place in the USSR as well as some personal features of Stalin, the decision gives a profound and completely satisfactory analysis of all the circumstances in which the cult of Stalin's person was able to develop. The decision quite rightly shows that the cult of the individual has done certain harm to the socialist society and to the cause of the Communist Party, but that it would be a mistake to seek the source of this cult in the nature of the Soviet social system.

In view of the fact that in the USSR the means of production and political power are vested in the hands of the working class, which is united with the toiling peasantry, the Soviet social and political system, differing from the bourgeois democracy, is truly democratic and of the people, because it genuinely reflects the will and the basic interests of the people and the interests of the workers. The errors and mistakes connected with the cult of personality could halt, particularly during the last years of Stalin's life, the development of the socialist system, yet they did not divert it from the path to Communism.

A great service of the leaders of the CPSU was that, by basing themselves on the principles of Marxism-Leninism, they corrected the errors and mistakes connected with the personality cult, restoring the Lenin norms of Party life, developing socialist democracy, strengthening still more the ties with the masses and still more closely rallying them under Lenin's banner, which has still further enhanced the trust which is enjoyed by the CPSU among the Soviet people and its prestige in the eyes of the international workers' movement.

The decision of the Central Committee of the CPSU stresses particularly powerfully the entire importance of international solidarity in new historical conditions. While the strength of socialism and the influence of socialist ideas in the world have grown considerably, the Marxist parties of the working class must really strengthen their ideological unity, preserve and consolidate their international solidarity in the struggle against the threats of a new war, in the struggle against capitalism, for democratic freedoms and socialism.

In their activity, the Communist parties must take into consideration national peculiarities and the condition of every country and fully represent the interests of the whole people. At the same time, they are aware of the fact that the struggle for the interests of the working class, for peace, and for national independence also constitutes the common concern of the entire international proletariat and that consequently they must unite their actions, being faithful to the scientific ideology of Marxism-Leninism and to the spirit of proletarian internationalism.

Believing that the decision taken by the Central Committee of the CPSU is a document of invaluable importance for the international working class, the Central Committee calls upon all members of the Party to study it seriously and to disseminate it widely. Such study will constitute a great contribution to the preparation and the successes of the XIVth Congress of the French Communist Party, which, preserving loyalty to the principles of Marxism-Leninism, will make every effort to implement unity of action among the working class—one of the most important elements of the victorious struggle for peace, democracy, and socialism.

17

Statement of the Executive Committee of the British Communist Party, July 14, 1956

DAILY WORKER, London
     July 16, 1956

A BRITISH Communist delegation was among the various groups of Western European Communists invited to Moscow in the wake of the CPSU resolution of June 30. After three of its leaders had returned from Moscow, the Executive [Central] Committee of the British Communist Party on July 14 adopted the statement printed below.

Similarly, the Dutch Communists professed full "satisfaction" with Moscow's explanations. The Amsterdam daily, *De Waarheid* (July 11), carried Paul De Groot's endorsement of them, along with the pronouncement that "there had been no mistakes in the [Soviet] system, but rather mistakes of policy and mistakes in carrying out correct policies."

The Austrian Communist Party likewise claimed to subscribe entirely to the CPSU resolution. After a speech by Johann Koplenig, the party's leader, its Central Committee, while admitting the "temporary difficulties for Communist parties" as a result of the new Moscow line, "welcomed" the Moscow text and pledged to "renew again our firm ties with the Soviet Union and our unswerving determination to struggle side by side with the Soviet Communist Party for the great ideas of Marxism-Leninism." (*Volksstimme*, Vienna, July 15 and 17, 1956.) Moscow radio, in reporting the statement, omitted the sole Austrian complaint that the CPSU had failed to consider in advance the effect of de-Stalinization on the foreign Communist parties.

THE Executive Committee has heard the report on the discussions between representatives of our party and the Communist Party of the Soviet Union. We fully approve of the actions of our representatives in these fraternal discussions and recognize the great value of such mutual exchange of views. Arising out of such discussions further steps toward strengthening relations between Communist Parties can come, and such a development would be of the greatest importance for the cause of peace, democracy and socialism.

In previous statements, the Executive Committee and the Political Committee of our party have dealt with many of the great political issues arising out of the [XXth CPSU] congress. In the course of these statements we raised a number of questions on which we considered further explanation was necessary. We therefore warmly welcome the resolution of June 30 of the Central Committee of the Communist Party of the Soviet Union: "On Overcoming the Cult of the Individual and Its Consequences." This resolution is of exceptional importance in its treatment of the main questions which have arisen in the course of our discussions.

The enemies of socialism have attempted to concentrate world attention on only one aspect of the XXth Congress of the CPSU—the reassessment of the role of Stalin. They want us to forget all the tremendous achievements and advances revealed by the XXth Congress—the fact that socialism is now a world system, the advance on the road to Communism in the USSR, the new possibilities for peaceful co-existence and for preventing war, the different forms of transition to socialism, and the new opportunities for achieving working-class unity.

We believe, therefore, that the resolution of the CPSU is absolutely correct to emphasize these questions on the background against which the negative features that had developed in the 1934–1956 period must be assessed. It deals frankly with these negative features, and does not attempt to hide the damage which they caused. It gives a far-reaching analysis of the historical and objective circumstances on which collective leadership was gradually weakened and the cult of Stalin arose.

The injustices and crimes associated with the 1934–1953 period caused grave harm to the cause of socialism and to the interests of the Soviet people. But it is not true, as the enemies of Communism allege, that they arose from the nature of the Soviet social system, or that they fundamentally changed its character. Political power and the means of production were firmly in the hands of the working people. Socialism was established in the Soviet Union and proved itself superior to capitalism in peace and war. These successes meant the ending of the exploitation of man by man, the ending of illiteracy and backwardness, the vast extension of education, the active participation of millions in social life and public work in town and country— in a word, a great human advance based on the economic transformation of society.

They would have been even greater but for the errors and abuses which had grown up in the Soviet Union. These errors and abuses had to be exposed, whatever the difficulties involved, in order to put an end to them and prevent such things from ever happening again. This the Soviet leaders have courageously done. We welcome this, and the far-reaching steps they are taking to rectify the past mistakes. The enormously beneficial effects of these steps can already be seen in the great successes of Soviet peace policy in the recent period, with the consequent relaxation of international tension; the prespectives of economic and cultural advance opened up by the Sixth Five-Year Plan; and the measures to safeguard socialist legality, develop Soviet democracy and protect the rights of Soviet citizens. As the CPSU continues the work of Marxist analysis of all the important questions involved in reassessing the past period, and the process of rectifying past errors and mistakes goes forward, further light will be thrown on some issues which are still not fully clarified.

Our party agrees with the estimate of the XXth Congress of the CPSU that the possibility exists of a peaceful transition to socialism and that there will be many different forms of transition to socialism. In 1951 we published our program, "The British Road to Socialism," in which we took into account the new world situation and the particular traditions, customs and institutions of our own people. But at the same time we believe in the vital importance of working-class unity, and of extending fraternal contacts, mutual discussions and solidarity between Communist Parties.

In carrying forward the discussion now going on in our party, we call on all our members to study and discuss the resolution of the CPSU. Our discussion has now reached a stage in which it is especially important to deal with our own policy and problems, in order to improve our work in the interests of the British people. We need to discuss how to develop the fight for working-class unity, which is vital for the defeat of the Tories and the advance to socialism. We need to discuss the role and organization of the Communist Party, in order to build our party and improve its work, structure and democratic functioning. This will greatly strengthen the fight for unity. We need to carry forward the preparations for a new edition of our program, "The British Road to Socialism," taking into account the many changes in Britain and in the world since it was first issued in 1951.

Already discussion is under way on these questions, and further steps are being taken to stimulate it. We ask all branches and members to make their contributions, while at the same time carrying out the policy and decisions of our 24th National Congress, so as to help the Party to become a more effective instrument of the British people to resist the Tory offensive and achieve socialism. The Tories and the employers are attacking the living conditions of the British people and creating unemployment. But just because of this they are arousing the opposition of wide sections of the people. New opportunities have emerged for defeating the Tory offensive and driving the Tories from office. Alongside our discussions and development of policy let us fulfil our responsibilities to the British people by leading the fight against the Tories, strengthening working-class unity, and building our party as the indispensable weapon of the working class in the fight for socialism.

18

Statement of the Secretariat of the Italian Communist Party

July 18, 1956

PALMIRO TOGLIATTI's stand (Document 12) was in effect approved by a resolution drafted by the secretariat of the Italian Communist Party and published on July 18, after the return of its delegation from Moscow. (The delegation, consisting of four leading Italian Communists, had been received by the Presidium of the CPSU on July 12, and had talked to Khrushchev in what TASS described as "an atmosphere of complete confidence.") Moscow promptly broadcast the Italian statement. However, the statement did not imply a full retraction of either earlier Italian Communist criticism or the concept of "polycentrism." In the wake of a meeting with Marshal Tito, Togliatti announced his plans to visit Communist China later in 1956.

THE leadership of the Italian Communist Party has convened to hear the report of its delegation which recently visited Moscow and had long friendly talks with the CPSU leaders. By approving the activities of the delegation the party leadership first and foremost expresses profound satisfaction with the cordial atmosphere and spirit of genuine friendship and mutual trust which prevailed during the meeting. This meeting reaffirms the friendship and fraternal solidarity of the CPSU and the Italian Communist Party, based on Marxism-Leninism, and the spirit of proletarian internationalism. The leadership of the party, in particular, again reaffirms that the Italian Communists fully approve the courageous and constructive activities of the CPSU leaders designed to overcome fully the consequences of the personality cult of Stalin both in the Soviet Union and in the international workers' movement.

The resolution of the CPSU Central Committee of June 30 is an important contribution to the elucidation of the causes of the origin of the inadmissibly prolonged and considerable violations of democracy and law in the Soviet state, which has always preserved its basically democratic and socialist character. This resolution is also an effective contribution to the genuine, open discussion now taking place in the international workers' movement, in which our party is taking an active part. This contact with the leaders of the CPSU yet again reaffirms the spirit of fraternal solidarity forming the basis of the relationship between Communist parties, each of which is struggling for democracy, peace, and socialism in the conditions prevailing in their respective countries.

19

Statement of the National Committee
of the Communist Party
of the United States, July 19, 1956

DAILY WORKER, New York

July 26, 1956

FOLLOWING THE publication on July 2 of the Central Committee resolution, the CPSU launched an effort to re-establish greater harmony between the Soviet and the foreign Communist parties. Three leading Soviet Communists, M. A. Suslov, A. I. Kirichenko, and B. N. Ponomarev, attended the Congress of the French Communist Party (see p. 319 above), and during the following weeks various Communist delegations from the West visited Moscow, where they were invariably received by members of the Party Presidium.

The Soviet press and radio gave emphasis to the resolutions and statements of Communists abroad endorsing or accepting the CPSU resolution of June 30. And in an apparent effort to overcome what ill feeling may have been created in the aftermath of the XXth Party Congress, *Pravda* on July 16 editorially blamed "reactionary circles" for attempting to sow disunity within the Communist family. While continuing to insist on the variety of "roads to Communism,"* *Pravda* declared that "the consolidation

---

* In addressing the French Communist Party Congress on July 19, Suslov urged ideological unity and close cooperation among Communist Parties, as well as tactics which uphold "the national interests of their country . . . [and]

of international contacts is a historical necessity both for the workers' parties of the lands of socialism and for the Marxist parties of all capitalist countries." Stressing that Communists in different countries "could not advance toward [their] great goal separately, in disunion," *Pravda* warned its foreign comrades against falling into the trap set by those anti-Communists who hoped that with the Comintern and Cominform dissolved, the national Communist Parties would "perhaps forget the great duty of international proletarian solidarity."*

Similarly, on July 24, *Pravda* printed a lengthy article entitled, "The Unshakable Unity of Countries of the Socialist System," which was widely reprinted and rebroadcast within the Soviet Union.** It endeavored to demonstrate that there was and could be no conflict between the outlook and interests of the USSR and the Communist parties abroad. "What helps one, helps the other; there are no opposing interests." Whatever the divergencies of tactics necessitated by differences in local circumstancs, Marxist-Leninist theory and goals remained common to all Communists; and "the natural march of history" drew all Communists more and more closely together:

The diversity of roads to socialism does not mean that the great idea of proletarian internationalism has been outmoded. . . . On the contrary, all these ways lead to a single goal. Loyalty to the great banner of proletarian internationalism and the constantly growing cohesion of the fighters for socialism are of paramount importance for the success of the great common cause.

By and large, the Communist parties of Asia and Africa refrained from making official pronouncements on the entire debate. Except for an article on April 5 in its official newspaper (cited

accord with concrete national peculiarities and traditions." The same line was expounded by Premier Bulganin in his speech in Warsaw on July 21. See also the editorial of the CPSU theoretical journal, *Kommunist*, 1956, No. 11 (August 7, 1956), "The Unity of the International Communist Movement is Unbreakable," devoted to the same theme but clearly restricting the differences from country to country to "tactical means of struggle."—*Editor.*

* See *Current Digest of the Soviet Press*, Vol. VIII, No. 29.
** *Ibid.*, Vol. VIII, No. 30.

above, pp. 298-99), the Chinese Communist Party avoided committing itself. Thus the Peking newspapers of July 6 carried, without
editorial comment, the CPSU resolution of June 30 as well as Togliatti's reaction. In a similar vein, it was announced that on July
16 a "Collection of Criticisms on the Stalin Issue" went on sale in
China. This publication contained the texts of resolutions and
articles by various Communist Parties and newspapers—again,
without indication of the Chinese Communists' own stand.

The first official reaction of the Indian Communist Party came
in a declaration of its Central Committee on July 12, which ignored the CPSU resolution of June 30. It applauded Moscow's
steps "to rectify the mistakes and undo the damage" caused by the
Stalin cult; but (according to Reuters) it also felt a one-sided
(i.e., negative) appraisal of Stalin's role would cause "bewilderment among the masses," and "it is also necessary to undertake a
fuller analysis of the causes which led to the arbitrary acts and
excesses." It reaffirmed, however, its fraternal solidarity with the
CPSU and its belief that the abuses of Stalinism were not intrinsic
to the Soviet system.

The Indochinese Communists showed no public dissent from
Moscow's stand. In April, the Central Committee of the Vietnam
Lao Ding (Communists) endorsed the stand of the XXth Party
Congress, and on July 10, its central organ, *Nhan Dan*, editorially
accepted the CPSU Central Committee's resolution. On August
3, *Pravda* carried a lengthy article by Ho Chi-Minh, in which he
gratefully acknowledged the "brilliant example" set by Moscow in
"sternly criticizing Stalin's mistakes," establishing collective leadership, and strengthening "ideological unity" of all Communist
parties.

There is no information on an official stand taken by the Communist Party of Indonesia. However, its General Secretary, D.
Aidit, on June 27 told a public gathering that along with the
"daring self-criticism" of its leadership, the CPSU would have done
well also to cite the meritorious services performed by Stalin and
to compare his "good and bad sides."

In general, the Communist parties of Latin America responded with noncommittal or vague statements, except for an explicit resolution of the Argentine Communist Party endorsing the CPSU decision (printed by the Buenos Aires *Nuestra Palabra* and reported by Moscow radio on July 20).

It took the American Communist Party several weeks to formulate a statement acceptable to the different factions which emerged in the aftermath of the debate on the XXth CPSU Congress. According to press reports (Joseph P. Lash, in the *New York Post* of July 22; William Z. Foster, in the New York *Daily Worker* of July 25; and *The New York Times* of July 26 and August 3, 1956), the national chairman, William Z. Foster, known as a veteran Stalinist, led a group loyal to the Soviet view; Eugene Dennis, the party's secretary, maintained a middle position (see Documents 5 and 15 above); and the editors of the New York *Daily Worker* represented a more critical wing. A party congress—the first in seven years—was to be convened in February 1957.

On July 19, the National Committee of the CPUSA accepted what was apparently a compromise formulation. The *Daily Worker* published it a week later, on July 26, as reprinted below.

THE resolution of the Central Committee of the Communist Party of the Soviet Union is a most valuable and important contribution to analyzing the origins, effects and lessons of the mistakes made by the CPSU under Stalin's leadership. We welcome it.

In responding to the discussion and views of other Marxist parties of the world, including our own, the resolution reflects the developing relationship of independent and friendly criticism which today marks the fraternal solidarity of Communist parties. The Communist Party of the United States took note of these new relations in the statement issued by its National Committee on June 25:

These relations must be based on the principles of serving the best national interests of each people and the common interests of all

progressive humanity; of the equality of parties; of the right and
duty of the Marxists of all countries to engage in friendly criticism
of the theory or practice of the Marxists of any country, whenever they feel this necessary. Far from weakening, this will
strengthen international working class solidarity.

The resolution of the CPSU is a timely and major contribution to a further strengthening of such international
solidarity. It assists all Marxist and working class organizations in their struggle to promote peaceful relations
among states, irrespective of social systems—the common
desire of all mankind.

Certain monopolist circles, in our country in particular,
are becoming ever more unscrupulous in attempting to
utilize the present new relations and friendly discussions
between the Communist parties for their own evil ends.
The State Department and the commercial press are trying
to suppress the historic contributions which the XXth Congress of the CPSU made, especially to promote peaceful
co-existence. In a vain effort to rekindle the cold war,
they are trying to twist the self-critical revelations about
the violations of socialist law and principle that took place
in the latter years of Stalin's leadership in order to incite
enmity toward the Soviet Union and the People's Democracies.

They are trying to fish in what they believe to be the
troubled waters of the international working class movement, hoping to sow discord and strife between the Communist and workers' parties of different countries.

The Communist Party of the United States denounces
these unprincipled maneuvers of the State Department and
the commercial press and calls upon American workers and

all other friends of peace to unite more firmly than ever in the fight for peaceful relations between states and against every attempt to revive the cold war. It declares that nothing will ever shake its firm adherence to the principle of international working-class solidarity.

We believe that the resolution of the CPSU provides a convincing answer to the Big Business enemies of socialism who claim that the gross mistakes made under Stalin's leadership are inherent in socialism. Not only does the socialist character of the system remain in the Soviet Union, despite the mistakes and injustices under Stalin's leadership, but during the past three years important steps have been taken to correct the mistakes of the past, to democratize further Soviet life and institutions, and to establish guarantees that such harmful injustices will never occur again. We greet these steps and are convinced that the Soviet Union, under the leadership of the CPSU, is moving ahead to a new period of unprecedented socialist progress.

In connection with the questions analyzed in the CPSU resolution, we believe certain aspects of the origins and effects of past violations of socialist law and principle need, and will receive, further study and discussion. Among these are: the question of bureaucratic distortions in a socialist society, as well as the happenings in the sphere of Jewish cultural institutions and their leadership. Our own party will, in the period ahead, continue to examine these questions with the aim of deepening its understanding of the profound lessons which must be drawn from the disclosures made by the Communist Party of the Soviet Union.

With renewed energy and devotion, the Communist Party

of the United States will put forth every effort to rally the American people to end the cold war and to ensure peace and good neighborly relations between the peoples of the U.S.A., the Soviet Union and all other lands. We shall continue to work for greater economic security, democracy and social progress and for the end of anti-Semitism and racism in our country.

It is our conviction that our country is on the eve of the broadest relationships of joint struggle between Communists and non-Communists for the present and future welfare of the American people. Our party pledges its continued self-sacrificing loyalty to the best interests of our country, its working class and its people—as its prime concern. We believe that the path is opening wider than ever today for unity with all socialist-minded groups to attain socialism by constitutional, peaceful means, expressing the free choice of the majority of the American people. This is the guiding aim of the American Communist Party.

Biographical Appendix

ABAKUMOV, VICTOR S.
Former head of the Soviet secret police, executed in 1954 as an accomplice of Beria.

ANDREYEV, ANDREI A.
Former Politburo member, relegated to relative obscurity after World War II.

BAGIROV, MIR DJAFAR
Party leader in Azerbaidjan, executed in 1956 as an accomplice of Beria.

BUKHARIN, NIKOLAI I.
Leading Soviet Communist theoretician and politician, leader of so-called "rightist" wing, tried and executed in 1938.

CHUBAR, VLAS B.
Soviet leader, member of CPSU Politburo, 1935-1938; victim of the purges.

DEGASPERI, ALCIDE
Italian Christian Democrat, Prime Minister, 1945-1953.

DENNIS, EUGENE
General Secretary of the National Committee of the United States Communist Party.

DZERZHINSKY, FELIX E.
Head of Soviet secret police after Bolshevik Revolution of 1917.

EIKHE, ROBERT I.
Former alternate member of CPSU Politburo, victim of purges.

GORBATOV, COL. GEN. ALEXANDER V.

Soviet army commander during World War II, now alternate member of the Central Committee of the CPSU.

IGNATIEV, SEMYON D.

Head of Soviet secret police in 1953 when "doctors' plot" was announced. Removed from office after Stalin's death, but now Party Secretary in the Bashkir Republic.

KAGANOVICH, LAZAR M.

Veteran Soviet leader, First Deputy Premier and member of the Presidium of the CC/CPSU.

KAMENEV, LEV B.

Outstanding Soviet leader in the 1920's, tried and executed in 1936.

KIROV, SERGEI M.

Soviet Communist Party leader and Politburo member, whose murder in 1934 is commonly regarded as the starting point of the Great Purges.

KOSAREV, ALEXANDER A.

Former Secretary-General of the Young Communist League (Komsomol), victim of the purges.

KOSSIOR, STANISLAV V.

Member of the CPSU Politburo from 1930 to 1938, victim of the purges.

KRUPSKAYA, NADEZHDA K.

Wife of Lenin, and an active Communist leader in her own right.

KUZNETSOV, ALEXANDER A.

Communist Party leader in Leningrad, executed on Stalin's orders about 1951.

MEZHLAUK, VALERY I.

Former head of Soviet State Planning Commission, purged in 1937.

MIKOYAN, ANASTAS I.

Veteran Soviet leader, First Deputy Premier and member of the Presidium of the Communist Party.

MOLOTOV, VYACHESLAV M.

Veteran Soviet leader, former Foreign Minister, still First Deputy Premier and member of the Presidium of the Communist Party.

ORDZHONIKIDZE, GRIGORY K.

Former outstanding Soviet leader, died in 1937.

PELLA, GIUSEPPE

Italian Christian Democrat; Prime Minister, 1953-1954.

POPKOV, PETER S.

Former Communist Party leader, victim of "Leningrad case."

POSKREBYSHEV, ALEXANDER N.

Stalin's aide and personal friend, apparently purged after Stalin's death in 1953.

POSTYSHEV, PAVEL P.

Former Communist Party leader in the Ukraine, disappeared in 1937.

RODIONOV, MIKHAIL I.

Former Premier of the Russian Soviet Federated Republic, victim of "Leningrad case."

ROKOSSOVSKY, MARSHAL KONSTANTIN

Soviet army commander during World War II, now head of the Polish armed forces.

RUDZUTAK, JAN E.

Former Soviet Commissar of Railroads and member of the Politburo, victim of the purges.

SCELBA, MARIO

Former Prime Minister of Italy, one of the founders of the Christian Democrat party.

VASILEVSKY, MARSHAL ALEXANDER M.

Leading Soviet military figure, First Deputy Minister of Defense.

VOZNESENSKY, NIKOLAI A.

Former chief Soviet planner and Politburo member, disappeared in 1949, subsequently executed, highest-ranking victim of "Leningrad case."

YAGODA, HENRYK G.

Former head of Soviet secret police, and one of the chief architects of the purges until his own arrest and execution in 1938.

YENUKIDZE, ABEL S.

A former friend of Stalin and high Soviet official, fell from grace in 1935, executed in 1937.

YEZHOV, NIKOLAI I.

Head of the secret police during the height of the purges, replaced by Beria in 1938, reportedly executed.

ZINOVIEV, GRIGORY E.

Outstanding Soviet leader in the 1920's, former president of the Communist International, victim of the purges in 1936.